MINE EYES HAVE SEEN

Books by Daniel A. Poling

Mothers of Men 1914

Huts in Hell 1918

Report on Steel Strike of 1919: Inter-Church World Movement (two volumes, arranged and edited with Robert Bruère) 1920

Learn to Live 1923

What Men Need Most 1923

An Adventure in Evangelism 1925

The Furnace (novel) 1925

John of Oregon (novel) 1926

Radio Talks to Young People 1926

Dr. Poling's Radio Talks 1927

The Heretic (novel) 1928

Youth and Life 1929

Between Two Worlds (novel) 1930
(reissued as The Romance of Jesus)

John Barleycorn: His Life and Letters (novel) 1933

Youth Marches 1937

Fifty-two Story Sermons for Children 1940

Opportunity Is Yours 1940

A Treasury of Best Loved Hymns 1942

A Preacher Looks at War 1943

Your Daddy Did Not Die 1944

A Treasury of Great Sermons 1944

Faith Is Power for You 1950

Prayers for the Armed Forces 1950

The Glory and Wonder of the Bible (with Dr. Henry Thomas) 1954

Your Questions Answered with Comforting Counsel 1956

DANIEL A. POLING

MINE EYES HAVE SEEN

McGRAW-HILL BOOK COMPANY, INC.

New York Toronto London

MINE EYES HAVE SEEN

Library of Congress Catalog Card Number: 59-14960

FIRST EDITION

This book is dedicated to my wife, Lillian Diebold Poling, who made two families into one and has made me a man immeasurably blessed

PREFACE

A life such as mine, spread over the world and so diversified that I find it difficult at times to give an account of it in chronological order, has been dependent upon many men and women for such measure of success and such avoidance of failure as may have resulted. As I think of those who have contributed directly to the preparation of this autobiography, I find myself a very humble man. I wonder how they have ever gone with me! But they have, and in such a manner as to place me lastingly in their debt. Of the many, I may mention only the few who worthily represent the others.

Ford Stewart, president of the Christian Herald Association and publisher of the *Christian Herald* magazine, has become to me as another son. For a long publishing generation we have worked together, and in these crowded years I have watched him rise to the first rank among all publishers and editorial executives. As no other one man could, he speaks for all my *Christian Herald* associates: the men and women at headquarters, in our great charities, and in all the other activities and interests that carry us around the world. Ford's relationship to this autobiography is more than casual. He gave it its title.

Estelle Feuille, the daughter of Judge Frank Feuille, one of the outstanding legal minds of his generation and an authority on Spanish law, was with me for twelve years. She is responsible for much of the material in this book, and though generally not of my political convictions, at the time of the Hoover-Smith presidential campaign she guarded my interests and protected my files as with her life. As all my secretaries have, Estelle Feuille became practically a member of my family.

Frances Sangster, now Mrs. Holingsworth Houston, had been president of the District of Columbia's Christian Endeavor Union before she came to spend twelve years directing my *Christian Herald* office and field activities. She married a member of my Philadelphia church, and when he went off to the South Pacific in an army uniform she continued to work for me and my causes with a devotion that was deep and constant.

Linda Halsted has been the indefatigable, patient, and ever-gracious secretary of this autobiography, and this volume is her major contribution to my editorial output.

The final paragraphs of this story have been written in a comfortable cottage by a beautiful spring-fed lake in the foothills of the Catskills, in the heart of the Rip Van Winkle country. I look out across the shimmering water to a densely wooded hill where deer may come down to drink and graze. Here, less than three hours from noisy, crowded Manhattan, my wife and I have found quiet and relaxation. Catherine and Herman Knaust, whose lake and retreat this is, are a long decade our juniors in years but in them Lillian and I have known that maturity of friendship that has kept our youth and now our middle years and beyond from fading. The life of Herman Knaust is another Horatio Alger story, and Catherine, beautiful, intuitive, and competent, is her husband's perfect complement. They have achieved a major success in the competitive world of business and, as I see it, an even greater triumph in sharing their success with others. They have brought to this country more than six hundred German and Baltic refugees, sponsored them, and found them jobs. Nearly all have now become American citizens, and among them, Herman insists, there have been no ingrates, no disappointments.

At this writing, one of the nation's leading scientists is collaborating with Herman Knaust and his brother Henry in a field of medicine and chemistry that may lead to almost infinite healing for the human race.

Catherine and Herman Knaust and their children came into our lives to enrich and bless us, and the last sentences of this autobiography are dedicated to them.

Savilla-by-the-Lake *Daniel A. Poling*

MINE EYES HAVE SEEN

1

Back at the gray dawn of memory is my mother, beautiful and loving, understanding and wise, and always equal to any situation. She is the first of all whom I remember.

Flying west a short time ago, I crossed the Missouri River at an elevation of eleven thousand feet. Seventy-five years ago the young bride who was to become my mother crossed it lower down, in a skiff. Far below my plane were the cities of Bismarck, with the white towers of the state capitol, and Mandan, across the river. When my mother first saw Bismarck, it was a frontier trading post at the end of the railroad; no bridge had yet been built to carry the Northern Pacific's trains across the water. Just a few miles to the south was Fort Abraham Lincoln, where Custer had taken command of his famous Seventh Cavalry and later ridden out to meet death at the hands of Sitting Bull on the banks of the Little Bighorn. Like most Western towns of the time, Bismarck, grandly named after Germany's Iron Chancellor, was not much more than a clump of cabins and shacks. In one of these, having ridden the train to the end of the line, my parents spent some rigorous days waiting for the Missouri's ice to melt and the spring floods to subside so that they might cross to the train on the western side.

Mother and Father were on their wedding journey, and a long one it was—although the plane I rode in so comfortably was covering the same route, from Canton, Ohio, to Portland, Oregon, in a matter of hours.

I have been reading in my mother's diary for 1884. On March 30 she wrote:

> Charlie went to the Methodist chapel this morning, and tonight he preached in the little sod church. I was not feeling well, and so I waited for him. Then, too, a young mother in our party has a sick baby and I have tried to help her.

Charlie—Charles Cupp Poling—my father, was a preacher of the Evangelical Church (later, after the unfortunate church division, of the United Evangelical Church). Now, at age twenty-five, he was traveling west to take up a new missionary assignment, and his bride was going with him. In the March 31 entry in the little red leather-backed book, this sentence appears:

> The baby died tonight, and we shall have a funeral in the morning.

And the day's record concludes:

> I wonder what I shall find in this strange new land to which we are going. I wonder what may happen to me and to the child I carry under my heart.

Looking back in time, I know that Mother found hardship and sorrow, sickness and death, but also love and great kindness, and a life of profound fulfillment with her large family, her church, and her friends. The child she carried and wondered about as she expressed her thoughts beside the frozen Missouri was the son who many years later soared across that once desolate spot in his plane and remembered the past.

My mother—Savilla Kring before she married father—was the first woman in the Evangelical Church ever to be ordained a preacher. A singing evangelist, she had the gift of stirring congregations. As soprano soloist with a vocal quartet, she traveled far from her parents' home in Pennsylvania. In the seventies she first sang the hymn "I'm a Child of the King" at Chautauqua, New York, and then went on to make it a favorite of the now long-forgotten camp meetings at Old Orchard, Maine, Round Lake, New York, and Ocean Grove, New Jersey. She sang it one Sunday morning in 1881 at the dedication of Ocean Grove's first pavilion. President James A. Garfield lay mortally wounded at Long Branch, only a few miles away. In the afternoon, Savilla was taken by carriage to the little seaside village, and the dying President, propped against his pillows, listened to the golden music of the eager girl:

My Father is rich in houses and lands;
He holdeth the wealth of the world in His hands...
A tent or a cottage, why should I care?
They are building a palace for me over there.

When I came to know Mother she had a voice like a gentle flute, and the memory of her singing this, her favorite, hymn still touches me deeply. One summer evening in 1932, on the moonlit roof of a hotel in Washington, D.C., I chanced to be conversing with Garfield's son. In 1916 I had campaigned with James R. Garfield in Ohio when he ran for governor, but only now did I tell him how Savilla Kring had sung for his father. "Was that your mother?" he asked in astonishment. "I remember her. As a little boy I stood beside my father's bed and listened to her sing just outside the door. She was very beautiful." I was able to tell Mr. Garfield that mother was still beautiful, and that she was still singing what had come to be known as "her" song.

Miss Kring, the daughter of an Evangelical pastor, was well launched upon what was then a spectacular career for a young woman when the proverbial penniless youth crossed her path in Canton, Ohio—or rather, blocked it. Red-headed, ambitious, and with the call to preach, Charles Poling was the son of a Virginia circuit rider whose parish extended from the Potomac across western Pennsylvania and eastern Ohio. Teaching school in the summer and attending Mount Union College in the winter, Father should have been discouraged when he met Mother, for he faced plenty of competition. An older man of wealth and piety had already told the young girl that after fasting and prayer he had seen in a vision that he was the man God had selected to be her husband. Mother was impressed but—quite reasonably, I think—insisted that since the matter was of some importance to her, she was sure she would receive a vision too. Until then, she said, she would not order her trousseau. Charles Poling could offer no visions to support his claim and he had no money; further, his piety, though genuine, was rugged. But he swept Savilla off her feet and almost before she knew it she was a poor preacher's bride, moving out of her glamorous life as an evangelistic singer into pioneer hardships, childbearing—and enduring happiness. When she told Father about the other man's vision, he said, "Wonderful—and I am yours!"

There was an uproar when the engagement was announced: much talk of "wasted talents" and the "sin of sacrificing a high calling" for such a marriage. Some of the saints were never reconciled. Father was not at all disturbed, however, nor were Savilla's parents, and the bride-to-be serenely answered her critics with, "Perhaps I shall raise a preacher or two." As it turned out, she did even better; she raised three.

Mother had a sense of humor that was second only to her radiant, mystical religious experience. Indeed, the two were often linked. "I used to be afraid of God until I heard Him laugh," she remarked one day, leaving me a puzzled youth until the laughter was pointed out, in Psalms: "But thou, O Lord shalt laugh at them."

And along with Mother's sense of humor went common sense. When a distressed young matron who had been too easily influenced by admiring, predatory males, came to Mother saying, "I have committed the unpardonable sin—my soul is lost," and then tried to tell Mother all about it, Mother had this answer for her: "Don't tell me another word, dear. We will just get down on our knees and tell the Heavenly Father—and *don't you dare* talk out loud." In this fashion, with my mother's arms around her, the young woman made her confession. The record shows that she lived the good life thereafter. When, at a rather worldly age myself, I asked Mother if she wasn't tempted just a little—whether she really wouldn't have enjoyed hearing the details—her brown eyes twinkled and she answered, "Definitely yes! Gossip is wonderful. But I knew that if she ever got started talking about it, she wouldn't be able to stop, and so many people would be hurt. Women are like that, you know." Well, aren't we all!

Mother's laughter, which was laughter with all the silver bells ringing, seemed to be an outward expression of the determination in her character. She *would* raise us so that we turned out at our best. Father's salary, when I first became aware of such things, was four hundred dollars a year. I remember my sense of affluence when it rose to six hundred: I wondered what we would do with the extra money. It was Mother, with her flying hands and fighting heart, who supplemented the income and held us together. We were never forsaken and we never begged, but we were undeniably outfitted from missionary boxes that came from the more affluent churches of the East. Some of the contents of those boxes were wonderful and others were not—garments frayed and faded, shoes without mates, games that lacked parts or directions, dolls that were losing their sawdust. Mother had all the answers. As she once remarked, she "died" with every dress she "dyed" and then made over. She invented new rules for the games; she stuffed the limp dolls; she converted the lonely shoes into sandals. I never owned an overcoat until I was in high school, and then one green with age came in a box. It fit me, and Mother dyed it.

From one missionary shipment a really fine fur cape emerged. Mother said, "But it's just *too* fine for me, and too rich for a preacher's wife." And so she made two small capes out of the one, and gave the second away. We children were terribly put out, for this had been the only chance our family ever had to lead the local fashion parade. Even so, we won in the end, for that very fall capes just covering the shoulders, with high collars coming up under the ears, became the rage.

Mother did something that was even more wonderful—she raised her "p.k.'s," her preacher's kids, without letting them develop inferiority complexes. Not one of us, such was her inspired way, ever had the slightest idea that he was unfortunate or to be pitied. We were taught to pray for wisdom and guidance, for direct help in practical, everyday matters. The example our parents gave us was, perhaps, a childlike faith, but never did those prayers for Heaven's aid conclude without the acceptance of responsibility for getting busy. "Pray without ceasing and work accordingly" was one of Father's mottoes, and one of his favorite texts was, "Faith without works is dead."

In one of our last conversations, Father smiled as he recalled his parents' firm reliance upon God to supply all wants according to the formula of "Ask and then go out for it." He added this: "Remember that promise, and remember that it never failed your father and his father and others before them. Your mother and I had more when she went on ahead than at any other time in our lives, and you children—well, you've never had to beg bread or anything else since you stopped pestering us for candy or ribbons long ago."

Mother was a very beautiful woman. As a little boy I knew it; when I was a man, and she had gone on to the house and lands she had celebrated in song, another woman, the venerable wife of a judge in Lafayette, Oregon, confirmed my memories. "Your mother," she said, "was the loveliest creature that ever came to this valley, and her voice made you forget about angels." Then she added, "But none of us could understand why she came here." To this woman it seemed a waste that Mother had hidden her gifts from the great centers of the East. Mother's answer to this point of view was in the fullness of her work, and I know that she would never have agreed that a day of her life was purposeless.

On my parents' golden wedding anniversary I surprised them by flying to Portland unannounced. This was in 1932, when people didn't take to the air as casually as they do now, and in Topeka, Kansas, my plane rose before dawn from a narrow strip that was illumined by automobile headlights. After the anniversary celebration, I talked Father and Mother into their first airplane ride. It was intended to be an ambitious one—across the continent to Long House, the summer home I had found for the Poling clan in New Hampshire.

At that time I owned and used in my traveling duties a Lockheed-Vega High-Wing Express, piloted for me by young Russell Thaw, son of Harry K. Thaw and Evelyn Nesbitt. Russell had been flying solo since he was fifteen, and he had my utter confidence although, looking back on some of his feats, such as landing me in an empty lot in Lima, Ohio, I find that I now shudder.

Starting east, we circled Mount Hood and looked down into its crater—Father suggested that. Thereafter, we followed the route of the wedding journey of half a century before. At Helena, when the brakes on our landing gear jammed, we went into a loop. I had strapped Mother by my side in the wide seat; Father sat in front. Russell did a remarkable job of getting us down; though shaken, none of us was hurt. "Our family never could do anything the easy way at first," was Mother's comment when Father, always solicitous, asked her how she felt. Then she turned to me. "I assume it isn't customary to come down like this," she said with a twinkle, "but I certainly enjoyed the ride."

My plane, its tail damaged, had to be left behind. I hardly expected Mother to agree to another flight, since she had been sick most of the way, but she insisted on our flying to Billings in a chartered plane, from which point the three of us took the train for the rest of the way.

As the seasons passed, Mother seemed not to grow older. Her mind quickened, her lovely voice remained. Only her body grew more fragile. In the middle 1930s, when the message reached us widely scattered children that she had passed unexpectedly into a coma, we all hurried homeward to Portland. And then, quite miraculously, she came back to us. For the first time in many years Mother's p.k.'s were all together, and again she was the heart of the family. She sang her song, "They are building a palace for me over there . . ." She queened the intimate scene. One evening we became hilarious. Any large and congenial family's reminiscences are likely to become loud as one leads to another. Ours did that night. Father was busy in his study. At eighty he was still preaching sermons to save the world, and that evening he was getting a new one out of his system. He stood the noise as long as he could and then came down to shush us. "What in the world will the neighbors think?" he asked. Mother had the answer. "Why, Charlie, they'll think it's the wake." And as he always did when Mother made her point, Father surrendered. He forgot his sermon and helped us make more noise.

Finally the day came when my duties called me back to my church in Philadelphia. I knew I was leaving the old home never to see it again as I had always known it. I lifted Mother from the davenport in the sitting room and carried her to her bed. Thoughtfully, the others left us there. Presently Mother said, "Put your head on my hands, for I can't lift them now." And, kneeling by her bed, I put my head down into her hands. They were working hands, and in their roughness was part of my life, for these hands had made me the man I was. They were also beautiful hands, infinitely gentle. She turned on her pillow until her lips were on my hair, and then she said:

"If, when you come again, I am not here to greet you as always I have been, then, my son, you will know where to find me."

With those words, her last to me, fixed in my heart, I went out and flew eastward toward the dawn.

Twice, in the years since that morning, I have dreamed about Mother when the dream seemed more than a dream. In both cases it was unmistakably a visitation to my subconscious. Once she moved with characteristic quietness and the ineffable smile that so often in life reassured me; she told me clearly that she understood the problem I faced and that my decision was pleasing to her. That was all. But when I woke—if I had been sleeping—I had the answer—her answer and mine—to what I had been searching for and agonizing over.

The second experience came after a recent major operation, during the days and nights that were rugged and seemed unending. Again I had the sense of Mother's presence, though now she was part of a larger company that included Father and the mother of my two sons, and others. My darkened hospital room became luminous and crowded. Sleepless, wide-eyed, I knew the presence of what the Scriptures describe as "a cloud of witnesses." There were moments when it seemed they must break through to me, become visible, speak. But this did not happen. Nor did it need to happen, for I was fully comforted. They were just there, to me as real as reality, "closer . . . than breathing, and nearer than hands and feet," as Tennyson puts it. I did not feel

I was on the way out and forward, but I did know that if that had been in God's plan for me, I would not have been lonely.

The first clear memory I have of my father is associated with an hour of terror. It was night and dark, and I was alone. Then Father came, lifted me from my crib, held me against his deep, warm chest, and laughed quietly and reassuringly. I had the croup, a scourge in those days, but in Father's comforting arms I relaxed and began to breathe quietly. Instinctively, because Father laughed, I knew that I need not be afraid.

Later, the first time I looked at death, Father again carried me in his arms and made it gentle. The tiny, still form lying in its cradle was my baby sister, Addie. In my lifetime I have seen death approach many times to claim those dear to me or, in the horror of brutal war, to strike down men whose names were unknown to me. But no matter the outward circumstances, the memory of my father's protecting arms has always come back to be part of my reassurance, my consolation.

Four strains converged in Father—Scotch, English, Welsh, Irish. I once heard him explain that he got his conservatism from the Scotch, his stubbornness from the English, just a suggestion of melody (he really had a fine tenor voice) from the Welsh, and his extreme modesty from the Irish. A sense of humor, obviously, went along with his sensitive and often unexpected tenderness.

Once while addressing a temperance rally in Topeka I overplayed my family hand—to my own confusion but to the delight of a self-respecting Kansas audience. Announcing the collection, I said, or thought I said, "When I first became well acquainted with my father, who was a clergyman in the state of Oregon, he was supporting a family of nine children on four hundred dollars a year." That night I learned the difference between being laughed with and laughed at—and believe me, there is a difference. My audience suddenly sat up, gave me one startled, concentrated look, and then went into near-hysterics. To me it seemed that the roof rose from its walls. For the rest of my speech, so far as I was concerned, it never came down.

After the meeting a friend, still laughing about my boner, told me that I had unwittingly transposed the quantities so that what I had wished to present as a hard fact of the preacher's life came out "supporting four hundred children on nine dollars a year." Father's response, when he heard about it, was, "Thanks for the compliment, Son, but why didn't you wait till you got to Salt Lake City where it might have done you some good?"

Father was not always the comforter or joker, however. He could be an angry man and a formidable disciplinarian. I associate his stern nature with the flaming red burnsides he wore when I was young. Particularly in dealing with me and my two brothers Father observed the wisdom found in Proverbs: "He that spareth his rod hateth his son: but he that loveth him chasteneth him betimes." I hasten to add that I never received a lick amiss.

My earliest recollection of corporal punishment is associated with my dislike of what today is called a baby-sitter. This particular character, an elderly neighbor, had tormented me beyond endurance, or so I thought. Faced with the prospect of more of her repressions, I bit her with enthusiasm and all my front teeth, then drove my four-year-old legs at top speed for the nearest exit. I was not fast enough. Father caught me. What he did to me made that the last time I ever put teeth into human flesh.

Another dandy whipping I arranged for deliberately. A dog-and-pony show came to the Marquam Theater in Portland. An advance agent appeared at the Stevens Addition school on the East Side and offered tickets in the top gallery to the four boys who would distribute fliers house to house. Somehow I was selected as one of the lucky four even though my father was known to be against theaters on principle, as was his church. At this point I talked myself into trouble. To my slipping conscience, I said, "This is different. Trained dogs and trained ponies—they're educational." I distributed the fliers, claimed my ticket, and went home to Father. He heard me through—he always did that—and then said, "No!"

So I went. I was nine or ten then, and I calmly assumed full responsibility and accepted in advance the penalty that would come. Later, when the punishment was over, I felt I had come out ahead. Today I am sure that my rewards were worth all that I received at home when I returned. I went early, without my supper, and reached the theater, as I had hoped to, in time to carry water to the ponies. Two of these sensitive creatures were in the midst of a feud and, approaching one of them from the wrong angle, I received a kick not intended for me. The blow landed on my shin and I fell in a heap.

A performer in that show, a young man who did tricks with a rope while he chewed gum, picked me up and calmed me. His name was Will Rogers, and from that night he was my idol. After making sure my leg was not broken, Will sat me on a chair in the wings and I saw the exhibition from there. It was wonderful, and doubly so because I was going to pay a price for it. Afterward, Will drove me home in a pony cart and explained my bruised shin to Father. Father was courteous with Will but firm with me. I did my best to keep my wounded leg in the foreground, but the paternal interest centered elsewhere. "Not because you went, Son," he explained, "but because you disobeyed."

In Lafayette, south of Portland in the Willamette Valley, Father built the little church that was the largest and most beautiful building in my small world. Much of the work he did with his own hands, and in the same way he helped build churches elsewhere in his wide parish. Stone upon stone, board above board, I watched our church rise, and then I saw it painted—white for the body, the tower in several colors. I played in the shadow of its walls and later worshiped at its altar. The faith my father declared from the pulpit he nailed together became my faith.

There was good and even great preaching in that modest sanctuary, and there were occasions when it was filled with the loveliness of Mother's singing. Then, too, there were lectures and commencement exercises, for the church became the chapel of a seminary that Father founded. I remember all of these—the sermons, the music, the commencements, the lectures, and the other community occasions that brought everyone together as perhaps only happened in pioneer towns. Memorable, all of it, but the best of all was when my mother prayed. She would talk about "unsearchable riches," this woman who was very poor of riches, and she would thank God for "many things," and her children wondered what they were, though today they know. Always Mother prayed to receive God's answer, whether or not this was the answer she thought she needed. And always, as I came to understand later, she found in prayer peace and the inner power that comes with peace.

The preacher who built that white church, and who filled it with the sermons of his faith, came back to it often for more than sixty years. I heard him last in that pulpit when he was nearly ninety. Today, the little church bears his name and is a memorial to him and to the woman who stood by his side and largely made him what he became. For Mother was the greater evangelist, imbued with the mysticism and power associated with motherhood. Father understood her loyalty and her faith in him, and generally sensed what she thought he should do even before Mother put her thoughts into words.

Ours is a preaching tradition. I have heard both my grandfathers, both my parents, both my brothers, and both my sons preach, and I hope to hear at least one or more of my twenty-one grandchildren. The preaching line runs unbroken for four generations through Father, for six generations through Mother, and of the nine males in the generations through Father, eight have been clergymen—not counting uncles and nephews.

Father was effective before any congregation, large or small. One Sunday afternoon when I was in my late teens, in a campmeeting tent with an Oregon rain pelting down, I heard him pour out his soul to an audience of less than fifty. A few years later, at a reunion of the Grand Army of the Republic in Ohio, I was present when he held more than seven thousand men and women spellbound. His text was, "And I, if I be lifted up from the earth, will draw all men unto me." One of his listeners, Major General Kiefer, a veteran of the Civil War and a former Speaker of the House of Representatives, said afterward: "Political or religious, I have never heard a more moving utterance."

An early recollection of my father associates him with a black horse: Father drawing on his rubber boots, getting into rubber garments, lifting me into his arms, and then mounting and riding away. He had a circuit that took him, through all weathers, deep into into the mountain country east and west of Lafayette. Father was a sound horseman. He came of a horse-loving family—its only male member in four generations who was not a preacher was a breeder and trainer of Morgans. But when the horse age passed for Father, and he dismounted and took over the wheel of an automobile, the change was not for the better. As an example of his style, which he considered the last word in prudence, he would drive into the center of an intersection, stop, and look in all directions before proceeding. Mother always insisted on riding with him. "If he does have the big accident," she said, when we remonstrated with her, "I don't want to be left behind." But he never had that accident. Once when he was with me in the East, his sons-in-law took his car out of the garage and lost it. "The law is on my side," Father fumed, when he returned to Portland and discovered the outrage, "and if it weren't for the humiliation of it, I'd have it on every one of you."

One of the most poignant of all the scenes from my childhood is that of the agony on my father's face when I came back from what he thought was my grave. We were living in Lafayette then, and I had learned to swim when he was not at home, disobeying his orders and going to the Yamhill River without his or Mother's knowledge. When the summer came that Father thought it was time for me to learn, I was already an adept. Rather than confess, I let him tie a clothesline around my waist and maintain the link between us while I struggled convincingly in the shallows. Pleased with my progress, Father sent me to the beach and admonished me to stay there while he demonstrated some real swimming.

It was while his back was turned that an evil spirit entered me. I scampered to the plank diving board, let out a wild yell, and fell off. Swimming underwater to the channel, where the current ran swift, I came up for air far below my point of disappearance. Then I saw Father in the water, calling my name and helplessly, frantically searching for me. My pleasure in my achievement was suddenly gone, and I was afraid. But the punishment I got that day was not from Father's hands; it was from the look on his face. When we were together again he sat with me on the sand and held me tightly. When at last he spoke, he said, "Sometime, my son, you will understand." There was something in his voice I had never heard before and shall never forget—the primal anguish of a father for his child.

Portland, when I first knew it, was a pretty tough place, a real frontier town, with bawdyhouses opening out on a downtown street and a congress of bums and hoodlums on most of the main corners. When the Salvation Army first came to town with its uniforms and bonnets, its tambourines and big bass drum and its hymns set to popular tunes, the loafers went into action. The Army's street-corner meetings were at first derided, then egged, then openly attacked. One evening we heard a cry of "Fire!" Father, who had defended the Salvationists from the beginning, ran from our house to the scene of the latest attack, a half-mile away. Against his orders, I followed at a distance. The Army's first small barracks had been set afire, and a large crowd had gathered to watch. Never shall I forget the sight of Father, hatless, his red burnsides bristling, wading in among the spectators to find the guilty ones and hold them for the law. The court action that followed helped create a new climate in Portland for the Salvation Army.

Since those days I have witnessed, and sometimes participated in, the activities of the Army in many parts of the world. It was a shipwreck in 1894 that started one of the Army's unique ministries. The survivors, brought to Portland, huddled, shivering and hungry, in a Salvation Army shelter. In the emergency, food ran out. An ingenious lassie seized a soup pot, carried it to a street corner, and on it placed the sign, "Keep this pot boiling." That night there was food for all. Now that kettle has come to be a symbol of the Salvation Army in its giving and receiving of gifts. I never hear the bells ringing at Christmas, or see the money going into the "boiling pots," mixed with love and good will to men, but I am reminded of my father tackling those hoodlums and fighting for the Army's right to exist.

What a man Father was! Even in near-poverty he could inspire his sons with the attractiveness of his high calling. Like Mother, he never really grew old. Sickness, major operations, and the inevitable disappointments of life left him still the incurable optimist. When he was past eighty-five he put a new roof on his house in Portland. It had been my joy and my privilege to give the house to my parents. Father loved his house. As we surveyed the finished job, he was clearly not pleased. "I made a mistake," he told me. "Those synthetic shingles look all right, but an Oregon house should be covered with clear cedar, and that's what I'll put on next." We discussed other matters for what I believed was a reasonable period, and then I asked, "Father, what's your guarantee on that roof?"

Like a flash came the answer: "Fifteen years—and I know what you're thinking!"

That was the summer of our last fishing trip. We packed into the Cascades, twenty-one miles over a mountain trail. Three days we fished for trout and three days it rained. I have pictures to prove that we caught the limit and that the big ones did not get away. Also, I caught a miserable cold. Father caught only fish. Riding out, he said, "Dan, do you know what's wrong with you?" "Certainly," I replied, "a cold." Father laughed, straightened himself in the saddle, and answered, "I'll tell you what's wrong. Your generation is soft." And his blue eyes flashed. That was our last ride together.

Father lived into his ninetieth year. Toward the end he was often confused. But when he went on his "big one"—he called it that—he was not confused. He died before I could reach his bedside from Philadelphia so that my last memories of him are associated with our fishing trip and other moments when he was vividly alive. Father's last words—they were written down for me—were: "I know that I am a dying man but I am a victorious man. I have a message for the Conference. Preach Christ, preach Christ crucified, buried and risen from the dead." Self-denying, ageless, indomitable Father—as he slipped away his thoughts turned from himself to his church, and his words were like the climax of a last sermon.

There were nine of us children eventually—five girls and four boys. The six of us who grew to manhood and womanhood—including my brothers Charles Samuel and Paul Newton, my sisters Ethel, Laura, and Mabel—all survive at this writing. All of us have raised families of our own and all of us have become grandparents, to the total of thirty-five grandchildren.

My brother and two sisters who did not live were casualties of frontier medical ignorance or neglect. None of their deaths, I am convinced, would have occurred in our present era of understanding of causes and treatments. My sister Addie came to Mother's breast when for the first time it was inadequate; the raw cow's milk she was given as a substitute was a liquid poison. Golden-haired May, the loveliest memory of my childhood, was stricken with what was diagnosed as "brain fever," and a few days before she was five she died with my name on her lips. I can hear her now: "Put the blocks away, Danny, I am very tired. May can't play any longer."

Rudolph, a dozen years younger than I, was a lad of great promise and I loved him dearly. His affliction was typhoid fever. The medicine Mother was instructed to give him burned holes in her apron. By the time she discovered this and discontinued giving it, it was too late.

The death of this brother was one of the crucial experiences of my life, for in his passing I learned a fundamental truth about prayer. I learned it in agony—and an agony that was twice bitter because the lesson followed another experience that had led me to think I knew all I needed to know about prayer.

Prayer is our inheritance. I received it from my parents as they received it from theirs, and with my face buried in the calico that covered my mother's knees, and with her worn, gentle hands on my head, I uttered the first prayers of childhood. Mother's low, armless rocker behind the airtight wood stove in the sitting room was an altar where we children were comforted and taught. Her open Bible lay upon that chair, and in the early-morning prayers she whispered there before the rest of us were awake Mother found the strength for her crowded day and the grace she breathed upon us all.

I grew up, then, to my junior year in college possessing the knowledge that prayer never fails. And now I was to pray to my first answer. The memory is sharp and clear.

I became the representative of my school, Dallas College, in a state oratorical contest. On Sunday before the Friday of the final event I developed a severe cold with a rising fever. "Grippe," said the doctor. Voiceless, I was in black despair at the thought of failing my school. The despair was half remorse: I had invited the disaster by going on an exhausting thirty-mile bicycle ride the day before the cold began. Wednesday night I began to be delirious.

Thursday morning something happened. First, I stopped my frantic regretting and began to think with a purpose. I was living at home, for our home at that period was on the edge of the Dallas campus. On the wall of my room hung a motto. I can see it yet—silver letters on a green card: "There Hath Not Failed One Word Of All His Good Promise." Mother had placed the message on that wall long before, and now it called me out of my despair and inspired me to action.

I rolled out of bed. On my knees, with my burning face buried in the covers that should have been over me, I prayed. I prayed to be ready and able to speak on Friday night. Whatever the cost might be, I asked for that. Not to win but to be there, in my place and with voice and strength enough not to let my college down. I did not ask for anything to the detriment of any other person. I asked only that I be able to do my assigned and accepted duty and that others not be the losers because of my weakness. Today, looking back, I know that prayer was right.

I got back into bed, pulled the covers to my chin, and had the answer for the doctor when he came again. I knew that I would speak. The doctor said no, but his word did not trouble me. A few hours later when the fever broke and I went into the great sweat that dropped me into the depths, I had a finish fight with doubt. I discovered the knowledge that I have never since lost: In weakness, God is man's strength, and His strength is matured and perfected for us in our weakness.

The physiologist and psychiatrist have their own answers for what happened to me that day—and, indeed, for much else that this book will relate. But with those answers fully evaluated, acknowledged, and appreciated, there is still something more—the truth that I discovered and experienced in my eighteenth year. It is this "something more" that I have endeavored to share with others throughout my career. It has given me not only peace of mind and peace of soul, but peace with power in and over every circumstance of life.

I delivered my oration, "A Vision for Service." The fortunes of the drawing made me the first speaker. I came on, was letter-perfect although wobbly in the knees, and got off the stage before I collapsed.

Of course I was gratified, later on, when I learned that I had won, but I had not asked for that. Even then I knew that such a prayer is always wrong, for it is a prayer against men who are your associates and comrades as well as your opponents. "May the best man win" is the thought that should go with you when you kneel as well as when you run, and I knew that.

And so my first answer, prayed to, was given me. My second experience came only a few months later when I was called home from my summer-vacation job to find my brother Rudolph with the fatal grip of typhoid upon him. I knew what to do—or thought I knew! I knelt again to ask God to keep His promise that had never failed, the promise of that old wall motto. With complete assurance I began that prayer.

But now it was different, altogether different. I got nowhere. There was no promise and no peace. I seemed as one standing before a wall of stone, or a gate of brass that would not open. I became increasingly importunate. I argued and made demands. Gradually, a hopelessness came upon me. First it was amazement or the shock of disillusion, then anger, and finally despair.

I wanted the life of my brother more than I desired anything in the world. I wanted his life so much that I was ready that night to pledge my own life for his recovery. But there was no answer and not the slightest intimation that I had been heard.

Would it have been possible for me to batter through that closed door? Does the promise "Ask it shall be given to you" strip down to just that? There are some who so affirm. I do not know, and if I thought I did, I would not assume the responsibility of speaking out. If finally God does not give me the keys, I shall not attempt to take them by force. I want *His* answer. Always I may have mine without going to the trouble of praying.

That night, hours after my return home, I left the house, which was then filled with the sounds of Rudolph's tortured breathing, and tramped alone through the countryside. I was alone now as I had never before been alone—helpless and without hope. But I would not concede defeat. The issue was too appalling. This was my first real bout with death, though death had come to our house twice before. Then I myself had been a child. Once I had barely been aware of the fact. The second time I had still been too young to feel I had a part to play. Now I was mature enough to feel responsible.

Tired to the bone, I returned to my room and to my knees. In the room next to mine the breathing had changed. No longer sharp and spaced, it galloped like a horse out of control. I could not pray again. Hours had passed since I first began to beat against that door that would not open. I waited there and at last in utter weariness fell asleep.

Dawn had come when I opened my eyes. Mother was there, and Father, but before they spoke, even before I was fully awake, I had my answer. It was as definite as the first answer had been, but much more vivid and compelling. The answer was "No."

The years that have passed since that morning when prayer led me to my first unmistakable negative have not dimmed the impression that came with the answer. I was satisfied, and with the answer came peace. It was the answer I wanted; it was my answer. There was no rebellion in me—none at all—and there was power, power that I knew was never to leave me, power that was to be my companion in sickness as in health, through war and peace, at birth and at death, all the way through life.

That morning I found the interpretation of Christ's incredible promise: "Whatsoever ye shall ask in my name, that will I do." Until then I had never really seen those three words "in my name." I had read only, "Whatsoever ye shall ask, that will I do." "But "in my name" now means to me literally "in my will." As I prayed for Rudolph's recovery, there was no "Thy will be done" anywhere in the anguished cry of my heart. I was ready to settle for nothing less than "*my* will be done."

But with the answer that came after I could no longer cry out my passionate demand, came also the assurance that "No" was not the only word God had for me. The affirmation in the answer was what I truly wanted. Yes, it was as definite and final as that. Then I would not have exchanged the "No" for "Yes."

Many particulars are still clouded; there remain many baffling questions. Some of them will not be answered, it appears, this side of Eternity. But through the years since I listened for my brother's last breath, I have been content to wait.

It was in that morning when he died that I came to know he had something better than I had asked for him; that, as Father told me later, our loss was his gain. Here also the details are clouded, but the reality is most real. I began to see even then that this life is the beginning and not the end, that it is, as has been said, "but the childhood of immortality."

Faith in its ultimate reaches cannot be rationalized, but my own children helped me understand something of the quality of what the truth itself is. I used to watch them when they dropped their toys beyond their reach, used to listen to their cries of anger or frustration or sheer grief. For young Daniel and Clark, or Mary or Jane, all was lost. For them the world had tumbled in. To me, the situation was considerably different. I could see that all was not lost, that the world for which my children lamented was intact and just about all ahead. And then I saw how quickly the child's memory of the event faded when its tears were dried. And so it is, I think, that God listens to our weeping when the situation is beyond our knowledge but still within His love and power.

There was an almost mystical relationship between Rudolph and me. At age seven he was a deep, quiet, radiant lad. He used to come and stand between my knees, without a movement or a word, as I sat studying at the table in my small room. He had never been robust, but we had learned to take that for granted, to accept him as he was, and it never occurred to us that he would not be staying. One evening he brought to my room a Kodak snapshot I had taken of him. He climbed into my lap with it while I sat studying, found a pencil, and laboriously spelled out his name in block letters across the picture: RUDOLPH. Then he slid down and went away, leaving the offering on my table. I still have that picture in an old trunk. When the mood is on me, I go to the attic and take it in my hands and remember the long night when in vain I battered at the door that would not open, but from which at last I turned away with the answer that was better than the one I sought—the answer that brought me peace with power.

2

Father's missionary assignments kept us going—in more senses than one—so that when we Polings sang "Home, Sweet Home," residences in Portland, Salem, Dayton, Lafayette, and nearby Dallas were all part of the picture. Though I was born in Portland, the little Willamette Valley town of Lafayette is the scene of my earliest memories, some of which I have already related. We lived there three different times. Father finally built us a small home on "Piety Hill," so called because two other preachers had homes there. When our house was finished, Father planted fruit trees in the ample yard and a row of maples down the grassy road out front. Some of these trees still survive, but our old house was sadly sagging when last I saw it.

That road in front of our house was the scene of a near catastrophe one day when I enterprisingly hitched the baby carriage to my play wagon and started coasting for the bottom. My newest baby sister, Laura, riding in the carriage, was too young to care when her part of the train broke loose and sped past me. Fortunately, I caught up and managed to be at the bottom of the pile when the upset came.

My closest companion of those Lafayette days was Chester Gates. We met first the morning Chester brought his small brown dog up from his house at the bottom of the hill; our friendship quickly ripened. Chester's father, a state senator, had been an officer in the United States Army during the Indian wars, and Chester could prove that his dad had been in the thick of some wonderful events, for on his old saber—I saw this more than once with my own eyes—was an awesome spot of red. Blood, of course. Unmistakably the blood of some ferocious Indian chief. Later, more mature consideration suggested that the breath-taking evidence was rust.

Senator Peter Gates was an important citizen in the town, and heavy black cigars were part of his political stock in trade. One bright Saturday afternoon Chester appeared at my house with two of these and, for a bonus, a half plug of Honey Drip chewing tobacco. We repaired to the shadows under the wooden bridge spanning Milligan Creek. There, reclining at our ease, safe from all unfriendly scrutiny, we seven- or eight-year-olds went to work on both the cigars and the plug. One or the other would certainly have sufficed, but the combination of riches was irresistible. Did you ever see the real Honey Drip, oozing under the knife of an old general store? For the unknowing, there was invitation in every drip.

Rather sooner than I had planned, I told Chester there were obligations awaiting me at home. Chester did not seek to detain me. Indeed, he and I started away together and with speed rapidly accelerating. As I ran up through Father's garden, I snatched a half-ripe tomato off a vine with the insane idea that something added might hold down what was already there. Swallowing the tomato all but whole, I fell in a heap against our kitchen door. When Mother opened that door, she was sure her first-born was hemorrhaging from the lungs. The doctor was hurriedly summoned, and there was considerable suspense before I was declared to be in basically good health. Bed rest and absolute quiet were prescribed, which meant that I had to miss the oncoming school party. It was some years before Mother learned the true cause of my illness. Then she laughed till she cried. "Oh, Danny boy," she said, "how you paid for that one!"

Chester got out of it a good deal better. First, he did not try the tomato cure. Second, he had presence enough to hie himself off to a friend's house for the recuperation period. As a result, when he appeared at home, his statement that he had no appetite for supper was not considered alarming, and Chester, though still groggy, did not miss the big doings at the schoolhouse.

When Father was building the church I have already described, Chester and I considerably delayed the program. There was a good-sized ditch running by the foundations and one afternoon during a thundershower we built a dam across it. By our lights the engineering project was a great success, for it quickly turned the foundations into a reservoir. Next day we took a different view. There was no way to drain the water and there were no pumps available. Chester and I had much less fun hand-dipping the water out than we had had watching it rush in.

After our boyhood experiences together, Chester and I together committed our lives to Jesus Christ. In the years that followed he became a successful pastor of churches, an inspiring leader of young people, a popular speaker at Christian Endeavor conferences, and a district superintendent in the Evangelical United Brethren Church. When he was about nine, Chester once told me in great confidence that he intended to become President of the United States. Eventually, as the outstanding representative of his denomination in the Pacific Northwest, I'm sure that Dr. Gates felt he had achieved a distinction even greater.

Another vivid memory of my Lafayette period is of Chester Gates's father the day his idol, John L. Sullivan, was defeated by Gentleman Jim Corbett in New Orleans. The senator was splitting rails and building a fence perhaps a mile from town, and Chester was to bring him the news just as soon as it was telephoned from Portland. The one telephone in Lafayette was in the saloon. Though our family hated liquor always, I remember my father remarking of this particular saloonkeeper, "If we have to have the place, there couldn't be a more decent fellow to run it." As soon as the incredible word of the great John L.'s defeat came over the line, Chester and I left on the run. When the senator heard our story he collapsed on the nearest stump. He just couldn't believe it—nor, of course could the rest of the country.

Sullivan later went off the scene delivering heavy blows against his real conqueror. In Camden, New Jersey, at a temperance mass meeting, I heard him thunder that "Corbett didn't defeat me—John Barleycorn did!"

In after years I became acquainted with Corbett in New

York. He was indeed a gentleman, and there were no noticeable marks upon his handsome face even after his career as the greatest defensive boxer in the heavyweight division.

Lafayette, when I was a lad, was a pioneer settlement, still conscious of its origins. I knew the wooden hitching post where Lieutenant Ulysses S. Grant, fresh out of West Point, had tied his pony during the period when he was located at the nearby Grande Round Indian Reservation. Phil Sheridan and O. O. Howard were later users of that same post. And one afternoon Father took me to a log barn and introduced me to the remains of a covered wagon. There in the old barn he told me its story. It had rolled down the Oregon Trail in a great train of wagons. He told me of how at night it was one in a circle of wagons, with the communal fire burning in the center while mounted guards rode out from the circle in all directions. After the simple meal, Father said, there would be prayers, following which the pioneers would sing together "Rock of Ages." In the morning, before dawn, the wagons would break the circle and roll on westward.

Father was a grand storyteller and I was an eager listener. He told me of the woman who had once sat on the wagon's high seat with a child by her side, another in her arms, and yet another under her heart, while her husband, riding close by the front wheel, directed the boy who drove the horses. During the years I was growing up in Lafayette, I came to know some of the pioneers who had ridden in that train. Their story is as vivid to me now as my memory of Father telling it. Once I climbed into that high seat, sat under the the torn, dusty canvas, and relived the heroic tale for myself. It was the story of those who opened the wilderness and possessed it at last. It was the story of the builders of our unique freedom with all its institutions of church and home and school, of industry and government.

My formal education, begun in Portland, continued in Lafayette. Maggie Boone, my teacher, was a proven disciplinarian, but somehow I was not deterred by my abstract knowledge of her firm wrist and hazel switch. One day, with a contraband blowpipe, I proceeded to plaster the schoolroom's fir-board ceiling with moist paper wads, just over the head of the lad known as Teacher's Pet (a title never applied to me in Lafayette or anywhere else!). Maggie caught me cold. Laying hold of my collar, she drew me to the front of the room where the rest could profit by an unobstructed view of my well-deserved punishment. When I went home that evening I did my best to appear the same boy I had set out. Unfortunately, Maggie had landed one of her wallaps off-target and nipped me under the chin. Father saw the red welt and I had to confess. The Boones, as it happened, were next-door neighbors and Maggie was Mother's close friend. Mother knew her to be a good and fair woman, with an unyielding commitment to what she believed was her duty. Father listened to my story, in which I tried valiantly to make wet wads on a schoolroom ceiling seem an important part of the curriculum. Then he turned me over his knee and added to the dose.

In these days of what is called progressive education a Maggie Boone, I feel certain, would find herself sued by irate parents and out of a job before the close of the term. However, I remember her only with gratitude. *Discipline* is too often the forgotten word in the vocabulary of the twentieth-century home and classroom. With discipline out, disrespect and worse move in. As will be seen later, I continued the example of my father when I paddled my own sons, and though one of them complained at the time that my method was unsound, as grown men they both thanked me.

Some other sounds and sights of those early Lafayette years carry clear in memory: The weird high calling of the peacocks on the Burbank place. The great white house in which old Mr. Burbank, a pioneer merchant, sat beneath the painted portrait of a girl—the daughter, it was said, who had tragically disappeared in the surf at Seaside on the north Oregon coast. The ringing sound of horse-hoofs on the planks of the bridge across Milligan Creek—a night sound; one I loved to hear as I drifted to sleep. My mother's gentle voice reading me stories from *The Youth's Companion.* Often she read me to sleep and sometimes, because she was utterly weary at the end of her day of children and house, she read herself there ahead of me.

Another memory concerns "Father" Moore, one of my earliest and best adult friends. Whenever a new baby was coming at home, I was sent to stay with Father Moore in Pleasantville. From him I learned three good things: how to weed potatoes, how to split knots, and how to phrase a concise prayer. In the morning, after he read aloud a chapter of the Book, he prayed, and always in his prayer was this sentence: "Help me to plow a straight furrow." Even as a youngster I was impressed by the inclusiveness of that one.

When I split oakwood for Father Moore it seemed to me there was a knot in every stick. "Give me the ax," he said one morning after watching my floundering attempts. He set the knot on edge, swung the blade high, and brought it down on the center of the knot. The halves flew apart. "That's the way to split a knot, Danny," he said. It was a memorable lesson, and somehow, though the old man said no more, I gathered that he wanted me to remember the technique for its figurative application to other problems.

Finally, I recall the night that was to have marked my first appearance as a public speaker. The occasion was a program at the Lafayette school. I had practiced my recitation in our chicken yard and cow barn and had it thoroughly committed, expression, gestures, and all. Even so, I felt flutters within me as I entered the schoolhouse for the proving. As the moment came near when I would be called to the platform, to be heard and judged by Maggie Boone and my classmates and all the assembled elders, I became increasingly frightened. Suddenly, I gave my parents the unmistakable sign and headed for the exit. When my name was called there was no Danny Poling present to respond. Alone, I walked the roads and paths around that little town until nearly dawn. Then hunger and weariness, a greater force than the fear that had sent me out, drove me home. I found a welcome there from my parents, and no other punishment than that which had been self-inflicted.

Mixed in among these Lafayette memories are the earliest memories of my life in Portland. One has to do with seeing, and disapproving of, my first United States President. After his election, Benjamin Harrison came to the city on a triumphal tour. The year was 1889 or '90. His Southern Pacific train, drawn by a flag-bedecked engine, stopped on the East Side. Father lifted me to his shoulder to give me a good view of the man over the heads of the crowd. Frankly, I was disappointed. As he stood on the rear platform, bowing and lifting his tall silk hat, there was a cigar in his left hand. This was several years before Chester Gates and I embarked on our brief careers as smokers, but still I felt that Harrison's stogie spoiled the picture. Nevertheless, I overcame my aversion, remained a Republican, and supported Harrison against Cleveland when he ran again in 1892. I wore the great man's button, parroted the arguments I had heard in favor of the McKinley tariffs, and, laboring under the belief that the same man ran indefinitely, informed everyone that I would vote for Harrison when I grew up. (During World War II, as we shall see, I helped re-elect our nearest approximation to a perpetual President.) When Harrison lost to Cleveland, the Democrat, I knew political defeat for the first time. Nothing, I was sure in my eight-year-old heart, could never be right again. But I was to experience defeat-by-ballot much more intimately in a later year when I ran for governor of the Buckeye State, and still later when I aspired to become mayor of Philadelphia.

Another notable American I first saw in Portland was William Jennings Bryan, certainly the most eloquent of the many political figures I have known. After McKinley had defeated him for the presidency he came to Portland and addressed an open-air meeting in Multonomah Field. Not a supporter of Bryan, I had worn a McKinley-Hobart button and marched valiantly in the Republican torchlight parades carrying the symbolic full dinner pail. Nonetheless, from a distance, I was already somewhat under the Bryan spell.

My earliest job, beginning in my tenth year, was as street salesboy for the *Oregonian* and the *Telegram*. The afternoon Bryan came to speak, I was waiting at the gates to the field with my papers under my arm. The distinguished visitor arrived in a shining carriage, seated with the governor of the state and the mayor of the city. I remember his striking handsomeness, his expansive, captivating smile, and the wide-brimmed hat that he continually lifted from his head to acknowledge the crowd's cheers. As the gates swung open a sudden impulse took hold of me. I dropped my papers, shot out of the crowd, and dove headlong at the rear end of that carriage. Catching hold of the axle, I swung up underneath and hung on. It was a stunt I was glad Father and Mother were not present to see. In less time than it takes to tell, I was in the center of the field, standing close against the dignitaries' platform, my chin level with the spot where Bryan stood to make his address. Do not ask why I was not taken in hand and led away; I can only report that I was not.

When the orator finished, he stooped and grasped my upstretched hand. I, Danny Poling, was first. What a moment that was in one boy's life! Years afterward, introducing Bryan at a Christian Endeavor convention in Ohio I told this story of our first meeting. It seemed to please him greatly. What I did not reveal was that I had not voted for him in the 1908 presidential campaign. Though I admired and loved the man, I had not agreed with his platform.

I met Bryan on numerous occasions during my mature years and heard him speak at least a dozen times. He was a matchless orator. During the 1904 campaign I heard him in support of Alton B. Parker, the Democratic presidential candidate, at an open-air meeting in South Bend, Indiana. Arriving late, I stood at the edge of the crowd, far behind Bryan. That day I paid particular attention to a certain quality that enabled incredibly large audiences to hear that golden voice even though it was never amplified artificially. Besides his inflection and his manifest sincerity, Bryan seemed to have the ventriloquist's power of projection, though on a grand scale. He could be heard perfectly by his farthest listener and, as I can testify, by those who could see nothing but his distant back. In the idiom of my college speech professor, David Metzger, Bryan "got it out."

Something Bryan said in that earlier Portland speech I still remember. He paid a tribute to America, land of free men, in which it was possible to survive an election without a revolution and then go forward without permanent bitterness. When he said that, the crowd was his. Years later, I heard Bryan in Canton, Ohio. Canton's favorite son, his opponent of 1896, was dead and buried but not at all forgotten. That day, on his first appearance in McKinley's home town, the Great Commoner was at his understanding best. As I remember them, these were his words: "Once I entertained the hope that I would be elected to the presidency of the United States. That hope was vain. But next to being elected was the distinction of being defeated by so great and good a man, your fellow townsman, William McKinley." Then and thereafter, Bryan owned Canton.

Portland, like Lafayette, was a rough frontier town in my childhood, and its toughness was not exclusively an adult characteristic. My East Side elementary school, Stevens Addition, would probably be closed today as a delinquent institution. When I first went there, trouble was more the rule than education. Across the gravel street was the firehouse; whenever the gong began to ring, all classes would surge to the windows to watch the smoke-belching engine roll out, drawn by its team of grays. Only after the last hoofbeat had died away would classwork resume. Things improved when the Board of Education made Professor Davis our principal. Although the memory of a six-year-old is perhaps not to be trusted, I remember Davis as a big man with a tight, scrubby mustache and his hair in a stiff pompadour. But physically big or not, the bad boys promptly moved in on him. The way he cleaned up the situation in that school made him a legendary figure. He seldom used the strap, although discipline by ruler and strap had been a substantial part of the curriculum heretofore. Occasionally he had to go the strap one better and resolve situations with swinging fists. His approach was the right one. Parents complained, of course, and one of the leading citizens even protested to the mayor. However, Davis was not intimidated, and he won through so completely that in less than two years Stevens became a model school.

Davis could be something more than a disciplinarian and an educator. The day my sister May died I was in the first grade at

Stevens. I walked in fear as my teacher led me from my class to the principal's office and to his desk. Though I had trembled on other occasions when he passed by, I found him now, in our first real meeting, one of the gentlest men I had ever known. He said little, but with one arm around my shoulders he comforted me as only a deeply understanding man could comfort a bewildered, suffering child.

Professor Davis went to Alaska a few years later, seeking his fortune in the gold fields. I never heard of him again and do not now remember that I ever knew the rest of his name, but among the many educators I have known he has a first place.

Two other Stevens teachers placed their signs upon me. Mary Donohoe made me into a student. She was a native of Virginia, born in the Valley, and her father had fought with Lee. Mary made me proud of my country without making me blind to its unfinished work. How deeply this gracious, beautiful, and wise young woman affected me may be suggested by the fact that my first daughter bears her given name. In the later years when I returned to Portland to visit my mother, Mary Donohoe was always second on the list. When Mother was no longer there to meet me, Mary was first. Her kind of teaching prompts a decisive negative reply to the question, "Do women teachers feminize boys?" She had her students going out to win victories on the athletic field, and afterward many of them went on to perform with distinction on the world's battlefields. In 1943 I spent an evening with Admiral Dan Barbey, a Naval hero of the Pacific landings. In the harbor at Hollandia, New Guinea, we momentarily forgot the war while we reminisced about brown-eyed Mary Donohoe.

From Mary's room in Stevens Addition I moved into the domain of Lilly Thomas—and a domain it proved to be, with Lilly ruling firmly. Her contribution to my life was both direct and indirect. She was a dedicated teacher and she could not be deceived. Either you had your lesson or you didn't. If you tried, she met you better than halfway; if you bluffed, she set you down with an irony that was something to experience—and avoid in the future. Today, having passed ninety, Lilly Davey Thomas is as dynamic and clear-minded in her Christian Americanism as she was so long ago when she first inspired me. A letter from her, written in the familiar, firm, sweeping hand, sends my head up and my eyes front as once her face and words challenged me in the schoolroom.

One deeply educational experience of my Portland period had nothing to do with school. With a half-dozen companions I stopped at an apple orchard I didn't own and climbed into one of the trees, intending to supply the waiting hands and pockets beneath me. Looking down from the heights, I suddenly found myself alone. Well, not quite alone. There, leaning on the fence, was George Ormsby, the Sunday-school superintendent in my father's church and just about the most important man in the community. The apples were his. "Come on down, Danny," he said. And I obeyed, even though his kindly smile did not entirely kill my desire to remain high in his tree.

"You like apples, don't you?" he went on. "But these are green, and anyway, you wouldn't want to take them, would you? Not without asking? Come with me." And we went together to his grocery store where I selected—reluctantly—some ripe apples. He sent me home with them, saying, "Give a couple to your father. Tell him Brother Ormsby sent them." That was all. But was it all? How I loved that man afterward! Had he been less understanding, I suppose that day would still seem among the worst of my childhood.

Outstanding among the friends of my own age was Ben Morrow. I first met him when, a twelve-year-old, he came delivering milk to our house—milk from the cows his family pastured in what is now just a crowded section of the old Stevens Addition. Ben was so thin then that he looked as if he might not hold together. Our friendship grew. We finished grade school together and went on to high school together. I enjoyed a memorable summer vacation with Ben. Today you can drive from Portland to the Salmon River at the base of Mount Hood in little more than an hour. In those days it was quite a trip. We started in the evening in a horse-drawn wagon and put up the first night with some of Ben's relatives. When we finally arrived at our destination, sweated and covered with dust, we looked not unlike the Indians who were huckleberrying about our campsite. The trout fishing in that beautiful river was a joy, and we had plenty to cook when we were hungry. One weekend Ben's brother came up to camp with a friend. Ben and I had a great time planting burrs under their cotton sheets and then listening to the comments in the adjoining tent when we all turned in. We got ours in the morning when, dragged suddenly from our beds, we were drenched with buckets of icy spring water.

Ben's path and mine parted when Father moved us back to Lafayette in 1898, but I found him again in France in 1918, where he had gone with the First Oregon Engineers. In Brest, Ben superintended the building of a great reservoir that remained as the American contribution to that city when the war was over. After returning to Portland Ben became the city's chief engineer, and the great dam that holds the flow of water from Bull Run Lake, the city's original supply, carries his name on a memorial plaque.

The first long journey of my childhood took me across the continent to visit Father's people in South Fork, Pennsylvania, and Mother's in Indiana. I was seven. Nothing suitable having been discovered in the latest missionary shipment, Father extravagantly bought me a brown derby hat. I detested it. Between Portland and Spokane I stuck my head out of the train window, and that, of course, was the last of the wretched thing. "Now, young man," Father said sternly, "you'll go bareheaded for the rest of the trip." and I did—carefully concealing how little I regretted the condition.

Grandfather Poling, born in Virginia, while still very young became a circuit rider with a tremendous parish that reached from the Potomac River to Lake Erie. The rigors of his calling were equaled only by the hardships his wife endured as she mothered his eight children in a log cabin while he rode the wilderness, preaching and ministering to the westward-moving pioneers. When I knew Grandfather he was an old man, austere but wholly lovable. I heard him repeat the scriptural passage that in the days of his youth and poverty had been his pillow text, the verse that had sent him off to sleep in his cabin. The same verse had been his comfort when he bedded down his horse and rolled into his blankets under some great tree: "I have been young and now I am old; yet have I not seen the righteous forsaken nor his seed begging bread."

Grandmother had her memories too, and she would smile and nod that her husband was right. "It was so," she said, "even when the salary he seldom saw was seventy-five dollars a year." Her hands, with those of her children, made up the deficit from the cow, the pigs, the garden, the orchard. Once, in West Virginia, I saw the spot where Grandfather Poling's cabin had stood, and I saw the stumps of the trees he had planted between his missions, and that his family had pruned and tended and picked the fruit from at last.

Grandfather Kring, Mother's father, was still an Evangelical pastor when I met him. He wore a full, dark, curly beard and was a gentler type than my other grandfather. He had Mother's intuitions with children. As we drove through the countryside together in his buggy, I listened eagerly to his stories that, like as not, would begin, "When I was a little boy your age in the Allegheny Mountains, the Indians would come to our cabin and I would play with their children . . ."

Two years later this gentle man was dead, and we again traveled east to be with his ailing widow. While Mother nursed her through that burning summer, I did light chores on Mother's uncle's farm, just outside Hicksville, Ohio. One experience there I shall never forget.

I had been set to planting pumpkin seeds in Cousin Wesley's corn rows when posters appeared announcing a circus on Saturday afternoon. It couldn't have been much of a circus, for Hicksville was a very small town, but to a boy who had never seen a circus it promised to be Barnum and Bailey and Ringling Brothers and all the rest combined. I knew there was no chance of my getting inside the big tent, since I didn't even have popcorn money, but I had a reasonable hope that I might see the parade. Cousin Wesley agreed that if I could finish planting the seeds in the field down the lane from the barn, I might walk the two miles to town. I redoubled my efforts at once, but it soon became apparent that I would never make it. Too many seeds, too little time.

Nevertheless, I appeared at dinner time, ready to go with or without eating first. To Uncle John's question (and he was a kindly man), "Did you plant *all* the seeds?" I replied, looking him in the eye, "Yes, I planted *all* the seeds." And so I saw the parade with its one mangy lion. To me, he was magnificent. I saw the one elephant and the one tiger and the beautiful ladies in short skirts on white horses, and I heard the calliope play. There were clowns too, although to me these foolish fellows were decidedly less interesting than the more serious attractions.

Encouraged by a friendly contemporary I met in the crowd, I followed the parade to the tent and made a try at entering same without payment. My new friend and I were achieving excellent progress (heads in, tails out), when we were detected and ingloriously pulled out.

Certain thoughts having nothing to do with the circus began to trouble me on my long walk back to the farm. But a boy's mind is versatile and his conscience may quiet down if he simply ignores it. I slept well. Some three weeks later Uncle John and Cousin Wesley cordially invited me to take a walk with them. I knew precisely where our stroll would end even before we headed in the direction of the cornfield down behind the barn. Across those ten acres of corn we traveled, an elderly man, his thoughtful son, and a small boy with heavy feet. In the field's far corner was a pile of stones and farm debris. Usually it presented an ugly, even depressing appearance. That day, pumpkin vines everywhere, it looked like the hanging gardens of old Babylon.

Ever since retribution came to me in that Ohio cornfield, the familiar Bible text "Be sure your sins will find you out" has read for me "Be sure your pumpkin seeds will find you out."

All of Father's p.k.'s who lived to the age of going, finally went to college, but Father had to found one college and preside over the destiny of another to get the lot of us through. Lafayette

Seminary, established by Father and his associates in 1889, had me for a student during the last two years of its existence. In 1900 the Seminary merged with another pioneer institution, La-Creole Academy, some thirty miles away in Polk County, and the result was Dallas College.

This meant another move for the Polings. I was made responsible for getting Daisy, our highly valued cow, safely and comfortably to her new home. Mrs. Mae Fletcher gave me a large breakfast and her blessing early in the morning, lent me the Fletcher pony, and off we started. Daisy and I covered the long distance—long for a cow, certainly—just before dark, arriving in Dallas as the train from Portland pulled in. All day I had been reflecting that driving a milk cow across country was not the most stylish occupation for a college man; the feeling was reinforced when the station crowd treated me and my waddling charge to a raucous, humiliating reception.

Up to June, 1904, when I graduated with the first B.A. degree that Dallas conferred, my scholastic record was not of the best. I never threatened a Phi Beta Kappa key, preferred double-breasted suits then and later, and wonder how I ever managed to finish. I did better in athletics, though I suppose I should hesitate to admit it. In 1904 our small school, whose coeducational student body never reached one hundred and fifty, scored an impossible track victory over Willamette University, and this occasion saw me at the high point of my athletic career. I scored firsts in the 50- and the 100-yard dashes, the 880, the broad jump and the high jump, ran anchor quarter in the winning mile relay, took third in the discus, and collapsed in glory. A few months later, the glory was gone. Having moved east in the meantime, I was persuaded to compete in an indoor meet in Johnstown, Pennsylvania. Alas, I had not kept in training, being busy with other matters, and the results were disastrous. It was a lesson for me. A fat and flabby Poling—whether the excess suet was physical or spiritual—would always run a poor race.

At Dallas, needing money to buy my clothes (now that I no longer dressed from missionary boxes!), I worked at various times on the right-of-way gang of the Dallas and Falls City Railroad, in the town lumberyard, on a threshing crew, at hoeing and harvesting in prune orchards, at delivering firewood, and at running the college's laundry route. Fortunately, I did take on one job that called for some substantial use of my gray matter. Carey Hayter, editor and publisher of the *Polk County Observer*, introduced me to journalism and opened the door to my association with the Portland *Oregonian*. As county reporter for that paper I was paid four dollars a column, and my published output was measured monthly. I soon learned that news which was wired in, rather than mailed, was invariably printed. I began to wire everything.

One morning I received a note from Harvey Scott, the editor. Revering Scott as one of the great figures of American journalism, I still treasure his communiqué, which came on copy paper, written and signed with his stub pencil: "Dan Poling, you are, of course, indispensable. How could the *Oregonian* get along without you? But if you don't cut down on the wires, we face the alternative of firing you or going out of business—and we shall hope to stay in business."

The *Oregonian* is still in business and I was not fired. I made the adjustment. Later, after I had moved to Ohio and had my first pastorate, I conducted a column of general-interest questions and answers for the *Oregonian*'s editorial page.

Of my Dallas teachers I particularly remember David M. Metzger—and across the world today I know there are men and women who recall him as fondly as I do. Metzger (who married the widowed mother of Chester Gates, my Lafayette friend) taught us half a dozen subjects, and it was he, more than anyone else, who developed my abilities as a public speaker. With the examples of my father and William Jennings Bryan before me, I might have adopted their styles, but I did not, thanks to Metzger's coaching. "Be yourself," he told me repeatedly. "Get it in, fill up with it, and then let it come out!" He never forced a gesture on me, never indicated the tone I was to use; the impulse was to come from within.

Other Dallas men I fondly recall were Herbert Dunkelberger, who nearly succeeded in teaching me mathematics and who rewarded my efforts by making me best man at his wedding, and C. T. Whittlesey, an Andover-Yale man who was the typical absent-minded professor. His chronic lateness to his classes inspired us to tie a cowbell beneath the chair he habitually shook before sitting down. This utterly sincere and selfless man was marvelously startled when the bell went off, but he took it so nicely that we felt somewhat ashamed.

One of my closest friends during these years was a man ten years older than myself, Fred West. Naturally talented, and a forthright Christian gentleman, Fred was the county seat's engineer, despite the fact that he had no technical training. Later, he owned and operated the electric light plant. He was a faithful confidant, a man with an understanding of younger men's problems. Our relationship was so close that Fred gave his only son my name. One Sunday afternoon on a South Pacific island, years later, just before Douglas MacArthur's return to the Philippines, I stood beside the commanding officer, General Boyd, while three of his young officers were decorated for courage beyond the call of duty. One of the three, a major, was an engineer. I did not hear his full name when the citation was read, but afterward, when he came and stood with me during the review, he asked, "Are you the Oregon Dan Poling?" He was Fred West's son, my namesake, Daniel Poling West.

As a young fellow, inspired by the examples I had seen within my own family, I came to the decision that I wanted my life to count for the most it could. To my mind this meant at first a career in law, and most of my thinking in college was directed to this end. Judge John Allen, of Portland, even had a desk waiting for me.

But this road I was not to take. In my senior year at Dallas I heard the high call of my Christian faith—a call that captured and mastered me. But even then, despite the number of Polings and Krings who had found their ways into pulpits, my serious thoughts of the ministry were associated with teaching. At this time my favorite aunt, my father's youngest sister, Irene, was an educational missionary in China. In the spring of 1904, at a

Y.M.C.A. conference at Gearhardt Park, on the coast, I became a student volunteer for overseas missions, fully expecting that I too would be sent out to China.

Almost at the same time, however, I was licensed to preach by the Oregon Conference of the United Evangelical Church. In those years my church did not absolutely require a seminary course. Although I had no formal theological training (and had little later on, for I was never a seminary man), I was considered to have some ability and consecration. As an unlicensed student, in the fall of 1903, I had briefly supplied the pulpit of the United Evangelical Church at Independence, Oregon, ten miles from Dallas. It was the custom to kneel. One Sunday after a Saturday-night basketball game, Dallas against Oregon State, I was so banged up that I could not get down to my knees. I remember wondering if my little congregation thought I was backsliding so soon. On Thanksgiving Day there was a blizzard, and I preached to three adults, including the janitor, and one infant. Since it was bitter cold, we forsook the benches and the pulpit and I delivered my carefully prepared sermon back by the stove where we could all sit in comfort.

It was in this background that the would-be lawyer became the committed preacher. I gave my first sermon as a licentiate in a little frame church at Rickreall, between Dallas and Salem, in the spring of 1904. My friend Professor Herbert Dunkelberger went with me to bolster my courage and to lead the singing. Not many of my texts do I remember, but that first one I cannot forget: "Let this mind be in you which also was in Christ Jesus your Lord."

My graduating class at Dallas numbered four, and I was definitely the fourth, preceded by my sister Ethel, who finished the music course with credit, and the two talented Allen sisters, who carried the honors. Dallas struggled on until the early 1920s, when it perished from lack of financial support, but not before giving infinite benefits to a goodly number of us. A. Ralph Van Orsdel, who graduated a year later than I and went on to become a distinguished lawyer, once said to me: "Dallas gave me, out of her limitations, values that the University of Nebraska and the University of Michigan could not duplicate." He was seeing beyond the college's shortage of materials and poverty of equipment to the spirit of the professors and the intimate ties that bound mind to mind and heart to heart. The small liberal arts Christian college is, beyond duplication elsewhere in the world, a unique American institution. If I owned a billion dollars, for the largest returns to God and country, I would conceive of no better place to invest them than in institutions like Dallas.

In the summer of 1904, Father, always a restless soul, decided it was time to break his ties of twenty years in Oregon and return to the Pittsburgh Conference, the place of his ministerial origin. Going east with the family, I intended to take post-graduate work at Johns Hopkins in economics, sociology, and philosophy, thus to prepare myself for my educational mission in China. As we shall see, these great plans came to naught.

Before we left my last Oregon home, the cottage on the high bank of the Rickreall, I made a pilgrimage to Independence, where I had preached as a student. My mission was to give my small white King Charles spaniel, Jolly, into the loving care of my friends and hers, the Boydsons. For neither of us was it to be an easy parting. Jolly had been with me since my seventh year. She had gone through college with me. I remembered the night we had first met, when she had begun by biting my finger as I tried to pull her out from under a sofa. I remembered the time in Lafayette when I thought she had run away, but she had only crept under the porch to have her first litter of pups. There were countless litters in the years thereafter.

At the Boydsons', though deaf and almost blind, Jolly became unusually alert, somehow sensing that we had taken our last journey together. As I held her in my arms, her trusting eyes turned to mine and I could hardly bring myself to leave her. Two days later, after we had departed from Dallas, Jolly disappeared from the Boydson house and traveled the ten miles to where she hoped to find me. Disappointed, she returned and died quietly before the fire in the friendly home that could not satisfy her.

Later, I put my recollections of Jolly into an admittedly sentimental poem. It never won me any prizes in verse competitions, but even today its lines bring that wistful little face vividly back to me:

> I remember well that first glad day,
> In a summer long ago,
> When she cuddled her way to my boyish heart:
> A queer little bunch of snow.
> I hugged her close in my chubby arms,
> And leapt for very joy;
> For she was a wee little puppy dog then,
> And I was a wee little boy.

After leaving the Willamette Valley, Mother, Father, my three sisters, my two brothers, and I traveled to Portland by train and then took a river steamer up the Columbia to The Dalles. Our stop here was for a farewell visit with our father's younger brother, Daniel V. Poling, who was pastor of the Congregational Church there, an historic institution that went back to the days of Marcus Whitman. "D.V.," as we and indeed most of Oregon called him, was more than an uncle to me. With his wealth of talents, he was the hero of my boyhood. His crooked mouth, oddly enough, made him especially attractive to me. He made the finest kites any boy ever flew. An accomplished pitcher in Pennsylvania before he came to Lafayette as a young minister under my father, D.V. introduced the curved ball to Oregon, and more important, taught his disciples how to control it. D.V.'s team stood all the neighboring towns on their heads. Again, he was an amateur boxer of no mean skill, and he owned the stallion Multonomah, a glorious Hambletonian. When sharp practices in harness racing brought discredit to the state fair, D.V. accepted the governor's frantic call and cleaned up the crooked business. He would even leave the judges' stand, relieve a driver, and drive the horse to its proper record. Because of these worldly activities, D.V. was condemned by some of his ministerial contemporaries and by other good people, but he was beholden to no man. He organized athletic teams and inspired boys to develop their muscles as well as their minds and souls. He lost an eye from a foul tip while umpiring a baseball game, and that in the end, I think, hastened his death. But his inspiration lived after him. From the pastorate he joined the faculty of Oregon State College, and his voice was heard at high school commencements and other convocations throughout the state. Today, on the campus where another Dan Poling, his son, is dean of men, a building bears D.V.'s name.

Soon after he came to Oregon, D.V. had married. Before I ever saw her I was sure I would hate his bride, because my hero would now have to be shared. But when I saw Alice Williams Poling, a vision of loveliness who swept me into her arms, I capitulated without a struggle. It was thoughtful Aunt Alice who gave me Jolly, my dog. Through the years, she bore with me on camping trips, encouraged me to dig out my ears, keep my shoes polished, and generally spared no pains to make a gentleman out of very raw material. My sometimes discouraged mother often remarked that Aunt Alice was her gift from heaven.

Our farewell to D.V. and his family was in effect my farewell to Oregon, and though "I knew it not, nor dreamed it," the parting was final. I returned there often on visits when Father and Mother finally moved back to Portland, and for a generation I looked forward to a time when I would live on the high ground looking up to Mount Hood. But it was not to be. Today, when I cross the Snake River in Idaho or when I fly down or drive through the great gorge of the Columbia, my pulse quickens and often my eyes mist, for always and forever I am a native son. The picture I offered in my high-school verses called "Mount Hood" is still before my eyes whenever I think of Oregon:

> She is monarch of the mountains
>   And sovereign grand sublime,
> Her crown the everlasting snows,
>   Her throne unfathomed time.
> Into the depths of heaven's blue,
>   Her ancient visage peers
> From earth below, from universe—
>   The homage of a million years.

3

The temperance movement in the United States grew out of the antislavery crusade; after the Civil War, almost to a man the abolitionists turned to the liquor problem. My own interest in the movement became strong during my college years. As a youth I had observed the effects of alcoholism both among individuals and groups. I had watched a brilliant young man, the son of a wealthy family, dissipate a promising career and die in an asylum for the insane. Unable to recognize me when I went to visit him for the last time, he sat tying and untying his shoes. I had seen the excesses of the Indians when they bought liquor during the hop-picking seasons and then fought with one another and threatened the peace of the community. The normal reaction to these experiences, intensified by my study of the problem in its general aspects, led me to the conclusion that the national leaders who advocated abolition of the liquor traffic were right.

The Intercollegiate Prohibition Association, which enlisted thousands of young men and women in its crusade, was presented to us at Dallas in the persons of D. Leigh Colvin, an Ohio Wesleyan graduate, and Virgil G. Hinshaw, a Quaker from Penn College, Iowa. The program these men advocated seemed tremendously important; it not only captured me completely but was responsible for some memorable events in my early life.

In July, 1904, after leaving the rest of the family at the old

Poling home in Pennsylvania, Father and I attended the national convention of the Prohibition party, held in the Claypool Hotel in Indianapolis. Here, though under age, I sat as a delegate from Oregon and helped nominate Dr. Silas Swallow as the party's presidential candidate. Swallow's opponent, one-armed General O. O. Howard, the famous Indian fighter and hero of Gettysburg, a great popular favorite, was eloquently supported by the Wendell Phillips of the movement, John G. Wooley. Wooley never recovered from the convention's rejection of his candidate, and he soon withdrew from the party to identify himself with the Anti-Saloon League, then and for another decade bitterly opposed by the Prohibition party as an "instrument of compromise."

Aside from the clash of personalities, the chief difference between the party and the League was the party's uncompromising insistence upon national prohibition as the only possible solution. The League advocated local option, leading to county option, state prohibition, and finally national prohibition. The eventual burying of the hatchet brought the party, the League, and the Woman's Christian Temperance Union together in the National Temperance Council, of which organization I became first chairman, serving through the campaign that resulted in the adoption of the Eighteenth Amendment in 1919. But this is running ahead of my story.

After the Indianapolis convention Father and I attended camp meetings in southern and central Ohio, Father as guest preacher, I as participant in the youth services. These meetings were held in huge tents on the outskirts of towns, and whole families came to them by train, trolley, or horse and buggy, sometimes staying for days at a time in cottages and smaller tents. There would be special play programs for the children while their parents took part in the big citizenship and temperance rallies and listened to addresses by state governors or other imported politicians who were known to be drys. It was in meetings of this sort—though not in the particular ones that Father and I were involved in—that Billy Sunday struck his mighty blows against John Barleycorn. I saw him in action numerous times in Ohio and elsewhere.

A tall, wiry man, he had been a professional baseball player, and his base-running record with the Chicago White Sox still stands after more than sixty years. More than once I saw him do a base slide halfway across a platform to make a point. He was easily one of the most colorful of all our evangelists. Once in Columbus, he stopped in the middle of a prayer, saying, "Pardon me, Lord, I'll be back in a minute." Then he called to the ushers to get some fresh air into the tabernacle. "Open up everything," he commanded. When the ventilation was improved to his satisfaction, he picked up his conversation with the Lord at the point where he had left off.

Some people thought that such tactics bordered on blasphemy, but from Sunday's great meetings, and from many other meetings of the same general kind across the country, there came much of the conviction about liquor that helped dry up three quarters of the nation's area well before prohibition became the national law. The crowds that attended our meetings in Ohio were sometimes overwhelming. I remember particularly a day at Highland Park, between Canton and Akron, when ten thousand people gathered for one Sunday service. Vehicles and horses converged upon that dedicated hilltop from a dozen miles around, and the dust hung overhead in clouds.

One day, between meetings, I drove with Father to the village of East Liberty, Ohio, which had been the parish of Grandfather Poling when my father, before his marriage, taught his first term of school in a nearby community. I had grown up hearing about East Liberty for this reason and for another, for it was the home of the Dutch-German Vandersalls. Their great brick house, built on a hill above a famous spring, had always been open to Evangelical preachers and their families. Father and Dan Vandersall had been schoolmates and close friends. My Oregon uncle, a good deal younger than Father, had been named Daniel Vandersall Poling.

Dan Vandersall's mother was still living, and Father wished to see her again and to have me with him. For Father, the visit was a welcome renewal of links to the past; for me, it proved a momentous glimpse of my future. At age ninety-five, Grandmother, as we both called her, was in bed with a broken hip, but she rejoiced in our coming and the hour of our stay soon passed. After Father read a lesson from the Scriptures, we knelt beside Grandmother's bed for prayer. As Father prayed, the outer door of an adjoining room opened and closed, and so it was that I rose from my knees that late afternoon looking into the face of the most beautiful girl I had ever seen. In that moment, before she even spoke, I learned that the idea of love at first sight was no mere flippancy.

Nearly two years older than I was, and gray-eyed, soft-spoken, with cheeks that dimpled when she smiled, Susan Jane Vandersall was the eldest daughter of my father's old schoolmate. Petite—one inch over five feet tall—Susie was as exquisite as Dresden china, and to me she was irresistible. As we stood talking by her grandmother's bed, I was completely won by her graciousness, her gentleness, and by a subtle something that was already calling us to each other. She made me feel that I belonged near her, and with an overwhelming rush of conviction I knew that I had met the one I would ask to become my wife. I wanted to linger, to know her better, but now Father's visit to the old house was finished and we drove away, back to our camp meetings. For a year I did not see Susie again, but I was filled with the certainty that she would one day share my life. The thought that I might propose and find myself rejected did not enter my head.

My plans for attending Johns Hopkins University collapsed when the Board of Foreign Missions of my church, which had complete charge of my career at this time, sent me, not to Canton, China, but to Canton, Ohio. Here I was given my first church—Trinity United Evangelical—as a young licentiate under Rev. Noah W. Sager. At first I was terribly disappointed, feeling that things had gone decidedly wrong; I had volunteered to be a missionary and a teacher, not a minister at home. But today, looking back on this and other sudden changes, I am struck by the mysterious way one event followed another to give a course to my life that I could never have foreseen.

Trinity was in Canton's factory district, and I was not only the church's pastor but its janitor and repairman as well, a combination that many people, including myself, soon regretted. One day, revarnishing all the benches, I used the wrong mix. It seemed to dry satisfactorily, but the following Sunday my congregation became almost permanently attached. Another time, while I was away on vacation, attending a series of camp meetings, my devoted friend Deacon Betz conceived the idea of papering the pulpit alcove. He selected a paper that he believed to be particularly appropriate, since the motif featured angels. Unfortunately, Betz was nearsighted, and the surprise he prepared for me was better than he knew. Returning from my trip just in time to hold the Sunday morning service, I, the unmarried nineteen-year-old minister, found cupids, complete with bows and arrows, swarming about my head. A repapering job was done on Monday.

Not all my experiences at Trinity were of a humorous cast. It was here that I had my first call to cope with the problems of death in one of its most heartrending forms. A little girl, a member of my Sunday school, came running to me one day, saying through her tears, "Daddy wants you to come quick!" When I reached the girl's home, I found her mother dying of peritonitis. The grieving husband sat nearby; the six small children were all weeping around the bed, the smallest one sitting on the pillow beside her mother's head. The young woman knew she was dying, and her mind remained clear right up to her last gasp. Feeling my inexperience and my inadequacy, I prayed with her. Afterward, I consoled the stricken father and his children as best I could, but this was an appalling load for an untried minister. The experience stays with me as one of the most difficult of my entire ministry, even though I found that the One whom I seek to serve gave me the answers.

Later, a similar case had a happier outcome. One day I was called to a home of great poverty where a little boy was suffering in the last stages of pneumonia. Unconscious, yet crying out with each labored breath, the suffering child seemed ready to die. The doctor, having done all he could, had already left the house. The distraught young mother cried out to me, begging for help, while her husband held her in his arms and tried to comfort her.

Only a few times in all my ministry have I ever felt impelled to appeal in prayer for an abrupt decision in a sickness, and then only when there was an irresistible "leading." Remembering the lesson I had learned when my brother Rudolph could not be healed for me, I have in all such cases waited for the word that Mary, mother of Jesus, said to His disciples at the marriage in Cana of Galilee: "Whatsoever He sayeth unto thee, do it!"

That day, in that humble home, I sensed the leading—a feeling that prayer would give me an answer for the boy. Kneeling, placing my hand on that fairly scorching brow, I prayed. I prayed not for the boy's healing but that God's will might be done. Incredible as it may seem, the boy began to grow better almost at once. Before I rose from his bedside it was apparent that the crisis had passed and that he would recover. But this brought up a new problem, which I only dimly foresaw as the exhausted mother poured out her thanks. Within a few hours the story had been told and retold around the community, the one significant recovery had mushroomed into a series, and I found that I had to deal with an undeserved reputation as a professional faith healer. And deal with it I did, for I was never that. I had done only what I learned to do the day my brother died—I had asked in Christ's name for the fulfillment of God's will.

Often through the years I have envied the sincere men and women who have been able to heal. Although the promise in James that "The prayer of faith shall save the sick" has been employed by many charlatans, it has also been the saving of countless "incurables." Jesus Christ, who healed in Judea and Galilee, is still the Great Physician, and God is not baffled even when our most skilled doctors and surgeons may be. But to me the healing gift was never granted, save in a limited way. Perhaps God had other tasks for me.

In the summer of 1905, at the annual conference of our church, held in Greensburg, Ohio, I again looked into the face that for a year had followed me in my thoughts. As I preached the conference sermon on Sunday night, Susie Vandersall sat with her Aunt Sarah directly in front of me. Later that evening we had our first real visit together. Susie promised to send me her picture, and the promise was kept. Years later, our son Clark, who loved this picture above all other likenesses of his mother, persuaded me to part with it. He kept it with him always, and I feel sure that it was with him when, in the North Atlantic, he went to his death in World War II.

After a year at Trinity I took a leave in order to accept the insistent invitation of the Intercollegiate Prohibition Association, which wanted me as a college visitor. For a brief period I toured the major colleges and universities of the eastern seaboard and the Midwest. In the late spring of 1906 the Board of Missions of my denomination sent me back to Canton, where I filled out the unexpired term of Noah Sager, he having followed my father's example and transferred to the Oregon Conference.

My ministry in Canton brought me near enough to East Liberty that I could press my suit with Susie Vandersall. Although we had been corresponding for some time, I was a late arrival in a crowded field and I knew it. One of my rivals, also a preacher, allowed it to be known that he was purchasing the ring. The news quickly reached me. The following Saturday I attended a Sunday-school picnic near Akron and took the East Liberty church organist for a prolonged boat ride on Cottage Lake—Susie being that musician. Afterward, I invited myself to her home for supper. Susie then offered to have the buggy hitched up so that she could drive me to Uniontown, from which point I could take the interurban electric car back to Canton. I accepted . . . and could have caught that train but didn't. Instead, I returned to the old brick house in East Liberty with my promised bride and told our glad story to her startled family.

While our courtship was brief, in reality it had been progressing through years—generation after generation. Our fathers had been friends, and although we grew up and went to school a wide continent apart, we "knew" each other, or at least we knew that the other one existed. Both of my preacher grandfathers had been ministers of the Vandersall family, and both had been entertained in that old brick house. In the few weeks after our engagement and before our marriage Susie and I had many happy times together, taking long walks across the hills and through the woods or buggy rides along the country roads, and visiting the Vandersall relatives and friends.

We were married on September 25, 1906. Two days before, at our church's annual conference, this time held in Carey, Ohio, I was ordained a deacon. From the conference Father and I, with Bishop H. B. Hartzler, went to the Vandersall house. Bishop Hartzler performed the ceremony. Susie came to meet me down the old stairway, looking lovelier in her wedding gown than I could have believed possible, even for her. Susie's sister Ora was the bridesmaid, and her cousin Stanley B. Vandersall, later to be my associate in the International Society of Christian Endeavor and in the World's Christian Endeavor Union, was my best man.

Our wedding trip took us to Le Mars, Iowa, where Father, having moved on from Pennsylvania, was now president of Western Union College (later West Mar College). We then returned to our parsonage in Canton. It was not our home for long, for in the fall of 1907 we were sent to Columbus, where I was appointed student pastor of the Wesley Avenue United Evangelical Church.

Entering Ohio State University as a graduate student, I found my program of advanced study broken off in less than a year when the pressure of my work made continuance impossible. My most valuable experience at Ohio State came from the work of Dr. William Henry Scott, head of the Department of Philosophy, who took me through Kant's *Critique of Pure Reason* and brought me out a more intelligent and, I believe, a more earnest Christian than when I went in. One of the treasured volumes in my library is Dr. Scott's desk copy of Kant's *Critique* with all his marginal notes. Another of those remarkable men who seem never to grow old, Dr. Scott had been president of the university until his retirement at seventy—after which he continued teaching in the Department of Philosophy for another twenty years.

When Susie and I discovered that the two in our house were presently to become three, I was receiving a salary of five hundred dollars a year, or a hundred more than Father had made when he was raising me and his eight other p.k.'s. But there was a signal difference: I got my salary while Father was not always paid. Still, I needed more money to make a proper reception for our first-born. I managed to borrow it, and, even better, I managed to repay it, which was harder.

Daniel Kring Poling made his appearance in our Columbus home on July 21, 1908. The so-called practical nurse we had engaged for the delivery impractically had hysterics when she was needed most and had to be dragged from the room and left with a bottle of smelling salts. This made me the doctor's assistant, a role which I learned as I went along. When slippery young Daniel was placed in my arms, I grabbed him by the heels and made him squall as bidden by the doctor, a practical father from the first moment possible.

Two years later, on August 7, 1910, our second son, Clark Vandersall, arrived under conditions that were only slightly less hectic so far as I was concerned. Assured that I could not expect to see our new baby for at least another two weeks, I had gone confidently off to a camp meeting in Pennsylvania. When the telegram reached me indicating the time estimate had been too generous, I began a hasty return to Columbus. In Pittsburgh, with fifteen minutes between trains, I rushed to a telephone and learned that Clark had arrived and that he and his mother were doing well. Relieved but rattled, I had to throw myself on the goodness of the stationmaster, for my baggage had been lost in the rush. He found it for me, with about a minute to spare before my train pulled out. My conduct obviously required an explanation, and when I offered it, the stationmaster slapped me on the back, crying, "Congratulations, son. Good luck to the kid, and God bless his mother!"

Susie, who knew my mother well, idolized her, and I saw them as spiritually two of a kind. They visited together all too infrequently, but letters and pictures kept my mother in close touch with our growing family. Susie herself was the perfect mother, suited to her role both temperamentally and biologically, and our years together were of matchless happiness. In 1914 and 1915, when I was serving as secretary of the Flying Squadron of America, promoting the prohibition program across the country, Susie was able to leave our children with her aunt and one of her sisters and go campaigning with me. She queened our travels, capturing everyone with her gentleness and thoughtfulness for others, and with her beauty and charm. Radiant and gracious, she swept young and old alike into her spiritual embrace. There was no hint in her luminous gray eyes, then or later, that her life was to be so brief a one.

In 1912, when our family acquired its first female member, Mary Savilla, we had a practical nurse for a few weeks. Daniel and Clark proved a handful for her. Each boy considered the new sister his own personal property, and the rivalry between them became dismayingly intense. The day Daniel, fleeing from punishment, took a short cut over a gas stove, Mrs. Livingstone indicated that I would either "straighten him out," as she put it, or she would leave us. Young Daniel offered me a theological explanation for the crisis. Mary, it appeared, was not Clark's sister but his. "*I* asked God," he insisted. "Clark couldn't pray for her—he can't talk! If Clark wants a sister, let him ask God for one." Somehow things were smoothed over and our family life went on, but at this point, as the harried father of three, I was increasingly grateful for the memory of how Father had handled his children when we "wandered off the reservation," as our family phrase for misconduct went.

Another day, eluding Mrs. Livingstone, Daniel made his way through the upstairs bathroom window onto the sloping roof of the kitchen. I don't think he had any clear idea of what he wanted to do out there—he was not yet four, remember—but when discovered by the neighbors, he was directing his unsteady steps back and forth in the gutter at the edge of the roof, fifteen feet above a cement walk. The gathering crowd told Daniel many things at once: He was to sit down on the roof and not move until he could be rescued; he was to go back in through the open window; he was to know that he was a bad boy who needed a thrashing. My son was not impressed, even when advised that the policeman was coming to get him. "He can't get up here, he's too fat!" replied Daniel, who knew his man. The situation was a stalemate. Then arrived motherly Mrs. Quinn, our good Roman Catholic neighbor.

"My, but you're brave, Daniel," she marveled. "You're just wonderful."

The boy began to listen. This was the mother of John Quinn, his playmate, speaking.

"And now you climb in that window and come downstairs, for I want to take you to the store and buy you a box of candy."

Hers were the magic words that led to action, hers was the imaginative strategy that won the devotion and respect of all who saw it. Daniel got his candy and he was not spanked. "Leave that part to his father if he still feels like it when I get through telling him the story," Mrs. Quinn advised Mrs. Livingstone. And that evening, when I heard the story of how the boy had been rescued, I did not feel he should be spanked. I was too relieved and grateful.

Bobby Quinn, the husband of our helpful neighbor, was then the manager of the Columbus Senators; later he became manager of the Boston Braves. He was one of the finest characters and business executives the great American game of baseball ever produced. His son, our boys' playmate, followed in his father's footsteps; today he is president of the Philadelphia Phillies.

About the time that Clark began to talk, I left my student pastorate to become the Christian Endeavor secretary for the state of Ohio. We then attended services in a small temporary church whose pastor, William S. Harpster, was my friend. These occasions were often an embarrassment, since Harpster usually insisted that I come to the pulpit and offer the opening prayer, and this meant leaving the two boys in the pew with Susie. Since Susie's attention was primarily centered on Mary, anything might happen. One day Daniel dogged my steps down the aisle and proceeded to put on a gymnastic exhibition before the altar, while I, with closed eyes, tried to lead the congregation in its morning devotions. I was told later that the show in front of me got most of the attention. Clark remained in his seat but wildly applauded his brother. This time Daniel got a good one when we all returned home, as did his brother.

There were times when the rod was applied and the results, at least with Daniel, were good. There were even times when Daniel would say to me, "Daddy, I feel it's time for me to be whipped." I could tell when these moments were coming, and the boy was generally right. They were the times when he had been most decidedly off the reservation. I never said to him that a whipping was going to be harder for me to give than for him to receive, because Daniel considerately beat me to it, generously claiming that the punishment was going to be much worse for me.

Clark, on the other hand, always let me know that my efforts for him were not appreciated. "When I become a father," he once told me, "I'll show you how it should be done."

Years later I visited white-haired Mrs. Livingstone in Columbus. Blind, but alert and full of memories, she quizzed me about "her" children. I noticed that she left Daniel to the last, and I detected a note of hesitation even then. When I told her that my first-born was attending Princeton Theological Seminary, she exclaimed, "Thank God! I knew that boy would either be a preacher or a convict!"

In 1908, when I became general secretary of the Ohio Christian Endeavor Union, I began a new phase in my life's work of helping bring together in a meaningful alliance the followers of Christ. This state organization, like those in other parts of the nation, and like the World's Christian Endeavor Union that ultimately drew together thousands of societies spread all over the globe, grew out of the original Christian Endeavor group. This was organized on February 2, 1881, after a young Congregational preacher in Portland, Maine, determined to activate and train the young people of his church. Finding them diffident and unresponsive in the presence of their elders, he had deeply felt his failure to awaken their interest in duties and responsibilities suited to their powers. The upshot was that, following a series of special meetings, a group of fifty-eight young men and women formally agreed to attend a weekly prayer meeting in which each one would take some active part, aside from reading a verse from the Bible. The organization was named "Christian Endeavor."

Francis Edward Clark was the minister whose organizational and inspirational spark fell upon dry tinder. In a phenomenally short time his Christian Endeavor society became the first world-wide Protestant ecumenical movement, and he had earned his popular title of the "good St. Francis of the world's youth." Caught up in his mission, Dr. Clark and his gracious, selfless wife, known to Endeavorers everywhere as "Mother Clark," spent practically all their time and effort organizing societies and unions around the world. Dr. Clark was one of the first million-milers, long before airplane travel made this record comparatively easy to obtain. Mrs. Clark, a small person physically, was a darling figure at Christian Endeavor conventions, and she continued to be the inspiration of the young people of the churches for more than a dozen years after her husband's death in 1927, in which year I became Dr. Clark's successor in leading the world movement.

My introduction to Christian Endeavor came during my Lafayette years when a gracious lady who was a member of my father's congregation, Martha Barden, organized what was, I believe, the first Junior Christian Endeavor Society west of the Rocky Mountains. In this society I learned the Scriptures and had my first experiences in speaking in public and in public prayer. My associations with Dr. Clark himself began in 1909 when we met at the Ohio State Christian Endeavor Convention. I came immediately under his spell. A benign, considerate, thoughtful personality, an inspirational speaker, and a fine administrator, he encouraged my interest in young people's religious activities, and I in turn saw the possibilities in his international, interdenominational Christian Endeavor movement. And so it was that in 1908 I began to engage in general church activities as a Christian Endeavor leader, and did not again serve a local congregation until 1920.

My relationship with Dr. Clark quickly became a close one, and Clark, our second son, was named for him.

As did most of the Protestant churches, Christian Endeavor

wholeheartedly supported the prohibition movement, and it was as a delegate to the International Christian Endeavor Convention of 1911, held in Atlantic City, that I heard the fighting slogan, "A saloonless nation by 1920, the three hundredth year from the landing of the Pilgrims at Plymouth." The conception made an even deeper impression on us than the presence and address of our guest of honor, President William Howard Taft. The authors of the resolution embodying the slogan were Dr. Ira Landrith, president of Ward Belmont College in Nashville, Tennessee, an heroic figure of a man physically and morally, and Dr. Howard B. Grose, the designer of the Christian Endeavor emblematic pin. The climactic phrase about the Pilgrims was added by Francis E. Clark. The slogan captured the imagination of the increasingly united prohibition forces, and I used it with telling effect in my first bid for elective office the following year.

In 1912 I was again in Atlantic City, this time for the Prohibition party's national convention. It was a meeting that saw the younger men taking over from the faction-plagued elders and electing Virgil G. Hinshaw as national chairman. As I have already related, it was Hinshaw who first drew me into antiliquor activities. For the next seven years, or until the Eighteenth Amendment was adopted, Hinshaw, a dedicated organizer, made the Prohibition party a power in the movement. It was his inspiration that led me to run for office in Ohio.

Although, under the state constitution, I was three years too young to serve as governor, I was not too young to be a candidate—and I was young enough and enthusiastic enough and even ignorant enough to jump into the fray when the Prohibition party drafted me. I immediately began an intensive campaign for county option—the right of a county to determine whether it would allow the open saloon. I spoke generally in the open air, averaging sixteen speeches a day through September and October of 1912. My companion and assistant was the dynamic young state chairman of our party, J. Raymond Schmidt. In a 1908 red chain-drive Thomas Flyer, Raymond and I, with our eighteen-year-old driver, Grant Gillenwater, and a cornet player, covered eighty-six of Ohio's eighty-eight counties. For me, used to getting from meeting to meeting by horse and buggy, the Motor Age had begun. Once our Flyer stopped dead in a stream that the poorest buggy could have traversed without trouble, and we sat there until a team of oxen could be mustered to pull us out. Nevertheless, by the standards of an earlier day, our campaign was a whirlwind affair.

Raymond, a recent DePauw University graduate, took collections in his leather cap while I spoke in halls, on street corners, and at crossroads. Our cause had its opponents, of course, and I remember that in Cincinnati we were treated to a barrage of mud. Most of it landed on our automobile, but in any case, though our appearances may have been damaged temporarily, our dedication to the prohibition ideal was untouched. In one small town the opposition sent the village inebriate out to heckle me. Talking gibberish as he walked up and down with me, he was heavy competition until I invited him to sit in the front seat of the Thomas Flyer. He had probably never been in an automobile before. Climbing in, he went happily and soundly to sleep—and I finished my talk to the electorate.

Our cornetist was an effective crowd puller. One day a deaf old man came up to our car. What I was saying about the evils of drink was lost on him, but the music was not. He put his ear right up to the bell of the cornet, and our musician blew with all his might into the old boy's ear. A beatific smile came over his face. "First thing I've heard in thirty years," he told the crowd.

One Sunday during the campaign, after preaching a nonpolitical sermon in the pulpit of the First Methodist Church in Greenville, Darke County, I went home to take dinner with the pastor, Charles Clifford Peale. His thirteen-year-old son assured me that he had not been bored as he listened to me in the family pew. Looking down on the lad from the summit of my twenty-seven years, I accepted his earnest compliment with something more than amusement, for there was a quality of sincerity about Norman Vincent Peale that won me then and there. I learned that Norman, rather than carry on the preaching tradition of his family, intended to go into journalism. Shades of Daniel Poling, the young *Oregonian* reporter who foresaw his career in the law!

Perhaps that day in the Peale home was born the friendship that has grown over the years until it resembles the relationship between blood brothers. Norman's father, destined to become distinguished in the ministry of the Methodist Church, was my campaign manager for Darke County, and it is pleasing to remember that his county was among the ones I carried.

Of course I was not elected governor of Ohio—there had been little or no thought that I would be—but there were some important consequences of my campaign nonetheless. State prohibition won, and the Prohibition party vote increased from approximately 2,500 to 47,000. The Republican candidate for governor, running on some innocuous issues and staging a routine campaign, was defeated. His party later underwent a shake-up, since it was now clear that the Prohibition party held the balance of power in the state. The man who beat me and the Republican aspirant was James Middleton Cox, a Dayton newspaper publisher. He was later a prominent supporter of Woodrow Wilson and the League of Nations, and was the unsuccessful presidential candidate (with Franklin Roosevelt as his running mate) in the race against Warren G. Harding.

In 1913 I became secretary of the Flying Squadron of America, under the inspiring leadership of J. Frank Hanly. A former governor of Indiana, Hanly had missed by one vote going into the U.S. Senate. He was, I think, the greatest natural orator of his generation. Born in a log cabin, self-educated, adamant in his convictions, he was Lincolnesque in his dedication to duty as he knew it. The hundreds of men and women he led in the Squadron's prohibition drive were almost all people of high culture and great eloquence, imbued with passion for their cause. I doubt if the United States had previously known a national speaking effort comparable to this, in which every community of twenty-five thousand or more was reached in a period of one year. The entire expenses of the campaign were paid for from collections taken at the public meetings, and it may suggest the temper of the times—both the zeal of the Squadron and the general interest in the adoption of a prohibition amendment—

when I note that this hat-passing operation raised a sum approaching four hundred thousand dollars.

To the human-interest side of the Flying Squadron story I can contribute at least one memorable bit. In 1914 we held a meeting in Syracuse, New York, in the largest auditorium in town—that of the First Baptist Church. My Oregon uncle, D.V., had come on to be our music director and vocal soloist. Ordinarily he had one of the greatest baritone singing voices I ever heard, but on this particular occasion he was suffering with a heavy cold. Accordingly, we arranged for him to sing at the beginning of the program so that he could go immediately to his hotel and rest.

I believe the baptistry of this great church is still one of the largest on record. It was a veritable swimming pool, and it was full. Curtains obscured the view of the audience on the first floor, but those who filled the gallery saw it all. D.V. sang with authority, despite his cold, and then withdrew through the door at the rear of the platform, assuming he could leave the church by a back door. It was a sad mistake. He found himself trapped. The light on the water in the baptistry reflected the tile floor, and D.V. essayed to walk across it. I had just begun to speak when he went in with wonderful form and sound effects. While the crowd roared, he managed to get ashore at his point of entry—and so, of course, he was still trapped. Something of order had been restored and I had facetiously remarked that Dr. Poling, as a Congregationalist, had no doubt become dissatisfied with his infant baptism and so taken things into his own hands—when the door opened behind me and out he came, dripping from every hem and crease. But even at such a moment D.V. was master of himself. Shoving one hand into his vest à la Napoleon and brushing back his hair with the other, he bowed himself off the platform and went *squash, squash, squash,* down the aisle to the exit. It occurred to me that he might get pneumonia, but it turned out the shock of his misstep seemed to bring about a quick cure of his cold.

The International Christian Endeavor Convention of 1913 was held in Los Angeles. One of the most moving experiences of my life occurred during this meeting when, following my citizenship address, the audience swept forward, gathered up the flags and banners, and staged a spontaneous marching demonstration, shouting our slogan, "A saloonless nation by 1920!"

Los Angeles of 1913 is far removed from us now, and national prohibition has long since come and gone, but it is worth remembering that just seven years after the adoption of the resolution in Atlantic City, the "impossible" was achieved and the amendment written into the Constitution. At this point the majority of prohibitionists considered the battle won and retired to the tents of indifference. The tragic failure of prohibition enforcement, accordingly, can be blamed in part upon those whose efforts ceased when their program was made the law.

If national prohibition is not the answer today for the rising tide of delinquency, accidents, and social waste that can be traced to excessive drinking—and I do not believe that it is—then the liquor interests and other parties concerned could well give attention to the *Christian Herald's* program, which I, as editor, have long endorsed: "We stand for the solution of the liquor problem through education." I have said and written repeatedly in recent years that if I had the power to bring back national prohibition I would not exercise it. Nonetheless, the harmful effects of drunkenness and alcoholism, with the resulting slaughter on our highways, cannot be wished away simply by closing our eyes to them, and I believe that the liquor traffic for private profit may well again become an issue in the United States.

4

In 1915 the International Christian Endeavor Convention, bringing together delegates from the United States, Canada, and Mexico, was held in the Chicago Coliseum. It was one of the last great gatherings I remember participating in before the advent of electrical amplification for the speakers' voices. "Father Endeavor," as Francis Edward Clark was familiarly known to his followers, was stricken with typhoid fever, and the heavy task of presiding fell on me, his young associate. Memories of my Dallas speech teacher's constant exhortation to "Let it come out!" returned to me, and I let it.

Regardless of its substance, my message at least carried to the farthest listener in that vast barn of a place, and I'm sure that my vocal performance, as much as anything else, resulted in my being elected associate president of the International Society of Christian Endeavor.

Shortly after the convention I was called on to render an even more important service for the still ailing Dr. Clark. As a trustee of Andrew Carnegie's Church Peace Union he was in the original group invited by Henry Ford to go on his peace mission to end the European war and "get our boys out of the trenches by Christmas, never to go back." At the Biltmore Hotel in New York I was unable to meet with Ford himself—few people got through to him at this critical moment in his ambitious preparations—but I observed the members of his party and decided for Dr. Clark that they were about as unimpressive a lot as could be assembled. The private session I had with William Jennings Bryan, who had recently resigned as President Wilson's Secretary of State, confirmed my misgivings. A Christian Endeavor trustee and a man as ardently interested in peace as Dr. Clark and myself, Bryan had at first taken Ford's invitation seriously—as had such other prominent Americans as Jane Addams, Thomas Alva Edison, Luther Burbank, William Howard Taft, David Starr Jordan, Julius Rosenwald, and John Wanamaker, all of whom were now withdrawing from the venture on one pretext or another. When Bryan followed suit, sensing that the Germans might exploit the Peace Ship to their own advantage, he supported me in my own decision to decline Henry Ford's invitation.

No one questioned Ford's sincerity, but his wisdom and judgment certainly sank to an impressive low. Religious fanatics and belligerent patriots moved into the ranks even before the responsible leaders moved out. One health crank turned up with a satchel of herb medicine to cure the doughboys' ills. Some members of the party took shameless advantage of Ford's dedication and generosity by purchasing all manner of things for themselves at his expense—even ordering household furniture shipped to their homes around the country. The newspapers made merciless sport of the whole project. One story, dealing with the president of the Anti-Tobacco League, sent the country into gales of laughter. This gentleman, who spent much of his time snatching cigarettes from smokers' lips, made himself obnoxious by insisting that there should be no smoking on the voyage. Though Ford himself was an unrelenting foe of the cigarette, his advisers were eventually able to persuade him that the man, however well meaning, was not an asset. Quite suddenly granted a personal interview with Ford, the zealot said, in effect: "I know that you do not smoke and that you detest tobacco. But something more is required. This prophetic mission must not be compromised. I urge you to speak a word. That is all that is needed now. Stop the smoking in this hotel and on the ship. Indeed, sir, I feel this matter so profoundly that I myself must resign from the party if tobacco is not prohibited." To the good man's dismay, Ford then and there accepted his resignation. Nor was he ever able to reinstate himself. An amused New York newspaperman reported that the president of the Anti-Tobacco League had withdrawn when he learned that both funnels of the ship would smoke all the way across the Atlantic.

By the time the *Oscar II* left the dock, Ford's project had become so discredited that Judge Ben Lindsey, one of the prominent men who stuck with Ford, felt obliged to insist that he was a patriotic American despite his presence on the ship. One newspaper quoted him as lamenting, "Oh God, why am I here?"

Not long after Ford abandoned his group in Sweden and returned secretly to the United States, I sat down with him in his Detroit plant for what proved to be one of the most unusual conversations of my life. The meeting had been suggested and arranged by a Canadian friend of Ford's, James A. MacDonald, a Presbyterian clergyman who had become the international-minded editor of the *Toronto Globe*. Under Dr. Clark's leadership, Christian Endeavor was enthusiastically committed to peace, and we were all hopeful of a quick and honorable end to the war without the further involvement of the United States in the rising tide of world battle. Now that Ford's great crusade was quietly withering away in the neutral capitals of Europe, MacDonald, a Christian Endeavor trustee, felt that the time was right for us to introduce Ford to our program for organizing the youth of the world for peace through international understanding. He hoped that we might win Ford's financial support for it.

In one of his other moments of poor judgement, the auto manufacturer had embraced the cause of anti-Semitism, even to accepting as genuine the spurious document known as the "Protocols of the Wise Men of Zion." It was Dr. MacDonald who helped Ford to acknowledge his mistake and extricate himself from his untenable position, and Ford never forgot his friend's sound advice and guidance.

When James MacDonald and I reached Detroit we did not immediately see Ford. First we heard Dr. Samuel Marquis, the Episcopal rector who had engineered the auto manufacturer's sudden return from Sweden, address a group of Detroit businessmen about developments in Europe. Heading what Ford called his "sociological department" at a salary of twenty thousand dollars a years, Marquis had been hostile to the whole idea of the Peace Ship. Now, praising Ford's grasp of international affairs, he insisted that Germany could not be conquered by force, that the war would end in a deadlock, and that it was imperative for the United States to initiate a program of industrial preparedness. It was not an auspicious beginning for our talk. Nor did MacDonald and I derive much comfort from our first words with Ford. He greeted us effusively, but warned us that he had his own peace plans and did not want to consider any others. Begging off from our appointment, he promised me a half-hour the next day. MacDonald could not put off his return to Toronto, and so it was that I presented the Christian Endeavor program to Ford singlehanded.

Our conference occurred in his private office in the presence of two secretaries and a stenographer, but these three were seated far enough away to give our talk at least a semblance of privacy. I began by placing MacDonald's letter, which he had thoughtfully prepared the night before, in Ford's hands. Ford hardly glanced at it, commenting, "I saw him yesterday and he said what he wanted to then."

Against these odds, I persisted until I had completed my story and felt at least the inner peace of knowing I had done my best.

Ford was a nervous man, and his eyes, hands, legs were constantly in motion. Swinging his feet under him and sitting on his ankles in his great chair, he opened up. "I have a machine of my own, and until it fails I won't consider another. No, sir! I know what I want. We are getting things started up fine now. I have two cablegrams from the party. I don't need any assistance. As to your young people, they are no good. I had them on the boat. They need to learn a lot."

Inveighing against young people in general, Ford was somewhat taking advantage of the Christian Endeavor's concern with all Protestant youth, but I was able to agree that the young peacemakers he had selected to go on his ship were not notable assets to his cause. Ford then went on at some length about a college education, although this was hardly our subject. He was against it. He referred to the fact that he had not allowed his son Edsel to go to college. After listening to this general assault on higher education, I finally felt moved to ask, "What about all your scientists, Mr. Ford?" He almost blew up.

I then learned that he considered the church an ineffective organization. "I have done more to get peace than all your churches and colleges and peace organizations," he declared, adding, "I am not financing things that I do not control." Several times he repeated, "I won't consider anything until I go the limit with my own plans, and we are going to do it. We are going to get peace!"

When I mentioned the famous men who were associated with the Christian Endeavor movement, among them John Wanamaker, William Jennings Bryan, and his own friend MacDonald, Ford fairly yelled at me, "Don't say anything about them. They need sand. They don't have nerve." All these men, of course, had refused to sail on his ship, but it seemed to me that the deep resentment apparent in Ford's voice and gestures may have related to the greater educational and social advantages enjoyed by these men in their early years. His mood, as I saw it, and despite everything he said to the contrary, was one of frustration and chagrin over the world's rejection of his peace bid. Even a more persuasive spokesman than I, I feel sure, would have gotten no further with Ford that day than I did.

And yet Ford possessed an undeniable greatness. Transparently vain and seemingly a superficial thinker on all matters outside the field of his inventive and business genius, he nevertheless had a great heart. Illustrative of his attitude toward weak humanity is an incident that happened at the time of my visit.

Some six hundred former convicts were employed in his factory. One was a man who had been sentenced for forgery. There seemed to have been extenuating circumstances, and when the man was paroled, Ford gave him a job at his precedent-shattering wage of five dollars a day. But after a few weeks the fellow went wrong again. When I conferred with Ford, his employee was back in the penitentiary. Later, I was told what Ford had said when he heard the news: "Make a record of the day when his sentence expires. Bring him back and give him another chance."

My work as associate president of the International Society of Christian Endeavor calling for me to be in the Society's headquarters, I said good-by to Ohio and moved our home to the Boston area. Eventually we settled in Auburndale, where we lived back to back with the editor of the *Christian Endeavor World*, Amos R. Wells. He and his family were the best of neighbors to us. Mrs. Wells and her daughter Elizabeth were constant in their thoughtful attentions to my beloved Susie, especially during the months I was overseas in 1918 and Susie was steadily failing in health. Amos Wells was one of the most persistent and voluminous writers I have ever known. His work for the Christian Endeavor's periodical took but a part of his creative effort. Besides writing a string of boys' adventure books, he wrote a popular geological account of New England, and humorous verse for *Life* and *Puck*. Whenever I saw him he was writing. Once, finding him scribbling away on the train down to Cape Cod, I asked him what his subject was. "An article on 'being an appendix,' for the *National Nurses Magazine*," he told me. Remembering this man's productivity and versatility, I hired him a decade later when I became editor of the *Christian Herald* in New York.

The Massachusetts scene was actually not new to us Polings when we moved there permanently. Our first extended summer vacations had been spent in the Christian Endeavor community on Cape Cod. It was here, in the summer of 1913, that my son Daniel, not yet six, enterprisingly made a raft of driftwood and with a friend his own age decided to try it out. The strong current swept the two boys a mile offshore before they were even missed. I was away from the Cape at the time, but my brother Paul pulled a strong oar and reached what was left of the raft just in time.

This experience taught me the infinite value of the "ones." Returning home, and having missed all news of the near-tragedy,

I found a new man driving the bus that took me from the station to the beach. I listened idly as he told a story about a couple of summer children and a raft, but my ears pricked up when he remarked, "One of them was Poling's kid." Then I wanted to hear everything he could tell me, and the rest of the ride was a torture of delay.

Ever since that summer evening, *one*—one human being as an entity—has meant more to me than any "one" ever meant before. Years afterward, in World War II, I read an English newspaper editorial about the loss of a troop convoy in the North Atlantic. I no longer remember the name of the ship, but it was a subject that had come to have a deep interest to me. Unlike the *Dorchester*, on which my son Clark had been lost, most of the men from this ship had been picked up. "And so, after all," the story concluded, "the loss was infinitesimal." The writer, of course, was thinking of the war's grand strategy, the total losses, the great issues at stake. But I could not escape dwelling on the individual lives, could not but think of the homes where now a man would be forever missing, and I remembered Daniel and his friend on that raft in the riptide of Cape Cod Bay. "Infinitesimals?" I asked myself. No, they were not infinitesimals; they were infinite ones.

The morning of Thursday, October 12, 1916, I sat in my office in Boston, signing my letters with unusual deliberation. The day was flawless; open sky without a cloud, air crisp without being sharp, and a sun that gave every blushing leaf an added tinge of gold. Boston, and a sizable portion of the rest of the United States and Canada, was stark mad with baseball enthusiasm. The preceding day the Red Sox had trounced the Brooklyn Trolley-Dodgers in the fourth game of the World Series. Awaited now was the umpire's announcement of the rival batteries for the last game.

With all my small tasks finished, I settled back in my office chair for a finish fight with myself. I wanted to see that game, but the day was also a school holiday, the first one of the year when chestnuts were on the ground. I knew that two small boys and their sister were waiting at home for the phone to ring and my voice to say, "Get your sweaters on; have the buckets ready; I'll be out on the one o'clock."

Then my telephone rang and a friend yelled in my ear, "Dan, seventeen thousand insane men and boys are trying to take this ticket away from me. Do you want it?"

But now the fight was all over. In a voice of sublime hypocrisy, I replied, "Sorry, old boy, but I have an important engagement."

I made the one o'clock after edging through the crowds bound for Braves' Field. Trying to feel cheerful, I found a seat. There were many; the car was not crowded. At Back Bay an old man came in and sized me up with amazement. "Well, I thought every man on the verdant side of seventy and not under legal restraint would be at the game. You are not seventy, and you don't look like an escaped inmate."

"Your diagnosis is correct and complimentary," I said, "but I am going chestnutting with my boys."

The old man dropped his jesting tone and said brusquely, "I would give a million dollars for the chance to go chestnutting with *my* boys. I used to dream of that sort of thing—but the boys never came."

There was length to my stride and a spring to my step when I turned into my street and neared our house. What an afternoon that was! I collected more thistle burrs than chestnuts. I lost my fountain pen. Daniel threw a club at a branch and it came down on my head. Mary lost one of her shoes and beguiled me into carrying her home. We were late for supper and anyway I was too tired to eat.

"We had a wonderful time," Daniel told his mother. "Feel the lump on Daddy's head!"

Susie, with small Mary standing by her side, looked at me with an understanding smile. "It was a little too much for you, wasn't it, Dan?"

Wearily, I shook my head. "I wouldn't have missed it for a million dollars!" And I meant it.

On July 29, 1917, our second daughter, Elizabeth Jane, was born under rather different circumstances than we had planned.

Our first three children had been received at home, "home grown" as the saying had it, and not entirely for the ordinary reasons of the time. A great many people in those days considered home delivery safer than a hospital delivery. Also, one heard stories of babies getting mixed up, and of course we were interested in having the originals. But our real reason for avoiding hospitals the first three times was a financial one; our children came into the world more rapidly then my salary increased.

This time, however, we planned to take Susie to the hospital in Newton. In fact, the taxi was at the door. But Elizabeth Jane moved her advent forward and we hurried back upstairs—just in time to encounter a temporary failure of the municipal lighting system. There were no other complications, thankfully, but even so our doctor was not amused. Muttering general criticisms of procrastinating parents, he suddenly became specific: "Another one like this and I'll take up preaching and let you do the doctoring!"

During these years, like most men whose field of concern was the conduct of life according to their concept of God's laws, I had increasingly to face the issues of what was then simply "the war," though now we differentiate it with a number as the first in a series.

Though I hate war utterly and have seen all too much of it in my lifetime, I have never been a pacifist. The militant pacifist who can state his reasons for his conscientious objections and then conduct his life consistently with them often seems to be in a far happier position than those of us who do not speak at all, or who, on their marching feet or on their knees, believe themselves to be among the peacemakers. In my student days, David Starr Jordan's *War and Waste* was my peace bible. From Jordan I learned why war should not be. I also learned that a great world war was no longer likely or even really possible. His reasons were convincing. Such a conflict could not be financed, Jordan declared, and the worker of one nation would certainly refuse to fight the worker of another nation. That book was the beginning of my education in war.

I took my graduate work in 1918 in the trenches. I saw men spitted on bayonets and scattered across a field. I saw white skulls plowed from their muddy graves by shellfire. I learned what it meant to be gassed.

In details I have again and again rethought my position on war, but in principle it has not changed since 1921, when I declined to sign a pledge of absolute nonparticipation. I was the only churchman at an Adline Club luncheon in New York who did not sign it, and I explained my position thus:

"As a Christian, and without prejudice to any other Christian, I cannot pledge myself to a specific action in advance of a particular event, the details of which cannot be known. I must keep my conscience free."

Sherwood Eddy, the Y.M.C.A. leader who had called us together, replied, "But, Dan, you as a Christian must have an absolute."

"I do, and here it is," I answered. "God helping me in my whole life and in all ordeals such as this, I will be Christian. Jesus Christ is my absolute."

Sherwood shook his head. "Too general, Dan."

"If my position is too general for you," I replied, "yours is too specific for me. For me, my position is comprehensive and complete."

And here is the sequel to that disagreement. A little over a decade later, when Mussolini began to menace Ethiopia, the question of sanctions against Italy came up in the League of Nations. Mussolini declared that if sanctions were imposed, he would invade Ethiopia. At this point, with but one exception, every man who had signed the antiwar pledge at that luncheon abandoned his stand and supported the League's sanctions. Dr. Eddy was among those who changed their positions; only Kirby Page remained consistent.

I am sure that in many important decisions of my life I may have been wrong, and it is certainly true that good men and true have often judged me unwise and mistaken. But with God helping me, up to now and at whatever personal cost I have followed the bidding of my conscience. And my conscience has never permitted me to be a pacifist.

In the early 1920s, of course, there was agreement everywhere that there would never be another world war. The Allies had won the "war to end war," the world had been made "safe for democracy," and we had President Harding's ringing word that "It must not happen again." However, I continued on principle to oppose the circulation of pacifist or absolute statements, particularly among young people. The futility of such stands was subsequently demonstrated when of the four million signers of the so-called Oxford Oath in Britain, less than fifty thousand maintained their stand after the beginning of World War II. The personal tragedies stemming from such pledges confronted me all around the world. Thousands of young people, persuaded by mature leaders whom they loved and trusted to take positions they could not ultimately adhere to, became disillusioned and embittered as they renounced their pacifism.

Particularly poignant was an experience I had early in 1936 when I visited Silliman University in the Philippines, immediately after the passage of President Quezon's defense bill. The bill called for selective conscription. Hundreds of the native students, having signed one of those sweeping statements, now found themselves confronted by an unforeseen dilemma. A large group of them came to me for advice. I told them that they had been misled, and that when they realized they had made a bad pledge they would have to break it. This would be an honorable action, I explained; upholding a position they now thought wrong would be dishonorable. In retrospect, remembering that a little more than five years later the Japanese overran the Philippines, the effect of that pledge seems even more tragic. I hope that my counsel, which had been tested in the trenches of France in 1918, may have helped those earnest, troubled young people find their way.

At the end of March, 1917, I was in Washington for a meeting of the National Temperance Council, and so it was that I had the privilege of being in the House of Representatives on April

2 when President Wilson called for a state of war with Germany.

I had had one previous experience with the President before I listened to him on that historic occasion. In August, 1914, I had visited him in the White House to plead for a young man who had been the cashier of a national bank in a Midwestern state. I knew the man well. He had been a state president of the Christian Endeavor Union and a highly regarded citizen of his community until he confessed to taking sums of money from his bank. The total amount was not large and not a dollar of it had been spent as such "withdrawals" usually are. Furthermore, the shortage had not been discovered. The young man, finding himself helpless to repay the money, had confessed. Had the bank been other than national, quite likely the matter would never have been made public. After a talk with the man I felt reassured as to his underlying moral worth, and I was convinced that the judgment rendered on him had been too harsh.

President Wilson was at this time a bereft man; his wife Ellen had passed away less than two weeks before. Sitting quietly in a chair beside me, he listened while I summarized the case and described what I considered the reasons for reducing the man's punishment. It seemed to me that the President was deeply moved, and his answer, I felt sure, would be a pardon. But then, as he leafed through the documents and supporting petitions and resolutions, he changed, and I felt the denial coming. Said he: "Mr. Poling, my heart and also my mind moves me to grant your well-stated and supported request, but my conscience does not. My judgment as a responsible man makes me take the hard course. If I were to allow other considerations to influence and determine my action, I would empty the prisons."

I went away disappointed, of course, but I had been given an intimate and memorable view of Woodrow Wilson the Scotch Presbyterian—adamant and committed, but also eager to live in a house by the side of the road and be a friend to man.

On the April day the President addressed the special session of the sixty-fifth Congress, I spent eleven hours in the gallery of the House, the chamber toward which the thoughts of millions all over the world were turning. My ticket of admission—they were priceless—was given me by Charles Randall of California, the only national representative ever elected by the Prohibition party. I saw Champ Clark of Missouri elected and sworn in as Speaker, then participated in the applause accorded Jeannette Rankin, the first woman ever elected to Congress. I listened to the long debate on the organization of the House and then, at eight-thirty in the evening, I saw the President received tumultuously as he came to present his message.

Looking stern and harassed, Wilson was unmistakably in a mood of determined conviction as he proceeded to the Speaker's rostrum. The cheers and applause of the senators and representatives, Supreme Court and Cabinet members, foreign diplomats, and crowded galleries seemed to inspire him, to lift him out of himself, and he spoke as the oracle of freedom and justice. "Our motives will not be revenge or the victorious assertion of the physical might of the nation, but only the vindication of right" —he spoke in a low, deeply vibrant voice, and his profound emotion in the weightier passages of supreme eloquence came through to all of us. Wilson believed that he was God's man for that crucial hour, and I thrill yet at the memory of his impassioned declaration that "The world must be made safe for democracy." When I left the House that night, I knew that for me there was no neutrality, and I sensed that I would soon find myself in the midst of war activities.

The following day I was in the Senate chamber when the war resolution was introduced and Senator La Follette blocked its immediate consideration. We observers in the galleries vigorously applauded the subsequent motion to adjourn, since it clearly meant the Senate would consider no other business before taking up the resolution and acting upon it. Vice-President Marshall called us to order sharply—after our applause had subsided.

As things turned out, I went to France with not one but two assignments. Under the supervision of Dr. John R. Mott, world leader of the Young Men's Christian Association, I was to carry on duties as a Y.M.C.A. secretary; for the War Department I was to conduct a program of morale-building, education, and inspiration. This second assignment brought me into close touch with Secretary of War Newton D. Baker, to whom I was introduced by Raymond B. Fosdick, Harry Emerson Fosdick's younger brother. I had admired Baker from a distance; now I came to know and love him as a friend. He was pre-eminently a man of peace, a man after Woodrow Wilson's own heart. Thrust into the boiling center of the war, he remained on the job to the bitter end, his ideals unimpaired, his soul untarnished. One of the finest, most objective and unselfish men I have ever known, Baker did a great deal to reconcile and confirm me in my own position as a nonpacifist. Today, I treasure a letter in his hand, written after he had read my little book entitled *Huts in Hell,* which I wrote after my return to the United States. "Thank you . . . for bringing this message home," he wrote. "It will lighten the hearts of a million mothers and secure for the boys in the army that confidence in their essential fineness which can only follow the testimony of witnesses who like you have lived the life and seen the conditions with anxious but unprejudiced eyes."

Much later, the year that Adolf Hitler became *Reichsführer* of Germany and warlike events increased their pace in Europe, I published a condemnation of pacifism that drew this endorsement from Baker: "The tragedy of the sectarianism of the peace movement has long lain heavily on my spirit . . . What you have written will help to make warriors for peace of some of these fine people who imagine they have done all that is necessary by vowing that they will not be warriors in war!" Newton D. Baker, as I knew and understood him, was one of our greatest warriors for peace and brotherhood. After the war he won my admiration anew when he helped to found the National Conference of Christians and Jews.

A little more than a month after I listened to the President call for war I stood on Fifth Avenue in New York. The city was riotously, gloriously alive, and a vibrant throng filled the space from building-line to building-line, leaving only a narrow lane where the hero of the day was soon to pass. I heard a confusion of tongues, saw a medley of people, a human flood fed by every racial fountain on earth. This was democracy's melting pot at its most exciting moment. The spot where I had waited for hours, it seemed, was directly in front of the reviewing stand at Forty-second Street. Obedient to the universal spiritual impulse, my eyes watched the billowing of a thousand flags. Old Glory was everywhere, and everywhere flanking her were the Tricolor and the Union Jack.

Now came the high, sharp sound of horses' hoofbeats. The throng surged against the officers who guarded the open way. The voices of those about me joined the wave of cheers that rolled upon us. There was a bedlam of horns and bugles. And then Marshal Joseph J. C. Joffre appeared. I shall never cease to see him as he was that day, an heroic figure in red and white beneath the sun-goldened sky. He passed very close to me. His military cap was lifted from his massive head. He was slightly smiling. His eyes were shining islands in seas of tears. His herculean shoulders were shaped for the load of a nation. His chest was broad and deep, to hold the heart of France.

The leader who had told his soldiers, "It was you who barred to the Germans the way to Verdun," fixed his eyes upon the place where I stood. While the question "Is he looking at me?" shaped itself in my mind, the cry "*Vive la France!*" rose beside me. Three times I heard it, in a clear, strong, unmistakably American voice. I turned. The face of the tall young American was deeply scarred; his right arm was bound against his chest. He wore the uniform of the Flying French Corps. His unmaimed left hand was raised as he cried again, "*Vive la France!*"

I saw Joffre lean forward, gaze intently, replace his cap upon his crown of white hair, and then, as warrior to warrior, salute. Then he passed beyond us.

It was a flash, but an eternal moment—this tender communication between the iron hero of the Marne and an American who, crossing the sea to fight in France, had honored the memory of Lafayette.

It had become increasingly apparent that my beloved Susie was not well. In spite of her courage, her determination to keep going, her old buoyancy of spirit was fading. In what was now a real and distressing family crisis, complicated by my overseas assignments, I called upon my youngest sister, Mabel. Not yet twenty, she came to us from Oregon to be Susie's companion through the next several months and to become our children's forever blessed Aunt Mebs.

I went to New York expecting to be shipped across on short notice. The day was repeatedly postponed. Shortly before Christmas Susie was able to come to New York for a weekend with me. She brought our ten-year-old Daniel with her. A glorious, unforgettable period that was for us as we forgot our concerns. It was like a renewed honeymoon. Soon after Susie and Daniel returned to Auburndale I received notice that I would not sail until the day after Christmas. My cup of happiness seemed to overflow as I headed for Auburndale on the twenty-fourth.

What a day that became! Daniel and Clark and Mary went with me to a friend's woodlot and there we cut our Christmas spruce. The boys insisted that I tell them war stories. A man who had not seen war, I did my imaginative best. A few months later I could have spoken with some authority. The children gave me enthusiastic but hardly efficient assistance as we carried our tree across the field, along the street, up our steps, and into the living room. That night all of us, saving only baby Jane, who was asleep in her crib, decorated the tree and fixed candles on its branches. Then, while the rest of our children made their heroic attempts to sleep, Susie and my sister Mabel and I arranged their presents beneath the tree. When I had been a boy in Oregon we had always had trees at Christmas, and we had always had presents—one to a child. Father and Mother would have liked to give us more, beyond doubt, but the realities of Father's salary made such extravagance impossible. Now, in Auburndale, how different it was! There were many presents for each child, for uncles and aunts and friends far and near had sent their offering to be placed beneath the tree with ours.

It seemed that God was very good to me, giving me that unlooked-for Christmas with my family. Susie, and this was so like her, never really let me know the extent of her suffering.

Therefore I did not realize how cruelly my going away pained her. The day after our wonderful Christmas, when it was time for me to say my final good-by, Susie looked so radiant and seemed so definitely improved that I went from our house with eager hopes for our future together.

My children accompanied me a little way as I hurried down the street to catch the suburban local to South Station in Boston. When they had reached the limit they were allowed to go by themselves, I turned back to watch them start home. In all her loveliness Susie stood framed in the white door of our house. I waved to her and hurried on. Only once more was I to see her as I saw her at that moment.

5

The great liner drove ahead through the night with ports closed and not a signal showing. Under the stars, Marines watched in silence by their guns. Each man wore or had by him a life preserver, and there was silence on the deck. I stood by the rail watching the waves break into spray against the vessel's bow. Phosphorescent glow bathed the sea in wondrous light all around. Only the stars and the weird illumination of the waves battled with the darkness; there was no moon.

It was hard to realize that out of sight in the darkness were silent watchers waiting for the opportunity to sink us. It was hard to grasp the stern significance of the men in uniform crowding the staterooms—the new army of democracy bound for the bleeding fields of France. It was difficult for me—the Oregon boy who had grown up on dreams of Indians attacking a wagon train—to realize that on my first voyage to Europe I was in momentary danger of death from a German torpedo. Our lives can encompass strangely diverse experiences. In my case the boy who had sat on the box of a dusty old covered wagon, his head filled with visions of the past, had now become the man who scanned the mid-Atlantic and pondered the survival chances of a troopship in enemy waters.

"Well, old top," said the British flier who was standing at the rail by my side, "I'm more nervous tonight than I ever was in the air. It's a jolly true fact I am. In the air you can see them coming, but out here you just wait." He was a captain and an ace. After convalescing from a wound, he had been sent to the United States to serve as instructor in one of the new aviation camps. Now he was returning to France to fight again.

We chatted, and then I turned in, fully dressed. In spite of the menace that charged the very atmosphere of my cabin, I was soon asleep. Moments later, it seemed—actually it was several hours—there was a frightful explosion overhead. I sat up in confusion, trying to get my bearings. Yes, I was at sea. Then I remembered the crash of a great stack of deck chairs that had awakened me a few nights earlier. Reassured, I lay down again. *Boom! Boom! Boom!*—three times in quick succession our six-inch guns spoke, shaking the ship from bow to stern. Before the third discharge I was jumping into my life jacket. Then, with my cabin mate, I hurried to the deck.

Eight times our guns were in action during that first attack. What the results were to the enemy I did not learn; the gun crews were not allowed to discuss such matters, and the ship's officers were reticent.

We underwent three more submarine attacks before we entered the Mersey River. Each time, unless we happened to be on deck when the action began, we were kept below until the action was over. Thus, there was little chance to observe the maneuvers of the enemy. However, I know exactly what a German periscope looks like at a distance of three hundred yards—one glimpse was enough to fix the image forever.

The last attack came at dusk, when we were not much more than thirty miles from Liverpool. Three destroyers had finally picked us up and the sight of the Stars and Stripes on their masts had given us a comforting sense of security. Cavorting like frisky young horses of the sea, these craft went into action with gunfire and depth charges, the latter dropped in the wake of the conning tower that had scarcely sunk out of sight when the destroyers dashed over the spot, one from the rear, another sweeping past our bow, clearing us, it seemed, by inches.

Later, in London, I was told that ours had been one of the most eventful crossings of the war in which the ship arrived with all hands safe. I could well believe it. The officer in charge of the blue-jackets on our ship was a friend of my cabin mate, and through him I learned his story. An Annapolis man, the officer had been compelled to resign his commission when his doctors assured him he was hopelessly ill with tuberculosis. The war need had brought him back to the sea. When I left him at Liverpool, he had been without sleep for two days and two nights, but he was happy. "I have my big chance now," he said, "and I'm getting well!" Thus does the spirit conquer the body when a crisis challenges the soul.

Persons about to be received by great or notable men—if my own experience is typical—go through anxious moments. There is the display of nonchalance, deceiving no one, especially the man who feigns it; there is the effort to convince the other fellow of your own importance or the importance of your mission—all very amusing to think about afterward but troubling at the time. Add a hand grenade to the mixture and the anxiety quotient can rise quite high.

In Chaumont I had stepped over from the Y.M.C.A. hut to "Black Jack" Pershing's headquarters in the ancient offices of the French commandant, wishing to learn when the general and I could confer about my War Camp program. Colonel Boyd, his secretary, suggested that I wait, and so I sat in the anteroom while the man whom our nation had made commander in chief of all our overseas forces wrestled with his problems. Three French officers were also waiting to see Pershing. One of them I took to be a general, although I had not yet learned to interpret French uniforms and gold braid: I had saluted letter carriers for a week before my mistake was pointed out to me.

Just behind the Frenchmen stood a table with four hand grenades on it. My eyes kept returning to them. Inexperienced though I was, I knew that a grenade was a formidable weapon, and it seemed to me that these samples had been placed on a very inadequate support. Sure enough, as my gaze went back to them for perhaps the twentieth time, one was rolling off the edge of the table. Powerless to shout a warning, I braced myself for the catastrophe.

The grenades, as it turned out, were unloaded, but their detonating caps were in place, and in a quiet room with everyone unsuspecting, a cap can sound like war itself. The three Frenchmen moved abruptly toward the ceiling, with imprecations, and Colonel Boyd, who had been working at his desk, joined the general movement. Only Pershing remained unperturbed; at least no sound came from his office and his door did not open. A little later, when I was ushered in, the general did not even refer to the incident.

Facing John J. Pershing for the first time, I found that the man looked exactly like his pictures. Moderately tall, exceedingly well proportioned, at age fifty-eight he stood erect without the conscious effort of those who begin their soldiering after years in the undisciplined pursuits of peace. His gray eyes were clear, deep-set, and penetrating. His close-cropped mustache accentuated the firmness of his mouth. When he shook hands he had a grip, and his conversation was the talk of a man who knew why he was, where he was, and what he had been appointed to do.

In the weeks I spent in France, the almost startling efficiency that I found everywhere, and in some instances under difficult and extreme circumstances, was at once associated with Pershing. The man's certainty of mind soon became proverbial. On October 19, 1917, he had been requested to pass judgment upon the sawed-off shotgun as a possible weapon for trench warfare. Seventeen days later the originator of the idea was notified that it had been adopted. Some of this speed of decision in the year 1959 would be welcome.

When our talk turned to the morals of the American soldiers in France, Pershing's face lighted; and well it might, for no nation has ever been served by cleaner-living men than the majority of those who wore the United States uniform, and the program of the American military authorities was a source of gratification and pride to all who believe that efficiency and morality are twin brothers. Our conference that day at General

Headquarters revealed Pershing's own firm religious convictions and his determination to give to the Army an outstanding religious leadership. He spoke with enthusiasm of what he hoped to secure for the men through his chaplains, and referred to the work he had committed to the care of his old friend Bishop Charles Henry Brent. Although the chaplaincy at the beginning of World War I was a very inadequately organized and manned corps, Pershing's words were those of a builder and prophet as well as of a driving warrior. Today, after its tentative beginnings, the chaplaincy has become a corps of career men, drawn from the clergymen of the three faiths, trained and equipped to render efficient, maximum spiritual service to the American men and women in uniform.

I already knew something of Pershing's religious background. His wife and children had been received into the Episcopal church by Bishop Brent when he was presiding over the Philippine diocese and the general was stationed in Manila. Then, in 1915, Pershing knew overwhelming tragedy when his wife and three daughters were burned to death in San Francisco, leaving him with a motherless son. It was a blow that would have finished a weaker man. Pershing not only survived but went on to play his glorious role as European commander in chief. After accepting his post in France the general was received into the fellowship of the church by Bishop Brent. To me there was something vastly reassuring in knowing that America's destiny was in the hands of a man who reached his great decisions so quickly and whose personal example was so high a challenge to acknowledge the authority of the spiritual.

It was after office hours when our first conference ended and I found my way down the ancient stairway of the officers' hostel at Chaumont. Out through the guarded gates I passed—the very gates through which Napoleon had marched his legions when he turned them toward Moscow and their destruction. As I thought of Bonaparte and of the insatiable ambition and pride that brought about the overthrow of the military genius no time of the past had duplicated, I was glad that America's man of the hour in Europe had not forgotten to place first things first;

that he had retained so clear a conception of relative values in so disturbed a time.

When Bishop Brent visited our forward positions at Toul and Nancy early in 1918, he had not yet been officially named Chief of Chaplains. I went along with him, at Pershing's request, as guide and companion. The bishop was a somewhat gaunt, stooped man, but he gave every sign of good health as we began our tour. As the day wore on, I became increasingly concerned about the condition of his feet. He was wearing a very fine pair of Cordovan cavalry boots laced over the insteps, and in the rain and muck I was afraid the leather must be shrinking. When I noticed the bishop beginning to limp I was sure of it, and when we came in from the trenches, I suggested he get out of his boots. He demurred, saying "I'm going to eat and then turn in early."

We were quartered in the archbishop's house in Toul, and Brent had the great bedchamber to himself while I had the antechamber. I offered to help him get his boots off but he declined with a smile, informing me that he could still take off his own shoes. However, that night he couldn't. First I heard him struggling, then floundering. Finally there came a knock at my door. I found the bishop in real trouble. He had unlaced and opened his boots as far as he could, but they held his ankles and feet in a viselike grip. I told him we would have to cut the boots open. "Oh, no," he protested, "I could not allow that!"

But he did, of course, and what a time we had even with that operation. They were *good* boots, made of two thicknesses of cowhide. I routed out two army nurses and with their sharpest instruments we slashed the leather with regard only for Bishop Brent's limbs. The ruthless business was finished none too soon, for one of the poor man's ankles was nearly black. With a little more delay he might have lost a foot.

A few years afterward, when Brent was presiding over the Episcopal Diocese in Buffalo, we sometimes met in New York at sessions of the Executive Committee of the Federal Council of Churches. Brent's usual greeting was, "Ah, here's the man who ruined the finest pair of boots I ever owned!"

Prayer has been and is my soul's breath, as indispensable to my soul as oxygen is to my body, and there have been stark moments when the immediate life of my body became dependent on prayer rather than upon physical breath. One such time occurred the night of February 2, 1918, when a gas alert was sounded in the Toul sector. With a dozen other men I was in a Y.M.C.A. dugout canteen. Behind the double gas curtains, wearing our English "box respirators," we stood for ninety minutes. For all of us it was the first experience of the kind. Coming as it did less than twenty-four hours after a major raid had penetrated our lines deeply at this point, it found us tense and afraid. We did not know what to expect; we could only wait.

The sweat ran from my armpits, and soon the desire to tear the mask from my face, to rush into the air outside and to breathe deeply at any cost, became all but irresistible. I knew terror as I had never known it before. Then I thought of home, remembered our children—and I prayed. Then, by the faith that rises to the listening God, I traveled home to peace and quiet. The guns were silenced. The batteries of 75s directly behind us and firing over us, were far away. In that humid, dark, crowded room, while the earth shook, I was alone, and yet not alone, because with me there was a Presence that filled the place. I was comforted. Whatever the answer of science—and I am sure science has an answer—breath from the soul saved the body. The rest who stood with me there were as conscious as I was of the something that came to us to make us adequate. "As thy days, so shall thy strength be" was the ancient promise that was fulfilled to us there in that quaking dugout.

God never promises exemption. He does promise companionship, which is better. He does not promise to deliver you or me or any other individual from pain, sorrow, or economic disaster, but he does give the assurance that He will help us through and that there will be compensations. "I will not leave you comfortless, I will come to you." These are the words of Jesus.

And this also needs to be said: Nowhere in either the Old Testament or the New are we assured special well-being because of piety. Indeed there are instances, as in the great drama of Job, when goodness itself is tested and made a vehicle of trial. Even Paul cried to be relieved of his "thorn in the flesh," but cried in vain; and his contemporaries, the disciples, including Peter and the faithful who were hunted through the Roman catacombs and burned along the Appian Way and fed to the lions in the Colosseum, were not relieved of their physical ordeals because they were holy. But that never-disregarded promise "I will come to you" was kept with each of them and it is written that they chose—it was their choice—to suffer affliction as the faithful had suffered in earlier times rather than to enjoy what Rome at her voluptuous best had to offer.

It is even more boldly stated, if you please: "For whom the Lord loveth he chasteneth, and scourgeth every son whom he receiveth." Surely these are words hard to understand. The problem of human suffering remains as one of the great mysteries, but this I do know: God comes to His people and grants them mercies and foreglimpses of that which will be theirs to possess. I have seen the evidence of such grantings in the veritable ecstasies of some sufferers upon their deathbeds. We might reasonably curse and die, as Job's wife recommended to him, if this life were all. Those who believe it to be all and who so insist are to be understood when they curse. But this life is definitely not all!

I believe in eternal life because it became a vivid personal experience for me on a certain February morning in 1918. With an orderly I waited in the rain at the head of a communicating trench north of Toul in France. A platoon of an American machine-gun company was coming out. The first lieutenant, bringing up the rear, recognized my uniform and stopped to ask the way to the nearest canteen. Fever burned in his tired face. "Tonsillitis," he croaked as he leaned on his stick, "and trench foot." Then, pulling himself together, he stumbled on after his men. When he had gone a short distance, a shell exploded in the middle of the platoon. Hearing it coming, the orderly and I flung ourselves flat in the mud. Then the screams of agony called us to the wounded and dead. First looking after those who still needed the little we could do for them, we began gathering the shattered bodies of the others.

There, on the blood-soaked bit of French soil I experienced the comprehension of immortality. I knew that the lieutenant with the aching throat, the lad whose sick eyes had looked into mine, the boy with whom I had just talked, was not in what I had just picked up. I had not talked to *that.* But also I knew he was somewhere. I knew that there had been authority enough to begin his life, to carry it from his mother's womb to this awful end. Short of immortality I had the choice of just two conclusions: Either the great creative authority had willed that this young personality be extinguished there in the blood and muck, willed to end it in such a sorry fashion; or the same authority was able to create but was unable to continue, was helpless before the event.

My heart and mind rejected both conclusions. I knew then that the young life did not stop where I picked up his body. I knew then, as I know now, that he went on. It was a conviction, an experience, so real that it left me at the moment all but unconcerned about the pitifully broken body.

On February 25 I headed for the front again, where for three days I was scheduled to substitute for a big-hearted Methodist preacher who had been several weeks on the toughest job of the division without a rest or a chance to clean up. His Y.M.C.A. canteen, the extension of a wine cellar under a ruined chateau, was less than four thousand feet from our most advanced position. The canteen itself did not measure thirty feet in its longest dimension; the space was too precious to allow for the presence of more than one man to run it.

The canteen services of the Y.M.C.A.'s Red Triangle, of which my project was typical, were an absolute necessity on the Western Front. There were no other places "alive" within miles. The ruined villages were utterly empty, and had been so for years. Nothing was left but rubble; even the broken furniture had disappeared. The Y.M.C.A. sold nothing for gain; it hoped only to keep its losses as low as possible so that its work could continue. Even so, tons of supplies were given away outright in the trips to the trenches, and hot drinks were daily served free. Now and then criticisms were heard, but they were usually traceable to the extreme difficulties of transportation, which in turn led to high costs. However, the commissary department of the Red Triangle gave vastly more than one hundred cents to the dollar in materials and services, and when I returned to America it was with no words of criticism for the organization.

In my canteen, "Jenny," the fifteen-dollar talking machine, was usually busy, the selections varying with the mood of the man playing it. I could have choked the fellow who put on Homer Rodeheaver's "Tell Mother I'll Be There," and then played it again and again. But I understood his obsession. A thousand things bring a man close to his mother in such a situation—the socks he tries to darn, the button he sews on, the food he eats. A letter from a mother made a lot of heaven there, when it was the right kind of letter: the kind that made a son proud of his mother—a message of courage, of cheer, of news, with details of the commonplace: the coming of the spring birds to the house he had made, the new paper on the wall, the new baby at the neighbors' house, the bright gossip of the street or town, the tragedy of the bread that burned while she wrote these things to him. Such messages built morale faster than all the flags or martial music or speeches by commanders.

My very first day in the canteen I watched a homesick lad from Montana finger through the records until he found the one he wanted. When he put it on, he removed his helmet to ease his weary head—regulations allowed uncovering while underground—sat down on a box directly in front of the sound chamber, and waited for the first word, his unshaven chin resting in his dirty, cracked hand. Then he and the rest of us listened in silence, spellbound, while Alma Gluck sang "Little Gray Home in the West." She had sung it to brilliant crowds in great halls, but surely with no greater effect than her recorded voice had in that dark old cellar filled with war-weary Americans, while the shrapnel and high explosives contributed their accompaniment overhead.

People at home wanted to know about the *spirit* of the trenches. It was one of rare comradeship. I never saw a man injure another up there, or seek to. Of course there were quarrels, but there were few opportunities for them and when they did happen, they led to words that did not have double meanings and to fists that came through the open and hit above the belt. Such moments were uncommon and did not last.

I saw a man carry, in addition to his own kit, the entire equipment of another man who was suffering from gas. Three miles and a half, through mud-filled trenches, he walked with his double load, helping a man he had never seen before.

In one of our companies were two Portuguese. One could not speak English. He was terribly dependent upon his buddy. While I was with the battalion to which his company belonged, the buddy was killed. The distress of the man who did not understand the language of the country he loved, and for whose cause he had volunteered his all, was most affecting. But how the other men of that company got about him! They swore that he should not have a single lonely minute. Indeed, they nearly ruined him with their attentions and destroyed his stomach with their gifts of food before a wise-headed corporal took command of the situation and set them right.

It was this spirit of man's thoughtfulness for his brother that reassured me when I asked myself, "How will this stupendous slaughter affect the heart of the race?" And the ordinary soldier himself was not unaware of the question. After I returned to America I heard a young Canadian major put it this way to a group of his friends at a church banquet:

"I go away determined, God helping me, to do my hardest duty: to render my country and the Empire an enthusiastic and utmost service; and to carry myself so that when I come back, if I come back, little children will run to me as confidently as they do now."

On my first night in my canteen, when the candles were blown out and all around me I could hear the regular breathing of the weary sleepers, I put on my helmet, pushed aside the gas curtains, climbed the steep steps, and walked for a while in the chill beneath the cloudless sky. The guns were going ceaselessly; back and forth the huge shells moaned, like tired and unwilling men. Down the line the *rat-tat-tat* of the machine guns, the explosions so close as to give almost the sound of ripping canvas, rang out at irregular intervals. The gunners were spraying no man's land, searching for enemy patrols. The huge trucks and great wagons that had been pounding the roads since early dark, bringing up supplies and ammunition, were still busy. It was a good night for the mule-skinners and the men at the wheels; they could move quickly since the moon reduced to a minimum the danger of accidents.

I stood for a moment by a battered pool in the center of what once had been a formal garden. Only the pool, the crumbled walls, and a few splintered trees remained of what had been the glory of an ancient name. A couple of weeks before this trip to the front I had received a packet of letters from home. One of those treasures was a letter from my son Clark, the first he ever wrote me. "Dear Daddy," it read in large block letters, "Gee, I wish I was where you are. Love, Clark." Thinking of his childish desire as I stood in that scene of desolation, I was glad that my boy could be with me only in spirit and that he, when grown, would never find himself in such a war—for surely, I told myself, the civilized world would never countenance another such conflict.

On my last day in that forward post it rained shells. The canteen entrance darkened as if the gas curtain had been dropped. It looked as if every man of General Pershing's Army was trying to come see me in a great hurry. For several minutes I had been aware of the quickened firing, noting that the explosions were unusually close; but, feeling safe and being busy, I had paid little attention to the noise. Now the big outdoors had suddenly become too small, and the men were taking cover.

One chap, taller and louder than the rest, came in waving a shoe above his head, and in his sock feet. When I inquired after his other shoe, he sang out, "Left it. Didn't need it anyhow." He had been cleaning his equipment in front of his billet when the Kaiser's guns began trying to disable the big batteries just behind us. A shell dropped in the pool I had stood by, and several others did spring plowing in the abandoned garden, but not one of our men was scratched and not a missile reached its objective.

I still have a souvenir of that day: the nose of a shrapnel shell that dropped by my foot in the dugout entrance. Sent to kill me or any other man it could reach, it became a paperweight that has seen peaceful service on my desk for over forty years.

As I look back on these war experiences another scene comes to mind that remains like a glimpse of beauty and tenderness in the realm of horror. On a train traveling from Saint-Nazaire to Brest, I occupied a compartment alone. From the window I watched the morning come across the rugged hills of Brittany. The thatched stone houses set in formal fields took shape out of the gray dawn. The unsightly, close-trimmed tree trunks, which were like the gnarled, twisted fingers of a heavy hand, became clearly defined against the sky. Cattle appeared in the meadows, and presently I began to see people moving along the roads and in the villages we passed.

The train stopped to take on passengers. My privacy was invaded by a most delightful French family: a father and mother and their daughter, an exquisite miss of five. The parents took the seat opposite mine; without so much as a glance at me the little girl established herself by my side with her two dolls.

Though I continued to watch the passing landscape, I was increasingly conscious of the child. Her rich brown hair and richer eyes, her delicately tinted skin, the deftness of her tiny fingers, the laughter in her voice all made her, for a father far removed from the children of his own fireside, a picture to revel in.

Presently our train stopped again. While we waited for the unloading of baggage and the changing of engines I amused myself by throwing walnuts to the children I saw outside. Scampering about in their wooden shoes, they tried to catch glimpses of my hat and uniform as I sat by the window. To them a uniformed American was a familiar and welcome sight. Ragged and dirty, they were very polite, and their thanks for the nuts were profuse.

My little traveling companion came to the window and, unconscious of what she was doing, stood with her hand on my knee while she watched the wild scramble outside. When the train started again, she discovered her closeness to me and blushed. My smile and the friendly recognition of her parents reassured her, and from then on we were fast friends. She received the candy I offered her with a curtsy and a "*Merci monsieur*," and then she told me all about her dolls. My attention was perfect, and the fact that I could not understand a word of her vivacious prattle, nor she a word of the English I had to speak in return, did not in the least discourage either of us.

What a glorious morning we spent together! When I brought forth the pictures of my children she commented volubly, both to me and to her parents. And then she became quiet and sat for several minutes looking at the picture in her hands and at me. Perhaps she sensed something of what my separation from my family meant to me. I felt her sympathy and was consoled.

As the morning went on, I saw the little head begin to nod. I made a pillow for it in my lap, and while the child slept I lost my fingers in her curls. It was with a pang that I noticed the father make ready to leave the train. The mother brought down from the rack my little friend's bonnet. The train slowed and stopped.

I stepped onto the station platform first and the couple's bags were handed down to me. Then the father descended, courteously thanking me for my kindnesses, and gave his hand to his wife. Then the little girl appeared in the doorway. With her pretty bonnet, her soft fur coat, and her two dolls, with her silken hair and her dimpled cheeks, she looked as if she had stepped out of a picture book. I held up my arms and into them she came. With an extra hug I set her down upon the platform.

For an instant she stood and looked at me. Then, to my disappointment, without an "*Au revoir*" or any sign, she ran to her mother. The mother listened to her, then smiled and nodded. The little one came tripping back, reached up her arms, and puckered her lips. Down went my arms in an eager swing. Close about my neck she threw her arms, and on either cheek she kissed me.

Only the guard's warning saved me from missing that train. From the window I watched the little group disappear, and for the rest of that day I was not lonely. The touch of a child's hands and the pressure of a child's lips had lifted me above high mountains and carried me beyond the sea.

At 10 A.M. on Friday, March 1, 1918, I started for the trenches with a fellow Y.M.C.A. secretary named Pest on what was to prove a big day for both of us. Our immediate destination was the ruined village of Seicheprey, beneath whose rubble lay the bomb-proof headquarters of our First Regular Army Division. Each of us carried a sack containing a hundred pounds of chocolate, nuts, oranges, and cigarettes—things that the Army's front-line mess could not duplicate. These trench supplies were "specials," our gifts to those who for days at a time had to bear the body- and nerve-destroying ordeal of the most advanced places.

For a mile the going was comparatively easy, with a firm footing beneath five or six inches of mud. At Dead Man's Curve, a bad spot which bent out from behind a great ammunition dump and passed between batteries and on toward Seicheprey, we took a short cut across a field. The road at the bend was stained with blood; an empty supply wagon had been caught there earlier in the morning and the two men on the driver's seat and all of the mules had been killed.

For five hundred yards we continued across the shell-plowed field, now and then turning from the direct path to avoid shell holes close together. Several times I saw as many as three craters with rims touching. All morning the firing had been heavy and the moaning missiles were now passing high above our heads. It was relatively easy to judge whether a shell would land to the right or left, near or at a distance. You judged a flying shell much as you would judge a batted baseball—by its sound. But judging and being unconcerned were different matters. Explosions churning the earth a half-mile away from us filled me with apprehension. Pest didn't seem to care for the spectacle either.

The air had been misty all morning. Snow began to fall as the two of us reached the great supply road that at this point paralleled the front line for fifteen miles. Passing in front of our most advanced batteries, it was camouflaged to a height of twenty feet with branches and painted canvas. This did not conceal the location of the road itself, but it did hide the movements of troops, munitions, and supplies from the German observers who here looked down upon our lines from Mont Sec, which towered nine hundred feet above our position.

Seicheprey, lying midway between Toul and Metz, was in the heart of the salient that, next to Verdun, had witnessed the bloodiest fighting on the French front. The village itself, with its single street and ruined houses, had been captured and recaptured a number of times. Out from it, or hard by, twenty thousand Frenchmen had been buried by the hands of their comrades or the shells of their foe. This place was almost holy ground, and many Americans sensed that it was an honor and a high trust for our men to be fighting there.

When Pest and I reported to Major Richard H. Griffiths in his candle-lit bomb shelter, we learned that the company we had planned to serve was digging itself out, reopening the trenches after the morning's intense bombardment, looking after the wounded, and clearing away the dead. Griffiths preferred that we take our sacks eastward to Company K, where things were in better order. He spoke with pardonable pride when he informed us that his men, even those at the most advanced listening posts, had already been served with food and hot coffee. Pest and I began to understand the heavy firing we had heard earlier. Our guns had been supporting the infantry, and the German guns had been trying to silence them.

Griffiths told us that the first American infantry captain to die in action had been killed that morning at the head of his men. Five out of the six lieutenants "up" at the time had been wounded, while the sixth had followed his captain.

We went on, then, to Company K headquarters, obtained a guide, and began our rounds. Our boots did us little good; the "chicken-ladder" trench floor had been badly smashed by the shelling and we often sank in the mud to our hips. A soft-voiced Southern lieutenant told us how the French, occupying trenches farther along, had moved several companies in behind us during the morning. There the men had lain in the open, some five hundred yards back, in case the enemy broke through our line. It all seemed rather unreal to me. No man's land, when I examined it from our parapet, seemed strangely peaceful, and the German barbed wire, beginning no more than five hundred feet from where I stood, looked more like loganberry trellises in Oregon than part of a war barricade in France. Thinking back on this trench warfare of 1918, now as obsolete as the crossbow, I am always astonished to recall how close to one another the opponents were for months and even years.

At about one o'clock Pest and I started back toward the low ground where we had originally planned to go. Surely things would have been cleaned up by now, and Major Griffiths' men would be glad to see us. I followed Pest but not without forebodings. There was plenty of noise in front of us, and I doubted that the enemy would cooperate with the engineers who were restoring our trenches by refraining from shelling them. The "little ones"—the three-inchers—were falling not far away as we crossed the low ground and followed the trench into a woods of shattered trunks.

At the far edge of the woods our way was blocked. Working parties filled the space. All about were the marks of the morning's bloody struggle. The wounded had all been started to the rear, but there were still dead about. Bodies hung in the barbed wire like ghastly scarecrows.

We emptied our sacks of their last oranges and chocolate bars and then turned back, hurrying our steps as the firing increased. When we came to the place where we had entered the woods, we found our way barred again. Two stretcher parties were resting in the cover of the ruined forest. One stretcher carried the remains of a second lieutenant who had been killed by a trench mortar; the other bore a German prisoner, a fine-looking, husky

Bavarian whose legs had been fearfully mangled. The bearers were worn out. They were within a hundred yards of the point where it was necessary to leave the shattered trench and take to the open. The snowfall had ended, the light had been growing better, and it was apparent that enemy observers, at this point less than two hundred yards away, would quickly spot any movement in the open. Pest and I volunteered to lend a hand, and together we carried the wounded German to where he had to go over the parapet. "*Schön*" (fine), he murmured, expressing appreciation for our efforts through his pain.

Still helping, we started across the open ground, carrying our stretcher at shoulder height to give the gentlemen across the way a square and open look. The going was heavy. After perhaps three hundred yards the four of us who had lifted the two stretchers at the parapet were relieved. Pest and I started for the shelter we would find at Seicheprey.

Suddenly, hell opened. A barrage was put down upon the field. I can hear today as distinctly as I heard it then the crash of enemy guns, and almost simultaneously with that the cry of the officer in charge of the stretchers, "*Scatter!*" Then all about us the shells dropped. I suppose that the barrage lasted five minutes, hardly more, but it was a kind of eternity. It seemed to my terrified eyes that no foot of ground about us was left untouched. That night an observer in our line, on his way back after being relieved, stopped long enough to tell me that more than two hundred shells had landed within a radius of fifty yards from the center of our party.

I sprawled upon my face and rolled over into a shallow hole. Not ten feet away, a man was suddenly lifted into the air; five feet he seemed to go up. He turned over and came down with a flop in a shell hole filled with water. Aside from the shock and bruises, he was uninjured. A three-inch shell had gone into the earth almost under him. But in the open and in soft ground these shells were not particularly dangerous unless they scored direct hits. They penetrated so far before they exploded that their effect was largely smothered.

Fortunately for our little party, this barrage had no shrapnel mixed with it; had there been shrapnel, my story would be of another sort and someone else would have written it. But I was so profoundly frightened that I made no distinction between high explosives and shrapnel. I found myself trying to hide behind a rock no larger than a baby's fist. I envied a white dog that suddenly appeared, wheeling about on his hind legs, barking angrily in a dozen directions at once, trying to cover each new explosion. I envied not his bark, but his potential speed, and called him a fool for not using it.

Then I heard someone say—or perhaps it was my own heart speaking—"Run for it!" Faster than I ever left the scratch on a cinder path, I got away. As I ran, I thought of two things. First, I breathed a prayer of thankfulness for the additional five thousand of war-risk life insurance that I had taken out just before leaving New York; and then I recalled the ancient tale of the colored brother who heard the bullet twice, once when it passed him and once again when he passed it. I did my best to emulate him. Only two of the stretcher party reached headquarters before I did; they were younger men and unimpeded by trench coats. Pest and I ran a dead heat.

Major Griffiths heard our report, smiled a trifle anxiously, told us of the comparative safety we had enjoyed because of the soft ground and absence of shrapnel, and then inquired, "Did the bearers stay with the prisoner?" Pest replied, "I am not sure, sir, I did not look around, but I am inclined to think that he is out there alone." Someone felt it in order to remark that if the enemy wanted to kill his own wounded, he ought to be given the privilege of doing so. Then the major said, "Yes, he's a Hun, but we're Americans. Go back and get him."

I am writing these lines more than forty years after the event, but again I am in that shelter, standing beside the rough table where I stood that March afternoon when Major Griffiths startled me out of my terror into sober reflection. I believe that I had tried to give the enemy the benefit of the doubt in conceding that he may not have recognized the nature of the party crossing the open field. But the major waived the whole question of enemy "frightfulness," and stated clearly and succinctly that heart of the American tradition at war. He saw only a prisoner, wounded and under fire, and he knew his duty.

We left headquarters with a lieutenant, and Pest volunteered to show him the location of the wounded German. I urged Pest not to go over the parapet again, pointing out that he and I were not soldiers even though we wore uniforms. Our soldier-like activities, I warned him, might lead to the trenches being closed to the Y.M.C.A. My friend acknowledged the warning and hurried on with the lieutenant. Since only one guide was needed, I waited at the head of a road leading through some tumbled walls and out toward some abandoned trenches with tangles of rusted wires above them. On beyond was the open field where so many brave men had fought and died since the Germans had first driven forward from Metz. Looking strangely out of place in a scene of such destruction were scores of wooden crosses: part of a French burial ground that had once been behind our lines.

"Poor place to spend a vacation," remarked the sentinel who stood post beside me. Scarcely had the words left his lips when that field again became an inferno. I could not see Pest and those who had joined him; a slight rise in the ground hid them. But as the air around me grew dark with earth and rocks, I was forced into the sickening conclusion that I had been afraid when I sought to dissuade Pest from going back for the prisoner.

Returning to headquarters, I found Major Griffiths trying to silence our batteries, for our fire was stirring the Germans to reply. Two runners had been dispatched, since our communication lines were down. Griffiths gave me permission to go down the road a way, looking for the stretcher party. As I reached the open place again, a new kind of fear possessed me, for there was no sign of life anywhere. The snow was falling again. I met a runner. He had not seen the party. I went on, and soon reached the spot where the first barrage had fallen. There was still no sign.

A second runner was skirting the woods we had passed through earlier. Yes, he had seen them. They had waited till the shelling slackened, and then from the cover of the woods he had watched them rush the stretcher back to the trench. They had taken a longer and more protected route toward headquarters. It was the way Pest and I and both the stretchers should have gone in the beginning.

The runner, a youthful veteran, instructing me to follow him at a distance of twenty paces, led me along a road that skirted behind our headquarters. Then, in that snow-powdered mud, I began to see the prints of French boots. I remembered what the Company K lieutenant had told me about the French backing us up. This, I realized, was the very spot where some of them had waited. Half-buried in the mud I saw a gas mask. A rush of emotion overwhelmed me as I caught it up and discovered spots of blood where a brave poilu had pressed his face into it only a few hours before. Somehow the thought of the young French soldiers dying on and for their native soil made me weep.

Now the German batteries became busy again. At first their objective seemed to be well beyond the village. Then the firing assumed the intensity of a barrage and the range was shortened so that the shells fell all over Major Griffiths' headquarters. Such a spectacle I had never seen before. It was as if the heavens had opened to precipitate an ocean of soil, boulders, and trees upon the earth. The earth itself seemed to open as the result of some great sickness and vomit this terrifying deluge. Deafened, rooted to the spot, I was conscious of no other emotion than complete amazement. I had been in the midst of the first barrage and close to the second one, so I had not *seen* them. We were perhaps a hundred and fifty yards from this one and could see it all.

Then a shrapnel shell burst not far away and we were roused from our stupor. The fragments flew all around us, spattering mud. We ran! Straight toward the barrage we went, without a word of discussion, for with shrapnel our one chance was to find shelter. That we were not hit before we reached it was one of the hourly miracles of the front. While the barrage was being pulled across the village and shortened in our direction, and with shrapnel bursting overhead, the runner and I dove into the first abandoned trench we spotted. A good eight-foot plunge it was too, landing us in slime and mud and, I am now convinced, something more that could not be seen or detected by two worried men—a residue of mustard gas. Our masks hung about our necks unused, and though I still held the poilu's mask in my hand, I was hardly aware of it.

Once in Oregon, among the dunes of the Columbia River, I had turned my pony's head into an approaching sand storm and flung myself headlong on the ground while with the sound of a hundred mountain torrents and in inky darkness a tempest of sand swirled over me. But the tempest at Seicheprey was a cloudburst of steel and iron, a continuous thunder in which were mingled the throaty roar of multiple discharges, the moan of shells through the air, and the shock of explosions. This appalling storm directed by men against men was "modern warfare."

And then, as suddenly as it began, the barrage ceased. After perhaps no more than ten minutes in that gas-poisoned trench the runner and I climbed out and hurried on to headquarters. Certain that I would find the shelter blown open and bodies scattered everywhere, I was surprised to find almost no damage. Three men had been wounded, some old house walls had been further broken down, and yards of camouflage had been destroyed, but this was about all. When I reported to Major Griffiths for the last time, he was sitting at his table in his bomb shelter, taking care of his communications as if nothing exceptional had been going on. For me the past few minutes had demonstrated the truth of the axiom I had often heard but scarcely believed: "It takes a thousand rounds to kill one man by shellfire."

Pest I found in a nearby communications trench, unharmed and waiting for me. From him I learned that the German prisoner had finally been brought in, suffering terribly but still exclaiming "*Schön, schön!*" at everything that was done for him. Every hand that had touched his stretcher had been a kind one, and the men who had risked their lives to save his had all expressed their admiration for his courage. The poor fellow breathed his last as he was being lifted into the ambulance that was to take him to the rear.

All in all it was quite an experience for a couple of men who had set out in a spirit of Christian fellowship to distribute candy and cigarettes to a few hard-pressed soldiers. In the morning, approaching Seicheprey, I had felt nervous when shells exploded a half-mile away from me; now, wallowing back through the mud and snow to the main road, I doubted if the physical side of war could ever upset me again.

The man who lingered in my memory that day, and still lingers with me, was Major Griffiths. I saw him during the course of that one day only, when his battalion had already come through a terrific shelling. I do not know how he looked in a dress uniform or when he was clean shaven; I have no conception of what his manner was in a drawing room; I am uninformed as to his church affiliation, if he had one. But he acted like a soldier that day and he spoke like a Christian. I'm sure that he was every inch a soldier, too, for after starting life as a newspaperman in Missouri, he had fought through the Spanish-American war and served in the Philippine constabulary. With the outbreak of the war in Europe he had enlisted in the British Army, but when the Stars and Stripes came to stand beside the Union Jack he moved over and was commissioned a major in our Army. This much I learned from him during our brief first meeting.

I intended to keep in touch with this leader of men, but our friendship was not to continue. Soon after my return to the United States I read a dispatch under the heading, "American colonel killed in action." The details were sparse: "Lieutenant Colonel Richard H. Griffiths, commanding a battalion of infantry has been killed by shellfire in Picardy. He emerged from a dugout just as an enemy shell arrived and exploded directly in front of him." Thus Griffiths went to stand at attention before the Commander whose orders, whether he thought of it that way or not, he so completely obeyed. Later, from a lieutenant I had come to know, I received a letter describing the circumstances of Griffiths' burial:

The regimental chaplain was sick. There happened to be a Red Cross chaplain visiting us from Paris, so he officiated. It was pitch dark and the boys had to be mighty careful to keep their shovels from clicking against stones. A lantern or a candle would have helped, but any light would have meant death. Twice the ritual was suspended while the mourners took to cover to avoid enemy bullets.

Some of the soldiers gathered wild violets and poppies at the rear of the trenches, keeping them fresh in a dipper of water in a dugout. These were laid on all the graves during the darkness.

The next night an enemy shell demolished the little cemetery, exposing the bodies. We had to bury Colonel Griffiths four separate times.

I still remember the last words I heard Griffiths say. There in his dim-lit shelter he smiled, threw up his hand, and said cheerfully—for all the world as if we were parting on some quiet street corner at home—"I'll be seeing you." The strange thing about this farewell—uttered so casually and yet so full of the confidence of enduring life—is that I heard it twice again during World War II in rather similar circumstances, spoken first by a young G.I. and then by our greatest leader of those years. Well, perhaps I shall indeed see Griffiths again, even as I shall again see the many whom I have loved and who have gone before me.

The first general gas attack experienced by American soldiers was directed against the sector held by our First Division. In the marshy ground to the right of Seicheprey one company suffered horribly. Men died almost instantly; others were carried back to die lingeringly, or to become permanent invalids. Early in the war both sides had sent gas forth from containers when the wind could be counted on to carry it to the enemy's positions. Later, the introduction of the gas shell gave this fiendish weapon a much greater reach. When fired alone, gas shells could be detected by the peculiar sound of their explosion, but when they were sent over in company with ordinary shells one had no warning, and during a general bombardment the safest thing was to wear one's mask continuously.

Mustard gas was so much heavier than the air that in some cases "active" trenches were cleared with shovels that were fitted for the purpose with canvas flaps. I saw soldiers lifting the invisible poison over the parapets, where the moving air could disperse it. Chlorine gas, unlike mustard, was dispersed by the use of a neutralizing solution in a special sprayer. Both these gases lingered in low spots, like the one I had plunged into during the barrage, and the casualties from this sort of accidental exposure were so great that at one point the French commanders issued a general order prohibiting their soldiers from entering shell holes.

Often gas poisoning was at first diagnosed as pneumonia, pleurisy, and even tuberculosis. My case was typical of the ones that developed slowly. At first I thought I had a cold. Then my lungs became sore, my throat burned, and I began to speak with difficulty. At times I bled from mouth and nose. My head ached constantly and I was tortured with coughing. To cap it, on the sixth day, my eyes crossed. At night, when I could sleep at all, I had horrible dreams and awoke struggling for a full breath. At such moments I sometimes had memories of my father's arms around me, as they had held and reassured me the night of my childhood when I was gasping with croup.

And perhaps I had breathed in no more than a whiff of gas in that trench! Gas was at least one horror not inflicted upon the soldiers of World War II. Both sides were fully prepared to use it. I saw containers of the stuff piled high behind our bases in Algeria. Mercifully, neither side was willing to begin the use of this frightful weapon.

As my condition worsened, I was evacuated to the naval hospital at Brest. There my trouble was diagnosed and I was given the absolute rest and protection from the elements that brought about my recovery. On the way to Brest, as I lay racked with chills in a canteen in Gondriecourt, still uncertain as to the nature of my sickness, an American appeared whom I quickly recognized. Harry Emerson Fosdick even then was a world figure of the Christian faith.

I had known and appreciated Fosdick through his writings, particularly his book *The Meaning of Prayer*. That dynamic and luminous treatise had made my life richer when I encountered it in 1915; I have kept it close at hand ever since. Scholarly, personal, and yet at grips with the everyday issues of life, it is a timeless volume. On theological matters and the question of pacifism Fosdick and I have had our differences over the years, but I continue to regard him as one of the great spiritual leaders of our time.

Early in World Wall II we had a serious correspondence, initiated by me, in which I urged that Fosdick not withhold from our servicemen the comfort and inspiration of his message and personality. I asked him to give to those in uniform what he had so richly given to others in an earlier time. He replied in effect that he would not ever again touch "the unclean thing" —war. He was, I felt, embarrassed and inhibited by the commitments he made in his famous sermon addressed to the Unknown Soldier. There is a wall of consistency that sometimes surrounds and imprisons sincere men and women. Consistency may indeed be a jewel but, as James Russell Lowell said in "The Present Crisis," one of his poems dealing with our Civil War, "new occasions teach new duties." We need not bless war to bless boys who through no wish of theirs are thrown into its ordeals and horrors—those who give their last full measure. We may refuse to touch war but war will touch us. And there is something more. Our sons may be at the controls of fighter planes "up there" but "down here" we feed gas into their tanks and shells into their cannon, and before God and man we have with them equal and perhaps greater moral responsibility for the result. This truth was borne home to me as I witnessed the horrors of 1918, and no experience I had in World War II or in the Korean War ever caused me to change my belief in the inadequacy of pacifism as an answer.

But such thoughts as these were not mine that bitterly cold March night in Gondriecourt when Fosdick and I met for the first time. Miserably sick, feeling like a stuffed toad in an icebox, I shook in my bunk and wished I could forget my troubles. Fosdick proved the Good Samaritan. The hot-water bottle his wife had insisted he carry overseas went with its comforting heat into my blankets; finally the good man himself crept into that narrow bunk and with his body warmth sought to stop the chills that racked me.

Another time, years later, Fosdick's spiritual presence came helpfully into my life. After a rugged football season, my son Daniel lay desperately ill of double pneumonia at Kimball Union Academy in New Hampshire. As I stood at his bedside, my hand on his head, I asked, "Is there anything I can do for you before I leave you for the night?"

Daniel was almost in a coma and fighting pleurisy pains, but he heard me. "Read something, Dad!" he gasped. I had just finished reading Fosdick's "Seeing It Through," a chapter from his *Twelve Tests of Character*, and I gave Daniel that phrase, "seeing it through," and the gist of Fosdick's message. Daniel whispered, "That's fine, Dad!" I said, "That's it, Dan—we're seeing it through." And my boy did just that.

6

There are times when the experience of the past can mean much to a man; or, to put it another way, when he can draw life-giving nourishment from his roots. Such a time was mine during the six weeks in 1918 when I convalesced in England and Scotland, trying to forget the horrors I had seen in the trenches.

It was early in the year, but England's fields had already begun to smile. The grass was green and presently the hedges began to bud. Birds were everywhere, and the khaki-colored lanes—for soldiers were on every path—were full of song. I wandered down streets immortalized by Dickens. I walked by the Humber, down which some of the Pilgrim Fathers had sailed. Later, in Southampton, I stood before the Pilgrim monument. Here John Alden, "a youth of the city," had joined the immortal company, and from the dock hard by the *Mayflower* had sailed. The Pownals, my father's mother's ancestors, had sailed from this land only a little later. Followers of Cromwell, they had fled following the Restoration. Landing in Boston, they had gone to William Penn's Philadelphia in 1663.

My footsteps echoed through cathedrals. That supremely exquisite creation at York, a spectacle of worship, burst upon my gaze like a palace from the celestial world. At dusk I followed Canon Braithwaite through the cathedral at Winchester, England's ancient capital. I thought of the twenty-three English kings who are buried within these walls; I thought of the Crusaders coming here for their parting consecration, ere they turned their faces toward the Holy Land. I thought, too, of the great Canute, whose kingly dust reposes somewhere beneath the nave, and of the lesson he learned from the tide that refused to obey his will.

The gray-haired canon showed me "Bloody Mary's" wedding chair, the gift of Pope Julius III when Mary married Philip of Spain. While the canon talked of the treasures for which he had long been responsible, the cathedral's choir began its practice. The music filled the mighty building and rang in a hundred echoes from column to column, and from the Norman tiles of the floor to the perfectly joined stones of the vaulted roof. The flare of our torch so lighted the sculptured effigies that they seemed to be living figures moving through the air, and the singing became the voices of England's ancient great, some of whom were good, all of whom were human. The voices that had spoken so long ago, I seemed to hear again.

In my study, as I write these lines, is a cathedral-shaped block of worm-eaten English heart of oak. It came from one of the original roof beams of Holy Trinity Church in Hull, the largest parish church in England. As the warden of Holy Trinity placed the memento in my hands on a spring afternoon so long ago, his arm swept toward the high vaulted nave, and he said, "Think of it, six hundred and thirty-four years ago it was placed here!" More than six centuries before I stood there, and more than two before Columbus began his voyage to the New World, that fragment of oak had been part of a mighty support lifted by the hands of dedicated men and fitted above an altar that even then stood upon the ruins of a more ancient altar. That bit of wood I brought home from England was not a jewel, nor was it a ransom in gold, but to me it has always been infinitely more treasurable.

My mood of exaltation in Britain's shrines of Protestanism was tempered now and then by my memory that the Puritans, the Pilgrims, and the Quakers—my own ancestors among them—had been forced to choose between their faith and their freedom. Cherishing both, they had been obliged to leave the inhospitable shores of England. I sensed the richness and continuity of England's religious traditions; at the same time I remembered the unbending authoritarianism that had led to the establishment of a freer Protestantism in the New World. Thus my heritage as a free Christian American was brought home to me as I wandered through the land that had contributed so greatly to that heritage.

I was particularly happy to tread the stones of Rochdale, for this was the city of John Bright, England's trumpet voice against slavery. Here, during our Civil War, Bright had inspired the cotton millers to support President Lincoln and the American Union. Despite dire want brought on by the closing of the mills, the workers had stood firm against any attempt to break the blockade of the South's cotton ports. As one of our most effective champions abroad during the Civil War, Bright's name should be better remembered by Americans than it now is.

In Scotland I caught a glimpse of the Robert Burns country at Dunoon, the home of tragic "Highland Mary," whose statue looks out across the Firth of Clyde. Here was the home of a later and living bard, Harry Lauder, from the depths of whose supreme sorrow was lifted a new song to comfort a weeping world. Some day Lauder's townsmen will rear another monument, facing out toward the sea. On it will be the name of Captain John Lauder, Sir Harry's heroic son.

It was my privilege to hear much of the story from Harry Lauder's own lips. On the afternoon of October 30, 1917, I was among the standees at the rear of the Academy of Music in Philadelphia. Lauder, then making his third or fourth "farewell" tour of America, outsang and outdid himself, stomping back and forth across the stage on his bandy legs, his kilt swinging to the tune of "Roamin' in the Gloamin' by the Bonnie Banks of Clyde." When he could sing no longer, and after repeated calls from the audience that had been brought close to his generous heart, the little Scot stepped to the front of the stage, stood quietly before us, and opened his soul for us to look into its depths. The story he told us was of his only son. John had been killed less than a year before, the day before Christmas, 1916, just as he was leaving the trenches for his first furlough home. Lauder had gone down to London to meet the young man, and there he waited while train after train came in with no John aboard. Many of the audience Lauder addressed that afternoon were soon to know firsthand the sensations of loss that were being described, for even then American soldiers were in France. By the time Lauder got to the end of his story the laughter and cheers that his earlier performance had evoked had given way to absolute silence. "I had three alternatives," he told us—and even as I write this I can hear the poignant burr in his voice—"For me it was drink or death or God, and I took God."

And so in the early summer of 1918, visiting Dunoon, I went with the pastor of the kirk to pay my respects to Harry Lauder and his wife. There was no false sentiment in them, only great and simple dignity covering two broken hearts, as the Lauders showed me the foundations of the house that was to have been finished for Captain John and his bride. Now no home would ever stand upon those stones. I came away from the visit carrying a Scotch thistle cane with Harry Lauder's name upon its silver plate, but even more than this souvenir I treasured the glimpse I had had into two lives scarred by tragedy and yet filled with the acceptance of the comforts of Christ.

My journey through England and Scotland was not entirely one of aimless wandering, inspiring though this part of it was. My physical strength and voice coming back to me, I took part in the National Temperance Crusade of the United Kingdom, a campaign sponsored by a representative group of men and women who felt the compulsion of an immediate problem. Witnesses from abroad were introduced in a great series of meetings. Prohibitionists and antiprohibitionists alike supported this effort, which, with its open forums and question-and-answer sessions, was really a gigantic educational clinic. The executive director of this effort was a gifted young Toronto journalist, Newton Wylie. He was a wonder! A broken back had kept him out of the armed forces, but in spite of virtually constant suffering he was a human dynamo, virile and indefatigable, with the double personality of inspirational leader and an administrator. The campaign he generaled, and into which I threw myself wholeheartedly, reached a million Britons from platforms and millions more through the daily and religious press.

One evening, after taking part in a meeting in a suburb, I returned to London and stepped out of my taxi before three old-fashioned houses. Dwarfed by the Privy Council building and the Foreign Office, they were decidedly strays of another century. Westminster Abbey and the Parliament buildings, looming nearby, seemed to give them their excuse for staying. Reading on one of the doors "The First Lord of the Treasury, No. 10," I knew that I stood before the portals of historic 10 Downing Street. I lifted the ancient knocker that had announced guests for perhaps three centuries and that had for at least a century and a half summoned attendants to usher in the world's statesmen and politicians. The door swung open and a quiet-spoken man in a business suit admitted me and took my card, bidding me follow.

Trailing my guide down the antlered hall, I ran head on into a well set up, youngish gentleman, Major Waldorf Astor, who was coming to meet me. He was delightfully without formality. During World War II, when he had succeeded to his father's title, I was to know him as Lord Astor, and be entertained by him and his brilliant American wife at their old home in Plymouth. Now, after we had made ourselves known to one another, Astor led me into the Council Chamber. Here, all the British cabinets had met since Robert Walpole established himself at 10 Downing Street during the monarchy of George II. As I looked about, I noted but one portrait. It hung over the fireplace: a painting of Francis Bacon. He was Lord Chancellor once, although he is better remembered as a master of human thought. For the rest, that historic room was stripped to essentials. Commanding the center was a great council table, covered with green baize and set about with heavy formal chairs. The walls were lined with bookshelves, but these were scarcely visible behind the many charts and maps that were displayed. On one large map of western Europe I saw battle lines that I had recently known more intimately.

William Pitt and his cabinets had sat here. In this room, when the terrible word of defeat came from Austerlitz, Pitt had pointed to the map of Europe and said, "Roll it up; it won't be needed for another ten years." Here the statesmen had stood with ringing cheers for the news from Trafalgar, and here, a decade later, had come the word of Napoleon's defeat at Waterloo. In this room Disraeli had won the Suez Canal for the Empire, and here Gladstone's mighty form had filled a chair before the fireplace. I saw the chamber as the spiritual home of indomitable leaders and conquerors, and I felt privileged to stand within its walls.

Turning to a stairway with Major Astor, I now beheld the man I had come to see. Halfway down the stairs, his left hand resting lightly on the banister, a smile of welcome lighting his face, stood Prime Minister David Lloyd George. The moment I first saw him answered any question that may have been in my mind as to the personal quality of his leadership. Square of shoulder, deep-chested, with an erect neck that gave his fine head its perfect placing, he was short and stocky, yet he had the appearance of added height that few short men are fortunate enough to possess. His clear eyes shone at me, and when he spoke, it was with one of the most musical and ingratiating voices I had ever heard. During the course of our conversation I learned that Lloyd George had been trained in the Christian Endeavor movement in his native Wales, and that his first speaking in public had been done for his local society. Then and later I found him one of those irresistible personalities who not only dominate others by the mastership of their own souls but bind men to them by their mental genius.

No other European political leader had been so long familiar and popular with the American people. The United States shouted its approval when he bitterly opposed the Boer War, and in his battle with landlordism, his struggle with the House of Lords, his championing of the rights of labor, and his unrelenting efforts to better the conditions of the poor, he had the heart of America with him.

The night I met the Prime Minister he had just returned from Versailles, where he and other Allied leaders had discussed and settled matters of vast importance to the armies on the Western Front. My mission was concerned with a matter vital to the prosecution of the Allied effort. In the United States, extremists among the temperance forces were pressing for the passage of a bill in Congress that would stop all grain shipments to the United Kingdom unless that nation immediately established wartime prohibition. It was a serious situation and one that gave me considerable embarrassment. Though I believed in prohibition for America, I did not condone attempting to force our views on Great Britain, against such age-old traditions as the pub and all it stood for. Lloyd George's lifelong and eloquent dedication to teetotalism had been a potent factor in America's own trend toward national prohibition. At the beginning of the war he had delivered one of his supreme philippics against alcohol, and perhaps his words had tipped the balance in a dozen states of the American Union. It was understandable that the American prohibitionists expected a very sympathetic reception from Lloyd George.

But the letter I now obtained from him was carefully worded for its effect on Americans, teetotaler and imbiber alike. It pointed out that although England did not have national prohibition, the manufacture of spirits in England had been entirely stopped, and the brewing of beer drastically curtailed. "Should the exigencies of War necessitate further restrictions," the Prime Minister concluded, "we shall follow with interest your campaign for the enforcement of War Prohibition in the United States of America." This statement, which I immediately carried back to America and gave to the secular as well as the religious press after presenting it to a specially called meeting of the National Temperance Council, fortunately proved effective in stopping a propaganda campaign that could, I believe, have seriously affected the unity of the Allies and the very course of the war.

I particularly remember Lloyd George's parting words to me that night as I left 10 Downing Street. He walked me to the door and stood with me for a moment before it was opened. Gripping my arm, he said earnestly, "This war is infinitely bigger than any one man's dearest principles. It is our all-out struggle to save freedom for all men." I could not have agreed more.

When my ship docked in New York in May, 1918, and my good Christian Endeavor friend Amos R. Wells was unexpectedly there to meet me, I was grateful but a little surprised. Soon enough I realized that there was something ominous about his coming down from Auburndale, for I heard him carefully explaining that I must not expect to find Susie in good health. "But she will be waiting for you in the white house," he remarked, obviously hoping to reassure me. However, I was not reassured, for I caught the implication that Susie had not been at home during all my absence.

Later, as Wells and I went up the tree-shaded street from the Auburndale station, my pace quickening to a run, I caught my first glimpse of Susie. She was standing in the open door of our home, looking as exquisitely beautiful as a picture while she waited to greet me on my return as she had been when we said good-by five months before. My sense of relief was infinite, for in that first moment there was not the slightest suggestion of illness or weakness. Susie was radiant—more lovely, if possible, than I had remembered her. Then our boys came rushing over the walk and down the steps to fling themselves on me. I was astonished to see how much they had grown since I had seen them last. Little Mary, grinning at her daddy, waited decorously near her mother, and behind her stood my faithful sister Mabel ("Mebs"), holding baby Jane in her arms.

All of this was the homecoming I had prayed for and dreamed of, and it seemed to me that my happiness could not be greater. Then the shocking and saddening truth was revealed to me. Susie had been in failing health for long months. Unbeknown to all of us, including Susie herself, the whooping cough she had contracted a few hours after Clark was born had opened the way for the chronic condition that became increasingly serious over the next eight years, leading at last to tuberculosis. It was not to be that I should ever again see the mother of my children as I saw her that summer day when she forced herself to stand in the doorway in order to greet me as she knew I would want to see her. She never stood again like that. It was as if she had willed herself to stay alive until I could return to be again the father to our children. In the quick days that followed I saw the mother of my sons and daughters slip away from us.

Susie died in a sanitarium at Attleboro, Massachusetts, following an emergency operation. We brought her body home to Auburndale, and my venerable Christian Endeavor friend, Dr. Francis E. Clark, conducted the simple home funeral services with tender understanding. Just before he read from the Scriptures and spoke his words of comfort, Dr. Clark baptized baby Jane, whose first given name, Elizabeth, was that of Elizabeth Wells, daughter of my faithful friends the Amos R. Wellses, and whose second name, Jane, was her mother's second name. Thus, three of our children were baptized by Dr. Clark. Daniel, our first, had been baptized by the man who had joined Susie and me in marriage, Bishop H. B. Hartzler.

After the services in Auburndale my sister Mebs and I took Susie's body and the children to Ohio, and there in a beautiful old cemetery in Summit County, only a few miles from the great house where Susie and I had first met and where we had been married, we turned back the sod and tucked her body under. It seemed to me that the girl who had been my wife had walked with me in life too short a time, and I regretted bitterly the long periods during which we had been separated.

One moment in Auburndale the night before the funeral services often returns to me. It is part of what I choose to call my own immortality experience. The feeling had first come to me outside that trench north of Toul when I gathered up the broken pieces of the body of the young lieutenant to whom I had just been talking. Now it came again. My children and their Aunt Mebs had gone upstairs to their rooms. Susie's sister Carrie and my parents—Father and Mother had come on from Pennsylvania—had also retired. I had asked to be left alone in the study just across from the room in which the open casket rested. Some time after midnight I went in and stood beside the quiet form that had been my wife. When my hand touched her face, I knew two things, and knew them with complete finality. First, she was not there; second, she still was there, but beyond my touch. There did not come to me the responding pressure I had known in happier times, but there did come to me the comforting knowledge that though gone, she was not away. Only the form remained before me, but I knew that there had been a divine miracle of survival, and that that which in Susie was destined to live forever—that which I had loved—was alive forevermore and would forever companion me. That night I knew, too, that much of our grief at death is self-pity. We grieve for ourselves, not for the loved one we have temporarily lost. If we believe as I do, then we cannot be grieving for the loved ones who have gone on ahead of us, for they have the better part, and we shall meet again just around the corner.

The reactions of my children to Susie's going were to me touching and typical. Baby Jane, hardly a year old, was of course unaware of what was happening. Mary, not yet five, was full of sorrow, though today she can remember her first mother only in flashes. Daniel, then ten, grieved deeply in what was for him an unnatural state of quietness, but he continued to be understanding about the sad event.

More than a decade later, when he was a student at Wooster College, in Ohio, Daniel hitchhiked and walked sixty miles to Susie's grave and spent a Mother's Day there with his memories of her. That evening he wrote a touching letter of appreciation and love to Lillian, who, as my second wife and his second mother, had long before taken Daniel into her great heart.

Clark took Susie's passing differently. At eight, he was deeply wounded and became rebellious. I remember him flinging himself into my arms and crying, "We'll never have another mother. No, never—and you see to that!" A little more than a year later Lillian entered our family and completely won Clark. "My Second Mother," the poetic tribute to Lillian that Clark wrote in his freshman year in college, suggests the healing quality that she brought to this relationship:

At your feet, my Second Mother,
This poor heart of mine I lay;
And the years will bring no other
Dearer than you are today.

For in years of happy living,
Since you came to mother me,
Always have I found you giving
Strength and love unstintingly.

In the summer of 1918, when I was attempting to find my way without Susie, my father and mother welcomed Mebs and my children with open arms in their own home. Father was then pastor of the United Evangelical Church in Wilkinsburg, Pennsylvania, and their modest home became ours for the next year. Mother gave my four the care and affection and training that the press of time and duty made it impossible for me to give them except now and then. Years later, Clark said of his grandmother, my mother, "Once I lived with a saint." Well, I had lived with her too, and Clark was telling me nothing new, but I was grateful that Mother's ministrations could come to my children at this period when they were so vitally needed.

All this is not to suggest that there weren't some lively moments in the home of Charles and Savilla Poling. Nine-year-old Clark developed the habit of trying to keep his grandfather in order at meal times: reminding him of a spoon that might remain in a cup of coffee a moment too long, or of an elbow resting on the table. If a crumb clung to my father's whiskery chin, Clark would let him know about it. Perhaps this reflected credit to the boy's home training, but on one of my stops at the house my sister took me aside and let me know that my younger son was being just a little disrespectful.

I had a private moment with the young man during which I explained fully what sort of behavior I expected in the future, and why. Always the casuist, Clark insisted that his grandfather ought not to have crumbs on his whiskers, that he often was unaware of such blemishes, and that no one else seemed to be thoughtful enough to tell him. I finished the discussion with the firm directive that a little boy was not the proper person to correct the manners of a grandfather, and I added the threat of suitable action if self-restraint were not imposed at once. Clark seemed impressed, and I had hopes. That evening we had apple pie for dessert, and a trifling flake of Mother's light-as-air crust went its own way and dangled on Father's chin. Clark's keen eyes fixed upon it. Raising his hand and pointing his finger, he started to speak. Then he became aware of my baleful eyes fixed upon him. Though he continued to point, his remark changed directions. "Daddy," he said, "will you please tell Grandpa to wipe his chin."

As soon as I was able to after my return from England, I reported to Secretary of War Baker and to Raymond B. Fosdick with reference to the War Camp Community Service program that I had been forced to relinquish when I was gassed. After that, I toured the country on behalf of the Liberty Loan drives and finished the writing of my book *Huts in Hell,* in which I offered to American readers my personal view of the war as I had seen it. People at home were much concerned about the moral stability of our soldiers overseas. Having observed these men both under fire and at liberty, away from the battlefields, I had seen good behavior and bad. I did not try to hide the bad any more than I tried to magnify the good. My conclusion was that Americans in France were pretty much like Americans anywhere: There were those who went to pieces and those who sought advantages, but there were also those who became greater because of the ordeals they faced and experienced. "For every man in the Army who is morally corrupted or destroyed," I told my audience, "at least five men are morally born again." I believed it then and I believe it today.

The International Society of Christian Endeavor was the publisher of my book, and we had a long struggle over the title I had chosen for it. Dr. and Mrs. Clark, among others, felt that it bordered on profanity. I stood firm, however, and while I was speaking at a Liberty Loan meeting in Omaha, Nebraska, was delighted to receive word that my associates in Boston had come around to my way of thinking. With its typical misspelling, the telegram said, DR. AND MRS. CLARK HAPPY AND THE TITLE IS NUTS IN HELL.

After the Armistice, having been certified as medically fit despite the presence of scars on my lungs, I returned to France to carry out assignments for the Y.M.C.A. and other social service organizations. I greatly appreciated the opportunity to travel over the battlefields I remembered so well, but I was even more interested in entering Germany and observing for myself the effects of the war. The defeated enemy was already at work rebuilding his nation. Recovery was in the air. Noting the determined spirit of the German rank and file, I reminded myself that in the past conquered nations had often risen from their ruin to destroy the victor's triumph.

In the hospital at Coblenz, recovering from his wounds, I saw the young German flier who was credited with having shot down Quentin Roosevelt, the youngest son of Theodore Roosevelt.

On New Year's Day, 1919, I had a memorable experience—my first airplane ride. My pilot was Lieutenant Colonel Beeman, one of Eddie Rickenbacker's men; our ship was one of the little Fokker biplanes that the Germans had surrendered under the Armistice terms. We took off shortly after dawn from Fortress Alexandria at Coblenz and flew to fabled Bingen on the Rhine. The distance was about thirty miles but we probably traveled twice as far in getting there because Beeman, anxious to treat a novice to all the thrills, did every turn and loop he knew. To me, clinging to anything I could find in the rear cockpit, his repertory of tricks seemed endless. Very soon I had no idea whether we were flying right side up or upside down, and it didn't really make any difference to me. In the freezing wind my face kept coming into violent contact with the front rim of the cockpit, and when Beeman finally released me from my torture I looked like a very red poppy on a wobbly stem.

After that experience I didn't fly again for seven years, and can't say that I felt deprived. Then, beginning in 1926, when I gathered my courage and took my family on a flight from London to Paris, I became a constant user of the airways.

My missions in World War II, during which I repeatedly flew across both oceans, made me practically a commuter to all quarters of the globe. After the war my journeys actually increased in number, and late in 1958, after my yearly visit to the *Christian Herald's* orphanages in Korea, my total air mileage reached 1,886,417, or an average of more than 53,000 miles a year since 1926. My Admiral's card with American Airlines is dated September, 1940, and I am now a member of Pan American's Clipper Club, a Million Miler with United, and an Ambassador with T.W.A. From that first Fokker plane of 1919, I have watched, and as a passenger participated in, the development of air travel. Keeping my engagements by jet these days, I look back and note that only twice have I ever missed an important engagement as the result of adverse flying conditions, and only once have I ever been hurt in an accident; this occurred in a charter plane and was not serious. When once a traveler becomes air-minded, it seems he can never again be satisfied with the slower ways to travel. This may be unfortunate. I confess to nostalgic emotion at the whistle of the old-time steam locomotive. Alas, these days, one has to go far to hear that bold yet mournful sound. Even in Korea the Diesel engine is replacing the kind I used to know and love.

Colonel Beeman, the man who got me into the air and did his best to kill my taste for it that January morning in Germany, gave up flying after he returned to the United States and became a shoe merchant in Boston.

When I was a little boy, aged seven, I met a girl named Lillian Diebold and made a very poor impression on her. It happened in Canton, Ohio, that first summer my parents and I traveled east from Oregon. For a couple of days we were house guests of Anton Diebold, one of the founders of the Diebold Safe and Lock Works. My mother's father had been the Diebold's pastor in the 1870s, and Mother had been an intimate friend of Matilda, the oldest of Anton's twelve children. Lillian, the girl I displeased, was the youngest. Slightly beyond me in age, she was immeasurably beyond me in her maturity.

I remember that as I sat in the Diebold parlor, Lillian appeared with a red balloon bobbing above her head. All my good home training suddenly forgotten, I demanded to have it. Probably it was the first balloon I had ever seen. Lillian was of course reluctant to turn it over, but she did so under pressure from her mother. Young Danny Poling was a guest, after all, and however thoughtless, he must be humored.

Gleefully, I drew that balloon to my room and went to sleep with it pressing against the ceiling above my head. That I had possibly offended its rightful owner did not seem to matter. Next morning I looked eagerly upward. The balloon was not there. I found it nodding on the floor beside my bed, its buoyancy and beauty gone. And somehow I began to feel as sad as that deflated balloon looked. Definitely, I had gotten off to a poor start with Lillian Diebold.

We met again when I had somewhat matured. This was when I returned to Canton as the youthful minister of the Trinity United Evangelical Church. Lillian was then a tall and beautiful girl, a perfect blonde. She laughed as she recalled our first meeting. Early in 1906 Lillian married Carl Heingartner, one of the finest men I have ever known. Carl was an automobile dealer in those early days when the horseless carriage was frightening though not yet displacing the horse. Quiet, loyal, always considerate of others, he was a man easily admired and loved. Carl and Lillian, though not members of my congregation, became attendants, and my friendship with both of them was of that intimate quality that brought them naturally close to me in the months just before my marriage. Susie and Lillian were dear friends. Carl accompanied me when I purchased Susie's engagement ring, and he and Lillian gave us our housewarming party when I brought Susie to Canton as my bride. We were a perfect foursome.

Then, soon after Susie and I moved to Columbus in 1907, Carl was stricken with cancer. After a brief interval of hope he died. I conducted the funeral services for my beloved friend, and I baptized his children, Rachel Katharine and Ann Louise.

The years passed. With my family I moved to Massachusetts.

Lillian, remaining single, established a unique home economics program in the Canton public school system. Having first taken a graduate course at Ohio State University, she raised the necessary funds to build a laboratory house, "The Little Nell House," and equip it fully from basement to attic. Here she guided the children of a depressed area of Canton toward careers as housewives and mothers, or as she preferred to describe it, "home executives." Active in many other community enterprises, she taught a girls' Sunday-school class in the First Presbyterian Church and, during the flu epidemic of 1918, directed an emergency hospital.

Our two families had grown together through the years as we visited frequently in both Columbus and Canton. Lillian and her sisters were with Mebs and me at Susie's burial. We had both gone through loss and sorrow, and after I returned from my second mission to Europe, it seemed blessedly inevitable that we should bring together our two broken families. With Francis E. Clark performing the ceremony, we were married in New York on August 11, 1919. Soon after, Lillian and I went to Canton to pick up eleven-year-old Rachel and seven-year-old Ann. To them I was to become the only father they really ever knew, and to me, from the very beginning of my marriage to their mother, they were as my own.

From Canton, Lillian and I took the girls via the Great Lakes and the St. Lawrence River to the house at Sagamore Beach, Cape Cod, where Mebs awaited us with Daniel, Clark, Mary, and Jane. Remembering now that first evening and the days that followed after my sister so wisely departed, I marvel at the veritable genius—the mingled love and administrative ability—with which Lillian took over and won her way into the hearts and lives of my four uncertain, questioning little people.

For my part, and knowing that Carl would have wished this, I formally adopted Rachel and Ann. As I look back on the successful beginning of this marriage, which had so many challenges facing it, it seems to me that the most difficult problem was the fact that Rachel, my new daughter, was a little older than Daniel, my older boy, and he was quite naturally irked to find himself moved down to second place. The fact that Rachel and Ann had always wanted to have brothers did not at first seem to make up for the displacement, at least in Daniel's eyes. That all our adjustments loom small in retrospect is the measure of Lillian's spiritual authority—a force at once tender and practical—which she brought fully developed to our marriage.

On July 27, 1920, our now indissolubly united family received a seventh member, Treva Mabel, or "Billie," born in our new home on Long Island. My ministry in New York City had begun then, and people who knew us only after we had come to this new scene were sometimes surprised to learn that our family had what was to them such a complicated past. But so complete and perfect was the blend that our maid, who lived with us for five years, was quite disgusted with herself because she could not unscramble us. The children were always delighted when they overheard inquisitive people wrongly deciding that all the "dark ones" must be "his," and attributing the "light ones" to "her." "Oh, yeah?" Daniel or Clark would likely reply, which meant, properly translated, "None of your business." Some well-meaning people are never happy unless they are fully informed, but such types received little help from our children. And when the situation demanded it, Lillian and I zealously guarded our family's unity. In 1954 we were driving around Hawaii with a Christian Endeavor party, one of whose female members began to show what I considered an excessive interest in our personal affairs. It was our wedding anniversary, and this gave her the opportunity she wanted. "Dr. Poling, how long have you and Mrs. Poling been married?" she asked. "Thirty-five years," I told her, "and our oldest boy celebrated his forty-fifth birthday in July." The good lady closed up like a clam, and I said no more either, knowing that others in the party would enlighten her with the details later on.

But it was our daughter Jane who found the way, long ago, to reduce our family relationships to a satisfying conclusion. One afternoon in New York, while the head of the house was away, I found myself baby-sitting. Trying to entertain all our children from young Dan down to Billie, our newest, I told a story of their antecedents. "Geographically," I explained, "we Polings are very representative. Your mother was born in Ohio. Your father was born in Oregon. Five of you were born in Ohio, one in Massachusetts, and one in New York."

At this point, Jane, who had been listening wide-eyed as she kept track, spoke out on her clear, high voice: "Isn't it wonderful how we all got together!"

Although the unexpectedness of the remark made us laugh, it certainly expressed what has ever been the feeling in our family.

Beginning in the 1930s, when our older children were more and more on their own, Lillian began a brilliant career in religious and civic affairs. Quietly and impressively, and I think unconsciously so far as she is concerned, she has continued to be one of the first church and community leaders wherever we have lived. In Philadelphia, after we moved there in 1936, she founded the Religion in Life Group, an organization bringing together Roman Catholic, Jewish, and Protestant women for the purposes of interfaith understanding. The organization has grown steadily in membership and influence in Philadelphia. Lillian also became president of the Council of Women for Home Missions, the first ecumenical organization among churchwomen, and president of Flowers for the Flowerless, another interfaith group that gathered and distributed flowers to hospitals and other institutions where shut-ins and the handicapped were cared for. Our daughter Jane, impressed by all this activity, once facetiously suggested that Lillian should organize a society to be called "Nuts for the Nutless."

For the past five years Lillian has been president of the American Mothers Committee, which selects the American Mother of the Year. In 1959, holding its conference sessions at the Waldorf Astoria Hotel in New York, the Committee celebrated its Silver Jubilee Anniversary. The Mother of the Year, selected from the fifty State Mothers—gracious and representative women all—was the distinguished Jewess, Mrs. Jennie Loitman Barron, the first woman superior court judge appointed in the state of Massachusetts, and one of the first women in the country to be so highly honored in her calling.

As I write these lines about Lillian, my beloved "Gene," whose spirit and gifts have now been everywhere in my life for more than forty years, making me a man immeasurably blessed, I am reminded of something I once said to my children. They never had any difficulty in appraising Lillian in the family setting as compared with their father, but she always lifted me before them and held me there so that they loved and regarded me beyond my real worth. On one occasion when we were all together, I said, "Give to your mother every credit but one. One I reserve for myself, and never forget it. I chose her—your mother."

7

In the late fall of 1919, granted a leave of absence by the Christian Endeavor movement, I moved my family to New York and became an associate general secretary of the Interchurch World Movement, an organization that represented practically all the American Protestant denominations. Thus it was that I learned the facts behind one of the most significant labor disputes of the first quarter of this century, namely the long and bitter strike against the United States Steel Corporation.

Today, people may find it hard to remember that the steel workers of 1919 were fighting for the eight-hour day and collective bargaining among other basic rights, whereas the steel industry, led by U.S. Steel's board chairman, Judge Elbert Gary, insisted on maintaining the twelve-hour day and the seven-day week. At the turn of the shift men were on duty for twenty-four hours, though of course not engaged in heavy labor for the whole period. The industry was using espionage and intimidation, and there was open violence to keep the workers from making an effective protest against their working conditions.

The Interchurch World Movement voted for an impartial investigation of the strike and the preparation of a report that would put the facts before the public. As an officer of a committee of eight church representatives headed by Bishop Francis J. McConnell, one of the most social-minded church leaders of his generation, I learned about the misunderstandings, willful and otherwise, the brutal disregard of human life and the bloody wrongdoing committed by both sides that made this strike both a blot and a milestone in labor history. The harrowing details I and others elicited from the aggrieved steel workers so impressed me that I later made them the basis of a novel, *The Furnace*, which reached a wide audience when it was published in 1923 and found the reviewers in agreement that it gave a realistic and fair presentation of a shocking situation.

Since the membership and motives of the Interchurch World Movement were utterly responsible and respectable, I was astonished when the steel directors went to work on us with much the same tactics they had used to discredit the strike leaders. Bishop McConnell and the rest of his committee were held up as vilifiers of patriotic Americans, as subverters of democracy. The charges were grotesque, ludicrous, and, I think, tragic in what they revealed of good intellects perverted to bad uses. Smear literature, put out by the deceptively named American Civic Federation and distributed in our churches, tried to brand us as German agitators. In these publications my name was invariably spelled *Pohling*, and the Reverend Fred B. Fisher's—he afterward became a bishop of the Methodist Episcopal Church—was spelled *Fischer*.

At least once this campaign to destroy the public's confidence in the findings we intended to publish caused Judge Elbert Gary a few moments of excruciating embarrassment. A copy of a document dealing with Bishop McConnell, myself, and some of the other committee members was sent to me by the son of a steel official who felt that I had been responsible for saving his life on the Toul front in the spring of 1918. He believed the document to be unfair, particularly so to me, and out of gratitude he mailed it to me. In his autobiography, Bishop McConnell told this story at some length and too generously. I gave the document to Bishop McConnell the morning we were to have a conference with Judge Gary in his office in downtown Manhattan.

Before we began our talk Gary informed us he wished to take up certain new information about the chairman of our committee. As we watched Gary feel in his pockets, McConnell and I exchanged a look. We had a good idea what his information was. Becoming agitated when he could not immediately find what he wanted, Gary sent his secretary scurrying to an outer office. When the man returned empty-handed and spoke in a whisper to Gary, Bishop McConnell smiled and said, "Please take my copy, Judge."

Gary, a dynamic man with a strong, stern face, turned several shades of rose when he saw the paper that had been given to me, and his promised discussion died right there. We had our conference and left. Later on Judge Gary told an associate that he had been "profoundly shocked by Bishop McConnell's unethical conduct in the use of a confidential document."

Students of labor history will recall that the steel strike was lost on all counts. The industry adamantly refused to recognize the workers' right to organize and protest, and finally succeeded in crushing the strike in 1920. What is less generally remembered is that all of the workers' just demands were granted by the end of the next seventeen years, when, under the chairmanship of Myron C. Taylor, U.S. Steel granted the last of these, collective bargaining. That lapse of time spells out in large letters much of the hardship and tragedy associated with labor-management relationships in this country. The steel workers' goals were certainly reasonable in 1919, and I am convinced that had industry, when it enjoyed full control, adopted some of the recommendation of our Interchurch World committee many of the strikes and lockouts of subsequent years would have been avoided. But the report of our investigation, though published in book form and widely distributed, was generally not effective.

As vice-chairman of the committee I had the task of editing the report and raising the funds to secure its publication. One of the central figures in my novel *The Furnace* embodied the character and civic statesmanship of John D. Rockefeller, Jr., who, though not originally in favor of our investigation, recognized the validity of our committee's achievement and insisted that the report be published. It was a mark of Mr. Rockefeller's wisdom that his Colorado Fuel and Iron Company, a steel subsidiary, granted the workers' demands before the steel strike began.

I feel certain that in some measure the evil excesses of labor leadership today reflect the intolerance and violent methods of industry of two generations ago. Though labor is now in the driver's seat, not all the drivers possess the courage, wisdom, and high Christian patriotism of George Meany, who follows worthily in the succession of Samuel Gompers, John Mitchell, and others of their kind. American labor and its leaders learned the hard way, and inevitably some men in the movement become hardened in their learning. It is my hope and my prayer that the learning period may presently be finished, and that we then may understand that though we are many in this nation, we are yet one. For the better future of America, may the day soon come when labor and management will take equal and full responsibility for the intelligent use of their privileges and freedoms—and their obligations to the general public as well.

On Sunday, January 4, 1920, I preached for the first time from the pulpit of the Marble Collegiate (Dutch Reformed) Church, at Fifth Avenue and Twenty-ninth Street in Manhattan. After twelve years of activities not directly connected with a church, I was again identified with a local congregation. Invited to serve as associate preacher, I later became co-minister with David James Burrell, who had begun his ministry in this ancient church in 1891; after Dr. Burrell's death in 1926, I became minister. I felt my privilege as well as my responsibilities, for the Collegiate Reformed Protestant Dutch Church of New York City—to give its full title—is the oldest secular or religious organization in the city and the oldest Protestant organization in North America with an unbroken ministerial succession, its career having continued from 1628 when it was organized under Peter Minuit, Director-General of the West India Company. The Marble Collegiate Church itself, opened in 1854, was the ninth place of worship in the succession that began in the loft of a grist mill in lower Manhattan. Sometimes, standing in the Marble Collegiate

Church's sanctuary, I thought of the succession of thirty-seven ministers who had preceded me, going back to Domine Jonas Michaelius, who had installed Peter Minuit as the church's first elder and instituted the line of elders and deacons that continued unbroken to my day. In such moments the continuity of God's inspiration and guidance became a lifting tide beneath and about me.

But even as my imagination was captured by my church's historic past, I was concerned with its services to the living. As I stood in the pulpit preaching as best I could the message of Jesus Christ, I often looked down at the pew where my family sat listening to me—or some of it. Lillian habitually and wisely placed herself between Clark and Daniel to enforce seemly behavior, if not total attentiveness, but sometimes her presence was not enough. I would see Dan reach over behind his mother and give Clark a poke. When the boys noticed my eyes fixed on them, they straightened up! My efforts must have done some good, for the boys grew up in that church in a double sense. As I shall relate in a later chapter, some of the crucial moments in young Clark's spiritual development were experienced within the walls of the Marble Collegiate Church.

There was an unwritten rule in the official family of this church that if a proposal could not win the unanimous support of the officers and minister, it would not be pressed. A sound rule it was, too, but I could not help feeling disappointed when I failed to convince the special work committee, made up of our elders and deacons, that we should open an outdoor pulpit and preach to the man in the street. Then, a little later, Senior Elder E. Francis Hyde came quietly to my support. Mr. Hyde, a banker, cultured gentleman, and man of reputation in the world of music, was in his late eighties when I became his "Domine." Perhaps he tottered a bit as he walked, but his serene mind never faltered. One morning I found him waiting for me in my study. With his characteristic chuckle, he asked, "How much did you tell us it would cost to establish that pulpit, Domine?" He already knew the answer, but I gave it to him again; three thousand dollars, I thought, would allow us to set the pulpit up inside the church's iron fence, at the corner of Fifth Avenue and Twenty-ninth Street, and to hire the additional preaching and musical talent we would need for an outdoor noontide service from Monday to Friday inclusive. The elder's gray eyes twinkled as he drew an envelope from his pocket and handed it to me. "When the special work committee meets on Friday night," he said dryly, "you tell us that if we change our minds and go along with you, you have three thousand dollars outside the budget to finance the project. Then perhaps *we* can be persuaded."

After the committee had heard this message, Elder Hyde added a few words. He had not been in favor of the wayside pulpit himself, he said, but he had been impressed by my enthusiasm for it, and also pleased by my patience. Now that the money was available, he felt that the project should be tried out for a season at least. And so our pulpit was established and manned. In my first message from it, I said, "If our ministry here sends a neglecting Jew back to his synagogue, an indifferent Roman Catholic back to his cathedral, or a forgetting Protestant back to his church, and ministers to all without regard, then we shall be happy and trust the Holy Spirit to complete any good work we may have begun."

As long as I remained at the Marble Collegiate Church that wayside pulpit ministered in several languages, served by preachers of many denominations. One day a young German, wandering up Fifth Avenue, stopped to listen. Today, after thirty years of loyal membership in our church, William Groll continues to be a fixture on our custodial staff. In the 1920s our church was in the heart of the loft district, and more of the garment workers spoke Yiddish than English. Accordingly we recruited a preacher who could carry our message to Jews. Some days people would come up to me after the sermons and tell me they were hungry. They never left without a ticket entitling them to a free meal at the Bowery Mission.

For five years my ministry at the Marble Collegiate Church was intimately associated with that of Dr. David James Burrell, a man I remember as the greatest extemporaneous speaker of his generation. Henry Ward Beecher, in one of the original Yale

Lectures in the series that bears his name, said in effect that great preaching comes not out of books but from the hearts and hungers of the people who come to hear it. In this sense, Burrell was Beecher's man.

On Sunday mornings, I used to go from my study to his a few minutes before service time, knock on his door, wait for his resonant "Come in," and then enter and assist him with his robe. One morning I forgot to wait. Barging in, I found the venerable man kneeling by a chair in a small recess, his calendar for the day before him, his face in his hands. Then I had his secret, or part of it. Always he went to his knees before he faced his waiting, expectant congregation. Always he indicated on his calendar sheet a rough outline of the sermon he was about to preach. That he took to the chair before which he knelt. There, burying his knees in a red cushion, his face in his hands, he sought the guidance and blessing of the One whom he loved, preached, and served. After this preparation, he carried no manuscript, no notes, into his pulpit.

Henry Ward Beecher made his point about great preaching, and great indeed by all the tests Dr. Burrell's certainly was. His method, with its freedom from notes, impressed me profoundly for it was also my father's. Following their examples, I made it mine.

In my early days at the Marble Collegiate Church I was involved in a storm that blew up over my good friend Harry Emerson Fosdick. Before it passed, I learned something about dealing with angry memberships.

As president of the Greater New York Federation of Churches, I invited Dr. Fosdick to speak at one of our annual dinners. At this period Fosdick, a Baptist, was guest preacher in the First Presbyterian Church of New York City, and by his presence there he was one of the focal points in the theological controversy that was then threatening a serious division in the Presbyterian denomination. Fosdick, who wore no man's collar, was not liberal enough to satisfy the liberals nor conservative enough for the conservatives. Some of our Federation's more conservative churches felt that Fosdick should not be heard at our dinner, and they threatened to resign if the invitation were not rescinded. My conscience said that this sort of pressure had to be resisted, my common sense told me it was unwarranted. I was reminded of the experience of a devout but dogmatic Christian woman who became almost hysterical when advised that her favorite organization intended to sponsor Dr. Fosdick in a series of lectures. The secretary of the organization persuaded the good woman that it was hardly fair to judge a man whom she had not heard speak. She went to hear Fosdick and her views changed completely. "He is so wonderful, so Christlike," she exclaimed, "it's just too bad he isn't orthodox!"

I stood firm and the Federation's invitation was not canceled. Introducing our speaker, I told the story of our fortunate meeting in Gondriecourt, not omitting mention of the hot-water bottle he filled for me. Fosdick spoke on this occasion with his accustomed eloquence and a reassuring note of brotherly love. He impressed all his audience—and no churches, I am happy to add, found it necessary to withdraw from the Greater New York Federation.

At the Marble Collegiate Church, Dr. Burrell and I enjoyed differences of opinion about Fosdick. Dr. Burrell was one of those who found Fosdick too liberal. "Dan, that fellow is your friend, and I respect friendship," he said to me one day, driving home the point with the remark, "One of my father's most intimate friends was Robert Ingersoll." Chuckling, Burrell went on to propose a gentlemen's agreement. "I will lay off criticizing Fosdick in this pulpit. It will cost me a struggle to do that, but I will do it for you. On the other hand, I don't want you to eulogize him in this pulpit. Now, what do you say to that?"

My answer was easy. "Since the only one whom I care to eulogize in our pulpit is Jesus Christ, I agree. In fact, I think I'm getting more out of the bargain than you are. You are going to be hurt!"

We left it at that. A short time later Dr. Burrell attended commencement at Princeton Theological Seminary. In the course of a characteristic evangelical address the temptation became irresistible and he referred to Harry Emerson Fosdick as "that Baptist bull in the Presbyterian china shop." The newspapers wouldn't let that one pass! Next morning, when Burrell's fighting words were on many a front page, he called me into his study. "Dan," he said, shaking his head, "this old man is heartily ashamed of himself. I apologize."

While I stood there wondering how I might reassure him without making an awkward situation worse, I saw his eyes twinkling. "But I was on the other side of the river when I said it!" he snapped.

Laughing, I was obliged to concede that he had been faithful to the letter if not the intent of our agreement, and anyhow I loved the way he said it.

One Easter morning at Marble Collegiate Church I committed a blunder that still haunts me. The church, of course, was crowded. After the Invocation, intending to begin the Lord's Prayer, "Our father who art in heaven," I said instead, "Now I lay me—" I recovered my senses at once and went directly into the Lord's Prayer, but my composure was gone for the day. I wanted never to open my eyes again! But I had to face the congregation, and there were broad and understanding smiles everywhere to greet me.

Following the service, a faithful parishioner, the widow of one of our elders, congratulated me in a way that took out some of the sting: "Domine, you were wonderful!" she said, as she held my hand between hers. "God must have made you say it. Now always we shall have another picture of our dear pastor—at the knee of his mother."

Long after this mistake had been largely forgotten, I made a second one, but this time deliberately. One of the good women of the parish had expressed what I thought was an undue amount of interest in my age. There came a moment when she pressed me with personal questions that were not warranted, and then admitted, "I have always wondered how your hair stays so black." Unwisely, I replied, "Why, I use my mother's dye." Though my father's hair had turned white before he was forty, at eighty-four Mother had practically no gray in her soft brown hair. This woman had never seen my mother, but I counted on my tone to put the idea across. The next meeting of Red Cross chapter heard the story thus: "The pastor dyes his hair. He told me so!"

Some of the most moving experiences of my ministerial life took place during my years in the Marble Collegiate Church. One of them was sparked by the simple invitation that I used to extend at the close of every Sunday evening sermon I preached. With minor variations, it went like this: "If there are those here who have burdens too great for them to bear alone, whatever your burden—sin, fear, sickness, doubt—if you would be remembered in my closing prayer, you may stand or lift your hand so that I may see you and pray for you." I always asked my listeners to bow for prayer first, so that when my invitation was extended it went out to an unseeing congregation.

One night a man who had raised his hand approached me in the chancel after the service. Well dressed, distinguished looking, he was a stranger to me. "Well, what can you do for me?" he asked.

The cynicism of his tone caused me to recoil. "Nothing," I replied. "I can do absolutely nothing for you, but I can take you to One who will answer your question."

We spent some time together that night, and a few days later we met again. The change in the man's attitude was profound. The cynicism was gone; in its place was humility. He offered almost no information about himself except his name, nor did I press for any. The information he conveyed unconsciously was all I needed. At the close of our third meeting, when we had prayed together, the man said:

"Listen to me, Dr. Poling. Years ago I made a promise, and so I've been attending church once a week ever since. But how does it happen that until last Sunday night I was never invited to do anything about it?"

I could not answer his question, but I could rejoice in his obvious happiness and relief that he had finally been "invited." My simple ministry has ever been based on the belief that the supreme business of the Christian Church is leading men and women to Jesus Christ, sustaining them and strengthening them in the Christian life, and training them for and engaging them in Christian service. My invitation—which I will continue to extend as long as I preach—is based on three assumptions: that in every congregation and group there are those who need and desire God; that God's spirit is always active and always God is present; that the least I should do and all I may do is make it possible for those who need a faith to live by—who want peace with power—to meet the One who is able to give them what they need and want. If it all sounds simple and easy, then I am glad, for Jesus Christ was like that. The common people "heard him gladly" for that very reason; they could understand him. Dr. Burrell expressed the matter memorably when he said, "Simplicity is rock crystal; profundity is mud."

On another Sunday at the Marble Collegiate Church a young man came forward after the service. He had been attending my services for three months, he said, and he had raised his hand a number of times. Now he wished an interview with me. We met the next afternoon. As is my custom, I told him that he need give me no information about himself, but that my ability to help him would be largely determined by his willingness to trust me. Taking me at my word, he refused even to tell me his name.

Two weeks later he came again to the church. This time he announced his name. It was one I recognized instantly; the family name is still well known throughout the Dominion of Canada. Then I heard the young man's story. He had flown as a Canadian combat pilot during the war. Shot down over France, he had all but died of his wounds. "But the scars on my body are nothing to the scars I carry here," he told me, touching his heart. And then I learned that he had taken to drink and a dishonorable way of life. Prayer led this boy to a reconciliation with himself, with his proud family, and with his God. I saw him often until he moved away from New York. One Christmas Eve the boy came to see me, bringing his father and mother. Only those who have experienced a moment of this sort can know what that meeting meant to all of us.

In the years I have been issuing that invitation, "Whatever your burden . . ." more than twelve thousand men and women have responded to it, and perhaps not one of them went away

The Oregon state champions of 1903. I'm holding the ball. Back row, left, Chester Gates.

Cincinnati, Ohio: the campaign of 1912. Sitting in back with me is J. Raymond Schmidt.

Ready for my assignments
in France; September, 1917.

The first two of my eight:
Daniel (right) and Clark.

Daniel, Clark, and Mary with their mother and me.

With Dr. Frances E. Clark after my election as president of the International Society of Christian Endeavor; Portland, Oregon, 1925.

Herbert Hoover receives the International Youth's Distinguished Service Citation at the International Christian Endeavor Convention of 1927; Cleveland, Ohio.

Wide World Photo

Father and Mother, with Russell Thaw, my pilot, as we greet a Spokane dignitary on our flight east in 1932.

Exchange of flags in the bombed ruins of City Temple, London, 1943. The British flag I was given hangs today in the Chapel of Four Chaplains.

With G.I.s on Bougainville, August, 1944;
an impromptu conference on spiritual problems.

Planting a tree in the Children's Memorial Forest; Palestine, 1947.

The Easter sunrise service, Tokyo, April 17, 1949.

U. S. Army Photo

Wide World Photo

President Truman presents an album of Chaplain memorial stamps to Clark Poling, Jr., May 28, 1948. Postmaster General Jesse M. Donaldson and relatives of Chaplains Washington, Goode, and Fox are among the witnesses.

President Eisenhower receives the pin signifying his honorary Christian Endeavor membership; Washington, 1954.

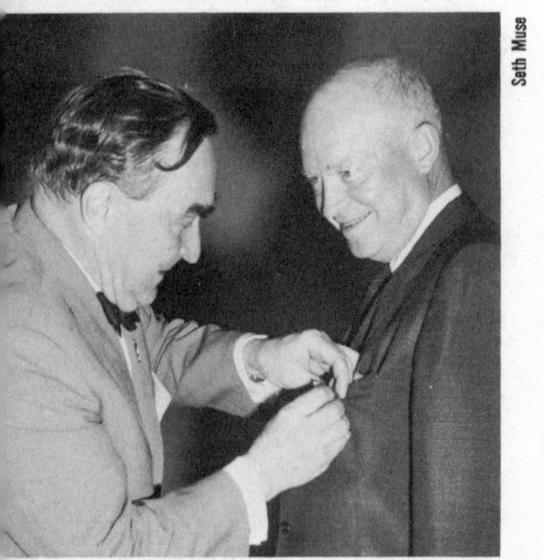

Seth Muse

The Evangelical United Brethren Church, Carey, Ohio: Norman Vincent Peale helps me observe the fiftieth anniversary of my ordination.

Newhard Stu

. S. Army Photo

Lee King Kow

With children of the *Christian Herald's* Korean orphanages, 1955 and 1958.

Religious News Service Photo

Walter A. White and I showing Billy Graham the mural in the Chapel of Four Chaplains.

Larry Keighley, courtesy THE SATURDAY EVENING POST

Baby-sitting with a few of my grandchildren. Clark's Corky and Susie are second and third from the left.

President and Madame Chiang Kai-shek surprise Lillian and me with a party for our wedding anniversary; Taipeh, Formosa, August 11, 1956.

altogether untouched by God's grace. At least a few thousand have certainly begun to live differently, have gone out to help answer my prayer for them that, "with God's help, tomorrow shall be different and better than today."

I remember another experience in which I had a part at the Marble Collegiate Church. A young man entered the building one evening and asked me for money. Rain had soaked him to the skin. He was brazenly drunk. As he looked at me with bleary eyes, he seemed tragically young; and to me this was somehow the important thing. His story sounded impossible. He was the son of wealthy parents and he had fallen among thieves and lost his money. Well, at least that part made him sound like the prodigal son, and he looked the part. His baggage was being held by his hotel for his unpaid bill. A member of his family was soon coming to the city to fix things up. Meantime, he needed fifteen dollars, only fifteen, to meet his immediate necessities, and he would repay me without fail as soon as his relative appeared.

I was convinced he was lying. One of the anxious deacons, who had previously observed his pastor's weaknesses in cases like this, started the boy on a swift march for the door. The boy broke free, turned back, and blurted out, "Take a chance, preacher!"

What it was that prompted me to give that lad another look I do not know, but I did look again and I did take that chance. The silent disgust of my friend the deacon was plain to see as he advanced the fifteen dollars and charged it to my personal account.

"I've taken the chance," I said, turning the money over, "and a wilder chance it is than any gambler ever took, but, O son, for the sake of many another needy fellow who will come here for help, as well as for your own sake, make good. Play the man. Go, and God go with you."

Half sobered by these parting words, the boy disappeared. Two days later he came back, clean and polished, and with my fifteen dollars. He took me to the hotel he had named at our first meeting, and there I met a gracious Southern woman who had come in place of the boy's invalid mother. The hardest heart would have melted at the story she told me of family tragedy and wasted youth. In that hotel room we prayed together. When I said good-by to the young man and his rescuer I felt that his reclamation had begun, and I was glad that I had taken the chance. He had asked, in words, for a few dollars, but I now understood that he had come seeking the help that only the One whom I serve could give him.

And so through the years they came to me: women and men, the young, the middle-aged, the old. Some were great sinners, others were only weak or sinned against. Some were wise, some highly educated. Some were little people by their own confession; others were smaller than they were at first willing to confess. All came looking for peace with power to meet and conquer life's problems and difficulties. I remember a charwoman from a nearby hotel who called on me one afternoon before going to her night's work. Hers was a poignant story. She was living in a common-law marriage with a man who loved her, and she had borne four children. "Could I be married?" she asked softly. "Oh, sir, would you marry us even now so that I could have a ring on my finger? We sit in the gallery and listen to you on Sunday night, and I have waited so long to get courage to ask you." Well, you may be sure I married the pair and gave them the full blessing of the old church. She went away with the ring on her finger, and it was still there when she died, some years later, and I read her burial service.

After ten crowded, fruitful years at the Marble Collegiate Church, during which I had been honored with the presidency of my denomination in the General Synod of the Reformed Church in America, I resigned my pastorate. It was a decision that gave my wife and me many a heartache, but in the end it seemed that the organizational and administrative responsibilities and travel that the presidency of the World's Christian Endeavor Union imposed on me made it impossible to serve adequately a church as pastor; I could not remain as a minister in New York City and continue to serve my world youth parish.

But though I believed I was leaving that blessed church, today, in a new relationship, I am "right back where I started from." Four years ago, my beloved friend Dr. Norman Vincent

Peale, my successor in the Marble Collegiate pulpit, invited me back for a six-weeks' period as Sunday evening preacher when he began preaching at two identical Sunday morning services. On Sunday morning Dr. Peale preaches to four thousand and more worshipers; the overflow congregations in the chapel, clubrooms, and parlors receive the service via closed-circuit television. As Sunday evening preacher, I am still there. Nostalgia and joy companion me as I keep returning to that pulpit and sanctuary and congregation. And one of the anniversaries I am looking forward to is January 3, 1960. If in God's will I should occupy the pulpit that night, it will have been exactly forty years since I preached my first sermon as associate preacher on the Marble Collegiate staff with Dr. Burrell. The chief compensation of this revived relationship is my continuing intimate association with Norman Vincent Peale, who, with his sermons, broadcasts, books, newspaper columns, and lectures, is literally a minister to millions.

Although this forty-year period is rather a long stretch, to a certain colonel in the U.S. Army it seemed much longer. In Seoul, Korea, in the fall of 1957, after I had preached in the chapel of the Eighth Army, the colonel, a former resident of New York, introduced himself. I noticed his eyes straying over me. "Dr. Poling," he said, "I used to hear your father preach in the old Marble Collegiate Church in New York, more than thirty years ago."

"You did not," I said. "You heard my father's eldest son."

The 1920s were for me indeed an eventful decade. One July 4, that of 1921, will be forever remembered as a day of near tragedy. That morning, with my wife, our eldest daughter, and our two sons, I was driving from Lake Sunapee, New Hampshire, to New York, where an International Christian Endeavor Convention, the details of which had been in my hands, was opening in the Armory on Park Avenue at Thirty-fourth Street. Between Greenfield and Northampton, in Massachusetts, just after I turned my wheel to avoid some children who were playing with firecrackers in front of a house, the steering rod pulled loose. While I still had the sensation of that wheel failing to control our car, a touring model with a soft top, we struck a telephone pole and turned over.

Our daughter Rachel was thrown clear. Dan received a broken shoulder; Clark a broken hip. Lillian, sitting beside me, went through the windshield and her right ear was all but severed. I was caught between the seat back, which broke off, and the instrument panel. When the car turned over and came down on me, I did not lose consciousness completely, thanks to Lillian. She crept back to me, pressed her lips to my ear, and called my name insistently, her voice staccato and commanding. I heard that call—how clearly I remember it after all these years—as though it came to me at the end of the world and from very far away. I could not answer but for ages I seemed to hear it, though it was only a few minutes before the men who were providentially at hand, working on the power lines along the road, lifted the car and pulled me out. Once I felt so free of pain that I almost stopped listening to Lillian's sharp summoning; then her voice called me back and would not let me go. Later, in the Northampton hospital, I was told that had I ever stopped listening to that voice, I would have died. But I knew that much before they told me.

My injuries were severe: two fractures in the vertebrae, three fractured ribs, crushed breastbone, crushed hips, a head wound, and unpredictable internal injuries. For ten days there was little to do but wait. Others waited with me. From Oregon my mother wired: I HAVE THE ANSWER. PSALM 91:15–16. Presently that text was read to me: "He shall call upon me and I will answer him: I will be with him in trouble; I will deliver him and honor him. With long life will I satisfy him and show him my salvation."

It was a command to recover. Mother knew, and I believed. My good doctors knew what *they* were waiting for, or thought they did, but I knew something better, and so did Lillian when she came to pray beside my bed. From the beginning she and I asked in God's will for the assurance of recovery. The answer came clear and without conditions attached: "Recovery." I never doubted the reality of that answer until the crisis was past, and then I wavered just a little. Weakness, it may have been. But

Lillian never wavered. She was like that then; she is like that today. And the promise came true for me and mine. Ours was a healing not without the finest medical assistance and care, but with these and also *beyond* them.

My recovery was complete. That mended back has carried me over the world. If anything, it became stronger after its injury than it was before. Not a scar from that ordeal was later visible above the collar on any of us who were in the accident.

Clark was the next most seriously injured after me. All through the hot July and August days he lay between sandbags with his leg suspended in traction. Like the rest of us, he never lost his confidence that he would recover. One day his uncle, Albert Henry Diebold, came up from New York to visit us. He informed Clark that our car could have saved us a lot of trouble by turning a little further off the road than it did. In that case, he said, it would have landed us quite comfortably in a tobacco field. Clark grinned up from his bed. "But, Uncle," he said, "you know how Daddy hates tobacco!"

Rachel's facial injuries, though painful, left no scars, and Lillian's ear healed perfectly.

For Daniel and Clark and me, the complete healing was a protracted affair. Clark's hip had to be broken and reset, and for a long period he used a crutch. But later he played football without hindrance, while Daniel was able to set a school record in the pole vault. I learned to walk again. At age thirty-seven such learning comes hard. Gripping the foot of the hospital bed with one hand, my other arm over my doctor's strong shoulder, again and again I lowered my feet until they touched the floor. I swung my legs, made the motions. Finally, I let my feet take just a fraction of my weight. It was agony. But it passed.

The words of the Apostle Paul have their bearing on all this: "Our light affliction, which is but for a moment, worketh for us a far more exceeding and eternal weight of glory." I know now that I would never have chosen that ordeal, particularly with its near-death for my dear ones. Even today the memory of its particulars and of the torture that followed is an ugly nightmare I do not enjoy recalling. But I also know that if what came to me out of that experience were now to be taken from me, I would suffer intellectual and moral losses that would be infinite. Even though I would not choose again what took me so near death, it does not seem that I could live without the riches that experience added to my life.

When I was a boy, the *Christian Herald,* along with *The Youth's Companion,* was one of the few periodicals I ever saw. Mother read to me from these magazines before I was old enough to read for myself. My first literary effort was some verses on Arthur Venville, the boy who became a hero when he passed ammunition for Admiral Dewey's men in the battle of Manila Bay. The poem, sent to the *Christian Herald,* was rejected so courteously that I felt encouraged to try again. I composed what I thought to be a touching and morally elevating story entitled "A Noble Horse," and this found ready acceptance in the columns of the Dayton, Oregon, *Journal.* It was quite a story! The horse was incredibly noble, the boy who rode him on a mission of mercy was even more noble, if possible, and of course the young author was completely in earnest. In 1926, after J. C. Penney persuaded me to become editor in chief of the *Christian Herald,* that youthful product had an unexpected resurrection. Someone who had learned of my elevation sent an ancient marked copy of the Dayton *Journal* to the editor of the *Christian Herald's* children's page, Margaret E. Sangster. The "contribution" was accepted. The proofs of that particular issue did not cross my desk—understandably—and it was a startled editor who later browsed through his own weekly and came upon " 'A Noble Horse,' by Danny Poling, age 14."

The *Christian Herald,* for which I began writing regularly in 1920, was founded in 1878 by Louis Klopsch, a converted Jew. A man who had made a comfortable fortune in the advertising business, Klopsch had become an admirer of Thomas De Witt Talmage, an eminent pulpit figure of his time. With Talmage's help, he soon found 250,000 subscribers for his magazine. Today, it is interesting to realize that this number was sufficient to place the *Christian Herald* sixth among American mass-circulation periodicals toward the end of the last century. The magazine was but one of Klopsch's projects; book publishing was another. Fifty years ago, hardly a church home in the United States was without a Bible or some other religious book that had come from the *Christian Herald's* presses. With the magazine well launched, Klopsch started a children's home at Nyack, New York; he took over and developed a struggling mission in Manhattan's skid row; and in the period before the American Red Cross became the dominant organization for international relief, the *Christian Herald* raised more than forty million dollars for relief of famine and flood victims in Russia, China, India, and many another needy nation. When Herbert Hoover made his appeal for aid for Europe from Brussels in 1919, the first ship to sail for Belgium with the needed food supplies carried *Christian Herald* banners on its sides.

Louis Klopsch is a man I regret having never known. He not only had a great vision but the ability to give it practical expression. The second layman to play a leading role in the *Christian Herald's* history I knew and know well—J. C. Penney, the distinguished merchant-philanthropist. Born in the stringent circumstances of a hard-shell Baptist preacher's home, and a frail specimen physically when young, Penney climbed to the heights of character and achievement. When I first met him in 1923 his social vision was already as broad as Louis Klopsch's had been. At his invitation I organized the J. C. Penney Foundation and directed its educational and philanthropic work. One of our most successful projects was the National Youth Radio Conference, the first nation-wide radio program featuring and supporting youth guidance. During the 1920s and early 1930s I broadcast this program weekly, first from the Marble Collegiate Church and then from the ballroom of the old Waldorf Astoria Hotel. Many hundreds of young people wrote in about their problems. We tried to direct them to institutions in their home communities. Generally, these people just needed encouragement, but some we helped in substantial ways too. One poor but ambitious boy in Leadville, Colorado, wanted to be a doctor; we made arrangements for him to go through medical school. A girl in upstate New York, a polio victim, did not even own crutches; she got around by pushing a kitchen chair before her. She was musical, and the National Youth Radio Conference helped her to go through teachers' college. Years later in Kingston, New York, this girl introduced herself to me when I spoke there. A fine high-school choir sang on the program. Afterward the choir leader, a lovely-looking girl, came up to me. Only then did I notice the crutch concealed beneath her robe. "Dr. Poling, I'm sure you don't remember me," she said, "but I'm one of the young people you helped through the National Youth Radio Conference." Well, I not only remembered her case, but now I shall never forget that brave and determined girl herself.

After the first World War, the *Christian Herald* lost many of its subscribers and supporters. It was close to failure when Mr. Penney stepped in and with considerably over a million dollars saved the situation. At this point I took over as editor in chief, and with Mr. Penney and his associates reorganized the journal. Occupied as I was with my duties at the Marble Collegiate Church and now also increasingly active in the Christian Endeavor movement as the venerable Dr. Clark drew near his retirement, I did not see how I could shoulder additional responsibilities. However, since that beginning I have been practically engulfed in the *Christian Herald* magazine and its associated activities. After more than thirty years of directing and managing the Christian Herald Association's affairs, always with the assistance of a large, able, and dedicated staff, I find myself today responsible in varying degrees for the continuance of Mont Lawn, our children's home at Nyack-on-Hudson; the Bowery Mission in Manhattan, with its clinic and employment agency; the Memorial Home Community at Penney Farms in Florida, for retired religious workers; our homes and orphanages in Korea, Formosa, and Hong Kong; the *Christian Herald's* new project, Long House, which I shall describe later; and our book club, the Family Bookshelf, which represents a crusade for decency as well as distinction in current literature and is generally regarded, I believe, as one of the most successful of the smaller clubs. The first extensive unit of the Memorial Home Community was erected by J. C. Penney as a memorial to his preacher father and mother; it has since been enlarged by the *Christian Herald* to include a million-and-a-quarter-dollar quadrangle with apartments for widows and widowers, and also a small hospital, a gift of the Olin Foundation.

The latest of our *Christian Herald* activities is the Christian Herald Tours, which operates successfully under the direction of Carroll M. Wright, who is also executive director of the Memorial Home Community. Mr. Wright has led more than a score of groups across Europe and through the Mediterranean to the Bible lands. He happens to be my one associate who has served with me in both Christian Endeavor and in the Christian Herald Association. Currently he is organizing the 1960 tour by sea, land, and air as far east as the Holy Land, and climaxing with a visit to the Passion Play at Oberammergau.

Our children's home, Mont Lawn, founded by Louis Klopsch, is now directed by Dr. Hubert Mott, who was for nine years superintendent of schools in Pleasantville, New York. In my opinion he is the most gifted, efficient, and inspiring personality in this field. The home is in an idyllic spot, high above and overlooking the Hudson River. One of its important features is a huge swimming pool, a gift made in recent years by my wife's brother, Albert Henry Diebold. More than twenty years ago Mont Lawn offered the first racially integrated summer camp in the greater New York City area, and now each summer eight hundred to a thousand underprivileged New York children of all races spend their two-week vacations at the home. Aside from its summer program, Mont Lawn fulfills a year-round ministry to smaller groups of blind and spastic children, and to the wives and children of inmates in Sing Sing, the state prison that lies just across the Hudson.

The Bowery Mission, the *Christian Herald's* establishment on New York's skid row, has quite a history. Just a hundred years ago John Parkinson, an American sailor, entered the mission and was converted—and so thoroughly that he went over the world telling his story. Parkinson founded a mission of his own in Smyrna, Turkey, and here it was that Louis Klopsch and his associate, Thomas De Witt Talmage, learned that Parkinson had been converted in New York. On their return to New York, the *Christian Herald* men visited the mission. Its founder and superintendent had just died, and it was about to close its doors. Louis Klopsch took the mission over, and now for sixty-four years the *Christian Herald* has carried forward its activities.

To me, that mission, with its kitchen, dining room, clothing department, delousing room, dormitory, and chapel, is a house of spiritual miracles. My connection with it is chiefly administrative. The man who does the inspired work of reclaiming souls is Rev. George Bolton. This man, a veritable saint, was once a skid-row derelict himself. He was converted in another mission, and today he is pastor and superintendent of the Bowery Mission. Recently, a malignancy made it necessary for him to have his larynx removed. Today he has taught himself to talk all over again. Meantime, with only a few weeks' interruption, George Bolton, continued to direct the mission's program. His faith is of the kind that moves mountains, and to me this devoted pastor symbolizes, as both giver and receiver, the whole meaning of the Bowery Mission.

The directors of the Christian Herald Association have no unrealistic notions about the possibilities of reclaiming the derelicts that come to the mission. We know that there will always be backsliders, but there are always some who will work their way back to a rewarding life, and these are the men whom we seek to serve. It was George Bolton who conceived of the mission's Uptown House. To this establishment go the converts who seem to be safely on their feet. Here they live under the honor system and have a better address from which to re-enter an active, productive life. Nearly 70 per cent of the men in the Uptown House succeed in their new lives, and George Bolton considers this figure one of his greatest rewards.

On one of my recent evening visits to the mission, I heard a trusted *Christian Herald* employee tell his story to the two hundred drunk or half drunk, unshaven, unwashed men who filled the mission's chapel. "Less than a year ago I too came in here" he said. "I was finished. I knew it. When I was sober I couldn't live with myself, so I kept on drinking. The night I came here

I was ready to write a suicide note. I had left my wife and three children three years before. I hardly knew where they were. I'd been successful enough—had run my own business—but drink got me and ruined me. I came in here just before the end. It was a last chance. I grabbed it. The man up front said, 'Jesus Christ will save you, drunk or sober, if you give him a chance.' Befuddled as I was, I said 'I'll take that chance.' I came to this altar, knelt, and Jesus Christ accepted my confession. He saved me. When I got up I was a changed man. I went out and proceeded to find my wife and my three children. My wife said, 'I'll go with you,' and she came to this mission and knelt with me at this altar, and our boy of twelve knelt with us, and we were again a united family. That's what Jesus Christ did for me, men, and that is what He can do for you."

When this man had finished his story, and the invitation, "Softly and tenderly, Jesus is calling, calling for you" was sung, I watched two burly men, one with heavily tattooed arms, come down the aisle to kneel at the mission's altar, and in humble admiration I watched George Bolton go on with his and God's unending work among the fallen.

As this book goes to press George Bolton's long-weary heart has taken its rest. Suddenly he left us, and he is now in his Father's house on high.

The Bowery Mission, the Mont Lawn children's home, the Far East orphanages—it is a large program. The masthead of the *Christian Herald* carries the significant words that pull all of it into a comprehensive unity—and, I am bound to add, give me a sense of consolidated purpose on occasions when I feel that I am flying off in all directions. "A Family Magazine, independent and interdenominational . . . dedicated to the promotion of evangelical Christianity, church unity, religious and racial understanding, world peace, the solving of the liquor problem, the service of the needy, and cooperation with all who seek a more Christian world." A skeptical reader of that dedication once commented, "Dan, that's just about as inclusive as the map of the world." "You hit it right on the head," I agreed, though in a somewhat different spirit, for to me the Christian Herald Association's activities have always been world-wide in scope and aspiration.

In 1930, when Mr. Penney was compelled to retire from his *Christian Herald* activities, he made me owner of the magazine. Understandably, I faced great financial obstacles. We soon completely reorganized and formed the nonprofit Christian Herald Association. For more than a quarter of a century now, all our earnings above expenses have gone toward the support of our Christian Herald charities at home and overseas. The *Christian Herald* found its second savior in my wife's brother, Albert Henry Diebold. Like Lillian, a product of a solid Evangelical Church upbringing in Canton, Albert Diebold developed into a social statesman to be ranked with his predecessors Klopsch and Penney, and today he and his wife Treva (after whom Lillian and I named our youngest daughter) devotedly give the kind of support and sound guidance that have allowed the *Christian Herald* and its far-flung projects a lifetime of eighty-one years.

In the summer of 1926 I took my entire family to England. My excuse was that I did not wish to be lonely while I attended the World's Christian Endeavor Convention, held in the Crystal Palace. This was an occasion of distinction in size and program. The tens of thousands of Endeavorers who crammed that famous old structure of Victorian days were mostly from the United Kingdom, but included representatives of some forty countries. We had a large delegation from Germany—the first group of Germans to attend such an international gathering since World War I. Among our speakers were Ramsey MacDonald, leader of the Labor Party, and Stanley Baldwin, the Prime Minister. Easily the most popular speaker was my great old friend of World War I days, David Lloyd George.

For our leader, "Father Endeavor" Clark, the occasion was one of farewell, though he did not know it. After his lifetime of service at the head of the movement he had founded, he had reached the time for retirement—but it was retirement forward and upward. The following year, after Dr. Clark's death, I was elected as his successor.

Our home that summer was the ancient rectory at Shuberyness, Essex, at the mouth of the Thames. While I occupied the pulpit of Christ Church, in Westminsterbridge Road, London (and the incumbent there, Dr. William Pool, preached for me at the Marble Collegiate Church in New York), my seven children became acquainted with something new—afternoon tea. Though the rectory trays came in heavily laden, I am compelled to report that there was never a crumb to be swept up afterward. By English standards it was a disgraceful exhibition of gluttony. My suggestions for restraint got nowhere. "What's food for but to eat?" Daniel inquired with the merciless logic of a fast-growing eighteen-year-old. Though I had to agree in principle, I'm sure that the Polings did terrible damage to the composure of the rectory's staff.

When we had departed for England, Lillian and I certainly had had no plans to add another daughter to our original five—and three days before we embarked for our return to New York we still had no such plans. Joan Poling became ours quite suddenly. Her story has a prologue.

In Canton, Ohio, during the flu epidemic of 1918, Lillian, as I have already mentioned, supervised an emergency hospital. One night she was summoned to the home of an Englishman named Bromage, an engineer who had been brought to Canton to supervise highly technical operations in the Duber-Hampton watch works. This firm had been taken over by the Government and was engaged in making precision instruments for the armed forces. A victim of the epidemic, Bromage was beyond help; he died, leaving three children, the youngest, Joan, less than a year old. Mrs. Bromage nearly died herself, and Lillian took care of her children while she recovered. Lillian and Mrs. Bromage became close friends in the ensuing months, and after the widow returned to England the following year, the two women kept up a correspondence.

Our last visit in England was to the Cheltenham home of Mrs. Bromage and her children. We were appalled by what we found. With British restraint, the widow had no more than hinted in her letters that life in postwar England was not easy for her. Now we found signs of want that could not be disguised;

Joan, a charming, dark-haired child of eight, was so pitifully undernourished and underdeveloped that she looked younger than our youngest, who was six. Profoundly touched, Lillian said, "Why don't we take her back with us, Dan? We can keep her until things improve over here." And Mrs. Bromage agreed that if we could do so, it would be wonderful indeed.

We made our plans, but our consul-general in Bristol soon informed us that our passports would not allow us to import a young house guest. An English judge to whom I explained the case said, "My dear sir, the only way you could possibly take that child to the States would be to adopt her."

It was a new idea, but by this time determination was mounting. "I'll adopt her," I said. The judge shook his head—it seemed that I would have to reside for six months in England before my application for adoption could even be considered.

To me, that was just about the end of the course, but Lillian would not give up without one last effort. "Do some pleading," she insisted. "Tell the judge that you adopted my two girls. You know how to plead, Dan." Thus urged on, I went back to see the judge. Perhaps it was the story of our marriage or perhaps it was his knowledge that Lillian had once cared for that same little girl in Canton, Ohio; perhaps he was persuaded by my ministerial credentials or perhaps it was his own fatherly heart. Whatever it was that tipped the balance, Lillian's faith was justified, and when I said good-by to that seemingly austere upholder of English law, I held in my hand a certificate of adoption dated back half a year.

It was a good while before my children could properly welcome our newest: Little Joan was desperately sick all the way across the Atlantic, with a combination of *mal de mer*, longing for home, and general poor health. Wondering if she would live until we reached New York, Lillian and I began to feel that we had acted rashly. But live she did, our daughter Joan, and today she is raising two fine sons of her own, Larry and Robert.

Lest it seem that we took a mother's daughter away rather peremptorily, this sequel should be added. We were all greatly pleased later on when we were able to bring Mrs. Bromage—

"Bromie" to the Polings—and her other two children, Muriel and Kenneth, to America. Though we didn't adopt them legally, they long ago entered the heart of our family, and they remain there today.

I remember that our little English daughter was uncertain and homesick in her new surroundings for some time. Once I was returning to New York from Cleveland on the train. Joan was in the upper berth and I had the lower. As I lay reading, I heard the child sobbing. I put on my robe, stepped into the aisle, and asked her what her trouble was.

She poked her head through the curtains and quavered, "Daddy Poling, aren't you lonely down there?"

"I certainly am," I replied. "I just can't stand it, Joan." And with that, I reached up and pulled her down. She cuddled up and quickly went to sleep.

Another vivid memory is of the first Christmas that we had our new daughter with us. We took Joan and the rest of our younger children to the church party at the Marble Collegiate Church. At the appropriate moment there was a loud knocking on an inner door, greeted by expectant laughter and a chorus of "Come in, Santa!" In came the old gentleman in his red suit and with his bag of gifts on his back. Standing where everyone could see him, he asked the usual questions: "How many of you children have been good this year?" Every hand in the room flew up. Santa was very impressed. "Now then, how many of you have daddies here?"

Up went the hands again—all but Joan's. Watching the proceedings from the sidelines with my wife, I saw that little hand start up, waver uncertainly, and go down. Joan turned, looking for someone. For me. The questioning look she gave me was eloquent. I nodded my reply. Wildly that hand shot up to join the rest.

Not seeing very clearly, both Lillian and I had to turn away for a moment.

8

In the fall of 1925 we bought a large old house and its tract of mountainous, wooded land in Deering Township, New Hampshire. Here, summer after summer, our children grew up, learning not only the eternal joys of country life but also some salient facts about American history from the traditions connected with our property. The original land grant had lain within the territory of the Massachusetts Bay Colony at the time the area was given to Ninean Aiken for the services he rendered to the Crown in 1758 when he took a platoon of Deering men to fight the French at Quebec. Some thirty years afterward, feeling that Deering was becoming uncomfortably populous, Aiken sold his holdings to Abram Gove and moved west. The Gove family eventually added a second complete house, attaching it end to end to Aiken's original, which suggested the name we immediately gave the property: Long House. I bought the property from heirs of the last of the Goves, the spinster sisters Sarah and Alzira, who died in the house of their ancestors.

Some of the original furniture remains in the house today: chairs, a settee, a lovely bookcase, a meal chest mentioned in a will probated a century and a half ago, family pictures, pewter pieces. The little square rosewood piano still stands where it was first placed a hundred years ago when it was hauled up the mountain by oxen as a Christmas present for one of the Gove women. As we remodeled the old place, we explored it from basement to attic and found many treasures. One early map showed us the original thirteen states and their territories. From another we learned the look of the United States in the year that Lewis and Clark started their westward journey of exploration; on it most of the rivers of the Pacific Coast are shown running in the wrong direction, and what is today the central farmland of our nation is marked "Uninhabited." Still another map we turned up showed the appearance of Deering Township a century before, and with it to guide our steps, my boys and I gradually explored every long-abandoned road and lane, and poked about the overgrown foundations of forgotten houses.

One old book on the Long House shelves proved to have unexpected value. A history of the Know-Nothing movement, it describes the political attempts to keep the foreign-born out of government office. Opposite the steel engraving of Daniel Webster, the golden-tongued hero of the cause, appears the watchword, "Let only Patriots be on guard tonight." Pasted into the front of the book we found the signature of an earlier American, Charles Cotesworth Pinckney. When our children began studying the Constitution in school, they looked at that signature and felt close to the man whose best-remembered words are "Millions for defense, but not one cent for tribute."

Definitely, Long House was a place in which to learn as well as to pass pleasant days. Many times I went to its ancient burying ground and stood looking at the crumbling stones covered with lichen and moss, and at the mounds blanketed with wintergreen. The Long House soil is stony, but it is ground not to be despised, for here lie men who fought at Bunker Hill and marched with Washington. Standing beneath the pines of this God's acre and looking out over Deering Pond toward Mount Crotchet, as did the earlier folk who came here to bury their dead, I and my family have often felt ourselves a part of a meaningful and continuing tradition. Who were these people whose memories we cherish? I used to ask myself. Sons and daughters of the soil, the answer came; men and women born of a humble folk who did their duty and passed along to me and mine a great heritage. By their silent presence they taught me and my family this lesson: *Do your best to keep free the nation that we gave you.* These ancient ones long ago accepted me and mine as one with them—or so I came to feel.

As I think back over the summer and winter holidays we spent at Long House, as I remember the intimate and larger gatherings of friends there—the parties, the weddings, the countless other happy events connected with the place—I rejoice in the fact that we were able to sink our roots in such a land. Once, we thought we would lose it. When the depression became severe in the 1930s, the two Morgans and the Shetland pony we kept for the children had to go—they were too great a load for us to carry. We took the horses out of their stalls to keep our children in school. Then came the day when Long House itself had to go on the block.

The children were wonderful. Children usually are wonderful in a family crisis. Oldsters crack before their young ones do. We had stripped the place—or thought we had—to the bone. Then, to pay the taxes, I sold off timber, sold oak and maple I had vowed never to cut. But we could not sell the property, even when we dropped the price. Prospects came, looked, and turned away. Other properties sold. All about us transfers were made. But the twenty rooms of Long House, so right for our large family and our many friends who visited us, made it too big for anyone who didn't want to start an institution—and in 1935 we couldn't even find an institution that wanted what we were almost willing to give away.

We prayed. It wasn't easy. Nothing is easy that bends you to your knees. But we prayed constantly that the place might be sold. Our answer came during the 1938 hurricane. That great storm showed us how strongly Ninean Aiken and the Goves had built their houses, but it pushed over one of the finest stands of white pine, spruce, and hemlock in southern New Hampshire. Nothing but that act of God could have ever persuaded me to sell those trees, for they were my pride and joy. It would have been a "sin" not to have passed them along with the property, had I been the one to make the choice, but it was not I who decided what should happen. The sale of that uprooted timber was what saved Long House for us and ours.

As I write these lines, it all sounds so simple, and in a certain way it was. When we turned to Him to "ask," we were once more acknowledging what we had always known: that we were not self-sufficient. God's hand, reaching to us and lifting us up, was the familiar hand of a friend. The ancient Scripture reads: "I have not seen the righteous forsaken nor his seed begging bread." Nor were we forsaken in a bitter time.

To bring the story of Long House quickly up to date, two years ago it was deeded to the Christian Herald Association. Lillian and I had perceived that none of our children, for various practical reasons, would ever be able to make it their home. With so many members of our own family treasuring its memories, we wanted other children to know its life-promising experiences, and so Long House is today a summer-vacation home for the teen-agers of Mont Lawn, the *Christian Herald* home in Nyack. Here, with some fifty carefully selected boys and girls who have passed the Mont Lawn age limit of twelve, we are going forward with a more advanced program of youth care and guidance leadership. We hope, as the program develops, to add scholarships for college. Already Mount Lawn's Dr. Hubert Mott has conducted two successful sessions of the Long House program. Lillian and I feel that we could not imagine or design a better use for the property we have loved for so long, and that has given so much to all our family.

Beginning in 1930, following my resignation from the Marble Collegiate Church, I took periodic leaves from the *Christian Herald* and went abroad to attend conventions and to organize or reorganize Christian Endeavor Unions in Spain, Italy, and the Bible lands. In 1930 the World's Christian Endeavor Convention was held in Berlin. Before I went to Germany I had a brainstorm. Up to that time, since the end of the war, there had been no exchange of any kind between the heads of the French and German states. Thinking that I might be able to make an impression on the President of the German Republic, Paul von Hindenburg, I obtained an interview with President Gaston Doumergue of France, with the idea of carrying some sort of helpful letter from him. Dr. William Cochrane, builder and pastor of the American Church in Paris, went along as my interpreter. Doumergue, a Protestant and therefore unique among modern French heads of state, was a friendly and delightful man, and though he was doubtful that any letter he could give me would be effective, he agreed that it was a move worth trying. Accordingly, he gave me a brief letter expressing his cordial sympathy with the aims of the World's Christian Endeavor Union. Addressed to me, it was so phrased that it could be shown to Hindenburg.

In Berlin, the German leader received the letter graciously and gave me a letter in reply. Though it was addressed to me personally, it was nevertheless another diplomatic exchange. Thus I was instrumental in bringing about the first communication between the heads of Germany and France following World War I.

Lillian acted as my interpreter with President von Hindenburg, and he was impressed with her linguistic ability. "Your German is High German," he said admiringly, and he complimented me on the selection of my *Frau.*

The German leader, then in his eighties, impressed me as being senile and at the mercy of venal, self-seeking men, particularly Hitler. Baron von Hene, Hindenburg's secretary, took me aside after my interview and told us with unmistakable despair in his voice that Hitler was on his way to power and that nothing could be done to stop him. Later in the year, visiting our United States Minister in Stockholm, I heard much the same word. "The Allies, particularly France," he said, "have insisted on rubbing the German nose in the dirt, and now Hitler has risen out of that dirt." Ten days later I heard it again from our Minister in the Hague—Mrs. Ruth Bryan Owen, William Jennings Bryan's daughter, and an old friend: "The German Republic had a real chance," she said, "but the Allies never allowed it to live."

It was in this ominous atmosphere, in July, 1930, that our World's Christian Endeavor Convention was held in Berlin. Over twelve thousand young people attended, and there were delegations and representatives from more than forty nations. During the day there were conferences and sermons, Bible study groups, citizenship meetings, and personal evangelism. At night, in the great auditorium, the convention sang to the music of a dozen massed bands and orchestras. The closing demonstrations of these world conventions are always very moving when the singing delegations march to the platform with their national flags. I remember the night at our Berlin convention when a German delegate rushed forward with the German national emblem and offered it to the leader of the British delegation. After those two flags changed hands on the platform, all the flags changed. Presiding, I was standing on the high podium watching the scene when Dr. Varcoe Cocks, president of the Australian Christian Endeavor Union, came leaping up the steps with his flag, the Southern Cross. He gave it to me and took in return the Stars and Stripes. Our meeting ended in this mighty and inspiring demonstration of unity that contrasted so strongly with the prevalent mood of the German Republic.

In July, 1934, I was again in Berlin, en route to Budapest. I sat within fifty feet of Hitler at the great mass meeting during which he told the people of Germany the reasons for his purge of June 20 that took the lives of former Chancellor Kurt Schleicher and Ernst Röhm, among others. For the first twenty minutes Hitler was comparatively calm, but from then on he needed only froth on his lips to complete the impression he gave of being a madman. I was sure that Germany was now in the hands of a power-mad ruler who would not hesitate to challenge France and England for his right to dominate the Continent. With the echoes of the *Führer's* harangue still ringing in my ears, I walked through Unter den Linden with two German Christian Endeavorers. They were less alarmed than I. Although they disagreed completely with Hitler's Aryan doctrine that sought to lift one race above all others—the German Christian Endeavor Union had already passed a resolution condemning the racist issue—they professed to see no dangers ahead. One of my young companions was a University of Leipzig graduate who had been my interpreter when I had previously been in Berlin. He insisted that Hitler, having won control, would now give Germany a moderate rule.

"But if you are mistaken," I said, "and the plan outlined in *Mein Kampf* presently becomes Germany's policy, what will you and our Christian Endeavor Union do?"

"Then," he said, "at whatever the cost, we choose Christ."

Today it may be hard to conceive of the fatefulness of such words. Such a moral crisis as these men presently faced has never arisen in the United States, and God forbid that it ever will. My two friends were not pacifists; they were Christians. To me, the outsider, it was already evident that Christianity and Nazism were not reconcilable. My friends and many of their associates learned this fact later on. Those who chose Christ, including my Leipzig interpreter, followed Him into Hitler's concentration camps, and there scores of them died, keeping their faith to the end. Today, with the agony of World War II past, those who survived, and their successors, are putting their lives into the building of a new and democratic western Germany. I met thousands of them in July, 1958, when our latest World's Christian Endeavor Convention was again held in Germany—this time in Frankfurt. Again there were delegations from many nations. In the night sessions there was music by a great choir and band, and addresses by government leaders and distinguished churchmen. The climactic moment came when Dr. Clyde Meadows, a master of assemblies and song leadership, in five minutes turned the eighteen thousand young people into one vast chorus, with each delegation singing in its own language "Blest Be the Tie that Binds," "Faith of Our Fathers, Living Still," and "A Mighty Fortress Is Our God." Dr. Meadows is today president of the International Society of Christian Endeavor.

In 1935, when delegations from thirty nations attended the World's Christian Endeavor Conference in Budapest, I became acquainted with Admiral Horthy, the Protestant leader of overwhelmingly Roman Catholic Hungary. A sparing eater and drinker, he was a splendid figure of a man, and he struck me by his positive approach to matters and his gracious personality. Though he ruled with dictatorial powers between the two World Wars, I believe that he was a good man, a patriot who served his country well, and against insuperable odds fought to save his fellow Hungarians from the wrath of Hitler and the terror that was later to come from the Kremlin. I was glad that I knew this man and saw the exquisitely beautiful capital of his country before the devastation of World War II all but destroyed it.

After the convention, Lillian and I went on around the world with Helen Lyon, one of the great spiritual leaders of the Christian Endeavor movement. In her whole life Helen was a vivid and happy demonstration of the Scriptural injunction, "When thou doest alms, let not thy left hand know what thy right hand doeth." One late afternoon in Syria we came to the top of a sandy hill. Below us, red in the sunset light, we saw a cluster of buildings. "There is my yacht!" Helen exclaimed. We were looking at a Syrian mission and hospital that Helen was supporting. This woman who could have afforded yachts preferred clinics and hospitals, schools and churches. When she gave the funds to erect the headquarters building of the World's Christian Endeavor Union in Columbus, Ohio, it was my thought that the building should bear her name. Instead, at her selfless insistence, and before I knew it, the building was given my name. Soon after we returned from our round-the-world journey Helen was happily married to Joseph Holton Jones, of Wilmington, Delaware.

On our travels around the world, Helen and Lillian and I visited nations that were soon to be involved in World War II. In Cairo, where we stayed in the old Shepheard's Hotel, there were student riots beneath our windows. Mussolini, having made his boasts against Ethiopia, the kingdom of Haile Selassie, was now about the ugly business of making them good.

We spent two weeks in Palestine, where we visited the holy places and saw evidence that pointed to the emergence of the great new nation, Israel. In Lahore, India, we witnessed riots in which Indians died in fratricidal strife.

In the whole course of my travels it seems to me that my talks and speeches have perhaps been translated into a hundred tongues, but I have never felt a real language barrier. Although I often could not understand a single one of the words that were spoken for me, or to me, I could never misunderstand the feeling in the voices that spoke or the emotions in the faces that were lifted to mine. In Bangkok, in the summer of 1935, my interpreter was a lovely and extraordinary young woman, a graduate of Silliman University in the Philippines. Her father, the Chief Justice of Siam's Supreme Court, was a Buddhist, but he had given his daughter freedom of choice and she was a Christian. This young woman sat directly in front of me and listened without taking a note while I addressed a youth group in English for twenty-five minutes. She then took my place on the platform and repeated the address in her own tongue—speaking for precisely twenty-five minutes. It was an uncanny experience to hear her using not only my inflections but to see many of my gestures repeated. I sensed that it was a phenomenal performance even before a teacher who was fluent in both languages informed me that the translation was perfect and that I had just seen as well as heard myself speaking Siamese.

The small ship that carried Lillian and Helen Lyon and me from Hong Kong north to Foochow had quite a history. Originally she was the lavish steam yacht of Jay Gould. After Gould's daughter Helen gave her to the United States Government in 1897, she served as a hospital ship through the Spanish-American and Philippine wars. Now renamed *Hai Ning*, she was in the China coastal trade under a British charter. Twice the ship had been attacked by pirates, and we traveled under heavy guard. The chief engineer, a rugged Scot, had been at Tientsin in 1900 during the Boxer uprising. I discovered that he was an eloquent admirer of the young American engineer who had organized the defenses of Tientsin against the Boxers—Herbert Hoover. "He is your greatest American, sir," the old Scot said, "and I knew that he would become your President some day." Well, I wasn't prepared to accept this sure foreknowledge, but since I had campaigned twice to put Mr. Hoover in the White House I was glad to hear the rest of his tribute.

In Foochow we visited the *Christian Herald's* orphanages, one for boys, the other for girls, and our industrial school. These installations, which the *Christian Herald* took over from their Congregational missionary founder in 1919 and 1920, had been thriving institutions ever since. My first visit to them in 1935 gave me an experience that I still treasure. Through an interpreter, I spoke to the boys at the orphanage, leading off with a feeble attempt at humor. "In America, unlike your country," I explained, "girls are much more valuable than boys, and I have six daughters, and each daughter has two brothers." This last was a joke I often used in those days. My audience listened closely but did not crack a smile, preserving characteristic Oriental calm. When I had finished speaking, some of the older boys went into a huddle at the rear of the chapel. Presently, one of them came down to the front and began speaking rapidly to the superintendent. The superintendent tried to shush him away, but I said I wanted to hear what he had to say. "Well, if you'll try not to be offended, I'll let him tell you," said the superintendent. "He speaks English."

The boy bowed to me. "Sir," he said, "we are sorry you are so poor a man in sons. We have decided to adopt you as a father. When you go back to America, tell your friends you have four hundred sons in China."

The story has a sequel. When I was in Chungking in 1943, I met again one of my Foochow "sons," Eugene Ting. He was graduating with a Ph.D. from Tientsin University, which had then, because of the war, been moved to Chungking. I learned from him that all the new boys who had entered the Foochow orphanage after my visit had been initiated into my family, and that I now had some twelve hundred Chinese sons.

Today, the Foochow orphanages and the industrial school no longer exist. The *Christian Herald's* property was confiscated by the Communists in 1950, and the children were dispersed. As quickly as we could, we opened an orphanage for refugee children in Hong Kong. The British Crown Government placed a loft building at our disposal on the mainland; modern buildings were erected later, and today Faith-Love, as our institution is called, is one of the best-run and best-equipped orphanages in the Eastern refugee world. In addition to Faith-Love, the *Christian Herald* now owns and supports eight orphanages in Korea and two on Formosa, and is responsible for feeding, clothing, and housing some sixteen hundred little waifs, many of them refugees from Communist China.

Some harrowing stories were told us by these refugees. One girl, eight years old when she came to our Hong Kong orphanage, had seen her father and two uncles beheaded when the Communists took over her city forty miles north of Canton. It was years before she lived beyond the memory of the horrors she had known, but when I last talked with her, on my visit to Hong Kong a year ago, she was growing into beautiful womanhood, her spirit strong and radiant. Two more of our children, a girl of ten and her five-year-old brother, were from a family in Canton whose mother was a Christian and whose father was a Buddhist. A remarkable man he must have been, because when his wife died in childbirth he resigned his position as pilot with China Airways and took a poorer-paying job on a Hong Kong newspaper that had a Canton edition in order to be nearer his little ones. He was one of forty-seven editors and journalists immediately arrested by the Communists. Later, his children attended his execution and saw his body with the head half torn away. The two youngest were brought to our orphanage by older refugees.

When we were in China in 1935, it was being taken over by a different enemy: the ruthless Japanese imperialists of that day. Japanese troops were everywhere. The little men sat insolently on their great Manchurian horses and ruled the streets.

One Sunday afternoon in Peiping I conferred with student leaders in a secret meeting in the basement of the Y.M.C.A. These young people came from the universities, colleges, and preparatory schools. I sought to dissuade them from their intention to stage a mass demonstration the following day. I reminded them that they had already made clear their opposition to the Japanese invaders; the continuance of their public protest would surely mean the closing of their schools and the end of all their organized activities. If they marched as planned, I said, the armed might of Japan would meet them.

It was at this point that a Chinese girl stood up to answer me.

"You are right, sir," she said. "We have made our purpose clear, and you are right when you tell us that we can accomplish nothing practical. But, sir, China needs martyrs, and we are candidates for that position."

And the next day she and the rest of the students marched through Peiping from dawn to sunset. Heavy streams of water drenched them. Soldiers with swords forced them into side streets. They re-formed and marched again. Again the Japanese soldiers met them. A few of the students were killed and many more went to hospitals, but they marched.

When I returned to the United States from this world mission, I wrote a little book entitled *Youth Marches*. I had seen tragic developments in country after country, all around the globe. I could not avoid the conclusion that the young people of the world would soon march to meet on the battlefield, and I knew that there was one and only one captain who could command them to march together instead of against each other. It was an ardent Christian's dream that led me to write: "Jesus Christ has the answer, youth's answer, time's answer, the world's answer. Jesus Christ is that captain." But the world, as we all know to our sorrow, was not ready to accept such a commander. Nor, alas, does it seem ready today.

From Peiping we traveled to Pyongyang, Korea, where we spent a memorable Christmas with Mr. and Mrs. Dexter Lutz and their daughters. Dexter was the agricultural specialist of the Presbyterian mission, and his wife, the daughter of William S. Harpster, my old Columbus, Ohio, friend, was the recognized musical leader of the missionary colony. Today the Lutzes are continuing their ministries in South Korea, under both the government and the Presbyterian mission.

In Tokyo, further along in our travels, Lillian and Helen Lyon were among a throng who watched Emperor Hirohito ride his white charger in the traditional New Year's pageantry that suggested the beauty and traditions of old Japan. I missed that spectacle because I was even then having an experience which demonstrated the power of the military clique that actually ruled the country. Invited to deliver a radio address to the youth of Japan,

I prepared my speech with care, confident that I could be helpful at least to the nation's Christians. I spoke as president of the World's Christian Endeavor Union and addressed myself directly to the very large Japanese Christian Endeavor constituency, discussing the brotherhood of man and the fatherhood of God, and expressing my fervent hope and prayer for world peace. After the broadcast I was complimented by the Japanese radio authorities and presented with a beautiful old ivory Buddha as an indication of official pleasure. I disposed of it without regrets when I was informed of how I had been tricked. The Japanese "translation" of my speech made me say what the Japanese government wanted me to say—or diametrically the opposite of what I had said in English. My salvation was that my missionary friends and others who understood both languages were not fooled.

Soon after the broadcast, my baggage was rifled and my diaries and other notes of our trip were stolen. My protests got me nowhere. My knowing Japanese friends assured me that in time, after the material had been studied, it would be returned with profuse apologies. But my friends were mistaken—I never saw my diaries again.

I cannot adequately describe the courage of my many Japanese friends, those heroic Christians and others too, who remained "loyal to the royal" in themselves and stood quietly and stoically against the rising tide of hate that led to the havoc of World War II. Again and again these glorious men and women, at the risk of losing their own freedom if not actually their lives, visited our American and other foreign missionaries to bring them food and needed supplies. I think with humility of their fortitude, even as I rejoice with them today in the better times of spiritual achievement and social and political progress that have come to their great land.

In 1936, not without hesitation in view of my many other commitments, I accepted the call of another church, Baptist Temple in Philadelphia, the founding church of Temple University. Both the church and the university, along with the three hospitals that were later united as Temple University Medical Center, were the creations of Russell Herman Conwell, minister, educator, and one of the greatest lecturers in all American lyceum history. "Acres of Diamonds," the lecture in which Dr. Conwell vividly illustrated his ideal of Christianized capitalism and the attainment of success over all difficulties, was first heard in 1888. He delivered it more than six thousand times, and from that one lecture alone made nearly six million dollars for his various enterprises.

Prayer was the heart of Dr. Conwell's message and the secret of his success. About all his concerns this man talked to God as to a friend. He believed that he prayed his church and hospitals and university into existence, and that again and again he saved them by prayer from bankruptcy. In 1912, for example, the university's trustees, their operating funds exhausted, voted to close the institution. The vote was taken on a Sunday when Dr. Conwell was absent—in church. The great man was not surprised when the trustees visited him on Monday with their news. "I knew something like this must happen. I prayed all night." (Dr. William H. Parkinson, dean of Temple University Medical Center, who told me this story, commented, "And that meant *all night*.") "But I know that God has not brought us thus far to have us fail," Dr. Conwell told the trustees. "Meet me here on Friday morning." In the interim, he put his case to the governor of Pennsylvania and then went on to address a joint session of the state legislature the day before it adjourned. The legislature did not let Dr. Conwell down. It voted him a hundred thousand dollars, which grant was instrumental in separating Temple University from the church and making it a state-supported university. It is today the largest of Pennsylvania's four state-supported universities, with more than twenty-six thousand students enrolled in its dozen colleges.

Conwell was a Hercules of a man physically, though as sympathetic and gentle as a woman, and his faith never went dead for lack of work on his part. He worked, as he said, eight hours a day for himself and another eight for Johnny Ring, the boy who had died serving him in the Civil War. It was the simple faith and steadfast praying of Johnny Ring that led Conwell from agnosticism to Christianity. Johnny was a simple lad who went to war with the "Berkshire Boys," the company of Union volunteers that Conwell organized. One night, in a surprise attack, the Berkshire Boys were driven across a stream. Johnny returned across the stream to fetch his commander's sword, which had been left behind in his tent. He brought it to Lieutenant Colonel Conwell through a flaming covered bridge. The Confederates who witnessed the brave deed held their fire in admiration, but the boy was so badly burned that he died with Conwell standing by his bed. That night, in his sorrow, Conwell gave his heart and life to Jesus Christ.

In his Philadelphia days Conwell was forever praying for something—an organ, the solvency of his university, or funds to educate young people toward degrees in law, medicine, and practically all the other professions. When this extraordinary character died in 1925, forty or more young men and women were being carried on his personal budget, receiving scholastic help from his lecture income. And yet this man who had made millions died practically penniless—voluntarily so. His entire estate consisted of his home, which was the gift of his church, and one of his associates later commented to me, "It was a great relief to find that Dr. Conwell hadn't gotten around to mortgaging it."

A sense of humor was another of Dr. Conwell's conspicuous gifts. When the Bok award of ten thousand dollars was given to him as the most distinguished Philadelphian of the year, a clergyman out West immediately wrote Conwell a letter explaining that he was building a church in a small, struggling community, and that God had revealed in a vision that the award money should be given to him to complete the project.

Conwell replied as follows: "Dear Brother, I am surprised at God. He knew that I gave that money away two years ago."

This was the man whose church I occupied as minister and pastor from 1936 to 1948. I met Dr. Conwell face to face only once, and then when he was advanced in years. Speaking at a patriotic youth mass meeting in Baptist Temple, I was presented by the great man. I found him truly great in mind and soul, and our one meeting confirmed everything I had heard or read about him. His personality was so impressive as he stepped to the front of his pulpit that he seemed to walk directly into my life. After Dr. Conwell had gone on ahead and I returned to Baptist Temple as minister, I renewed my acquaintance with a certain brown tile the church's founder had placed in his pulpit. It was a memorial to the Italian Roman Catholic nun who had nursed him, the Baptist preacher, when he fell dangerously ill on a mission to Italy. Dr. Conwell was an interfaith man before there were organizations carrying that name, and always his shoulder brushed that tile as he came into his pulpit, and always mine brushed it too in the years that I served his great church.

Though I became officially a member of the Baptist Temple congregation, I did so without changing my pre-existing denominational status as a member of the Reformed Church in America, Classis of New York, and as Honorary Member of the Evangelical United Brethren Church in Ohio—the church of my father's and of my own ordination. Such denominational crossings have ever been of less moment to me than the work my Master gives me to do. At Baptist Temple I was always convinced that my ministry, with its emphasis on personal evangelism and on prayer, with its faith in immortality and with its simple formula of "Faith without works is dead," followed the pattern that Dr. Conwell had established.

My outside duties and activities frequently took me away from Baptist Temple, even as they had accounted for my absences from the Marble Collegiate Church, and the situation did not improve when I began going overseas on various missions before and after the United States entered World War II. What made the situation tolerable was the absolute support of my parishioners and of the officers of the church. On the occasions when I departed, my decisions were not questioned; when I returned, it was to a congregation of love and loyalty. Through those busy and often difficult years Baptist Temple remained always a blessed place for a minister to come home to from London, North Africa, China, the South Pacific, and the banks of the Rhine.

My congregation included two remarkable men, both of whom had known firsthand the inspiration of Dr. Conwell. As I greeted the worshipers after the morning service on my second Sunday at Baptist Temple, a towering, slightly stooped man looked down upon me, smiled, and extended his great hand. "Call me Pat," he said. Thus I met Harry T. Patterson, one of Russell Conwell's "boys" who had been inspired by his "Acres of Diamonds." An immigrant from Northern Ireland, Patterson had begun his business career with John Wanamaker and then gone on by himself to become a successful linen merchant. Pat and his gracious wife were not only loyal parishioners; they quickly became Lillian's and my intimate friends. We were often entertained in their lovely Germantown home, which, I was pleased to learn, had been the home away from home of Harry Lauder. Pat and Lauder were fellow Scots of the blood, though born with a sea between them, and the house had actually been designed with the comfort of Lauder and his good wife in mind. After Pat's death, his home became ours for the duration of my Philadelphia ministry.

Pat had an impaired heart when I first met him, and it was not to be that I should know him for long. What a triumphant experience his death was! Many years before, on the grounds of the old Miami Chautauqua, south of Dayton, Ohio, I had conceived the idea of putting our young people into a circle with shoulders touching as they faced inward, and then having them cross their arms and clasp their neighbors' hands. Standing thus, we would begin our prayers. During the years since that time, in small groups and great, I have "made the circle" in countries all around the world. Today, that little ritual has been adopted by many different youth groups. Harry Patterson and his wife were captivated by the circle when Lillian and I made it with them the evening of our first visit in their home.

Then came Pat's last night on earth. I was with him in his bedroom at home. The tall man lay propped against his pillows; his face was ashen but his eyes were bright. He smiled up at me. "Pastor, this is it," he whispered in the lilt of his homeland.

"How do you feel, Pat?" I asked.

Like a flash came the answer: "Wonderful, Pastor, I feel wonderful. Why, if I felt any better, I just couldn't stand it. Make a circle!"

And we made it, around and across the bed. His wife, Frances, held one of his hands; I held the other, and Lillian and the nurse completed the link. And in that happy communion, as I prayed, Pat left us, moving from the house he loved into the house "not made with hands."

The second of my links to Dr. Conwell's service of prayer was Dr. Temple Fay, brain surgeon, practical psychologist, and pioneer in the use of lowered body temperatures in surgery. It is only a coincidence that his name also links him to Temple University, where he was a distinguished member of the staff.

Our friendship began the night Lillian and I invited the Medical Center's freshman class to our home on North Broad Street. Dr. Fay, one of the Center's senior surgeons, came with Dean William Parkinson as our guest to speak informally to the young men and women who would soon be his students. He was, and is today, universally popular as a class lecturer. Among other things that night, he told us of an experience he had had when he was a young resident in an upstate hospital.

"I had a desk at the entrance to a ward," he said, "and one day I watched a charwoman enter that ward and move quietly from bed to bed. At each bedside she would take the hand of the patient, who seemed to welcome her, between her two hands, stand with closed eyes for a brief interval, and then move on to the next bed. I felt that I had to do something about her, for she was clearly out of her place. When she passed near my desk, I said, 'You know, do you not, that you do not belong here? What you are doing is very irregular.' And she replied, near to tears, 'Doctor, I meant no harm. Always when I have finished my work I come here like this, and always I do just what you have seen me do, and the patients tell me that I help them.'

"I went brusquely to the first bed," Dr. Fay told us, "and asked the man lying there whether he had been helped by the visit of this woman. The man replied, 'Yes, Doctor. She has something in her hands.' " Dr. Fay let the end of his story sink in. Then he resumed. "Young gentlemen and ladies, Temple University has much to give you, much that you will get out of books, and much more, perhaps, that you will get from your associations with members of your faculty. But if when you leave you do not have that *something in your hands*, you will not have enough, for you will not have all that you should and may have." And that night Dr. Fay concluded his remarks with the statement, "Russell H. Conwell, the founder of this university, had it in his hands because he was God's man."

Through the years that followed, I came to regard Dr. Fay as a mystic as well as a scientist, and a man with the insight of a seer. There came a time when a dear relative of ours, Mrs. Dorothy Hostetter, was faced with a decision of unusual poignancy. Her son, born with a heart defect, at age twelve faced the prospect of physical degeneration and even early death if his condition were not surgically remedied. The mother was torn by doubts, accentuated by the fact that her husband had died at thirty-nine with a thrombosis. I came to realize that her decision would rest very much on the advice I gave her. Instinctively, I consulted Dr. Fay. He made the problem appear simple.

"I know the surgeon," he said. "The young mother could not have chosen a more competent man. I know the hospital too, and I know the technique of the operation although I do not perform it myself. Tell the mother she has these alternatives. First, she may go ahead with the operation as called for by the diagnosis. Always, of course, an operation may fail, however simple it is. Even a tonsillectomy has its hazards. But there is every reasonable hope of success in this case. Second, she can wait, with deterioration steadily progressing." Here my friend got to the heart of the matter. "If she does nothing but await the inevitable, she will spend the rest of her life regretting her decision. If the operation is a success, she will be overjoyed, but she must make the decision. Don't advise her. Tell her to go out to her lonely hilltop, even as you and I have gone. Tell her to go there and wait expectantly. She will receive her answer. Then she will go forward. And whatever the result—operation or no operation—success or failure—she will know that she made the right decision."

The mother followed that prescription. The answer she received was to operate. The operation was apparently completely successful.

I realize that it all sounds very easy. And it *was* easy, in the hands of the Great Physician, whose assistant Dr. Temple Fay was and is. Like the charwoman he had once questioned, my friend long ago found power in his hands because he possessed it in his mind and heart—because he had taken it from the hands of the Great Physician himself.

My memories of Baptist Temple come close to home, for here it was that I performed the marriage ceremony for our daughter Treva Mabel, or "Billie," when she became the wife of Philip H. Roy, who had been her fellow student at Bucknell University. They were a pair in music. Billie was the university's soprano soloist and Phil was its tenor soloist. Phil, who holds the one Phi Betta Kappa key in all our family, is an important junior executive with the Merck Chemical Company.

Rachel, our eldest, was the first of our children to marry. She persuaded me both to perform the ceremony and to give the bride away. "You can work it out," she insisted, and I did. The ceremony took place at Long House, in New Hampshire. The groom, just Bill Van Note to us then, but today Dr. William Gardner Van Note, president of Clarkson College of Technology, waited in what we called the Arizona Room, with our son Daniel as his best man. Rachel entered on my arm. When I asked the fateful question, "Who giveth this bride to marriage?," I answered myself with, "I, her father," and went on from there.

That established the precedent. Billie insisted on the same double-duty ceremony when she married Phil. Joan married Reid Malcolm, a member of Baptist Temple and a University of Pennsylvania graduate, at the time of his graduation as a naval air pilot in Pensacola. With Reid's mother I went to Mobile, Alabama, and in the historic Presbyterian church there I again doubled as father and minister. At this writing Joan's husband is a top department executive in the Olin Mathieson Chemical Corporation.

Our daughter Mary and Lyman Philips Wood were married by our son Daniel while Lillian and I were traveling around the world in 1935. Though I was not able to give Mary away, she had our blessing. Mary's husband, managing successful enterprises of his own, is also a consultant in the broad field of mail-order sales and buying. Their two children, Nancy and Phillips, ran off with prep-school honors. After three colleges had accepted her, Nancy chose Wellesley. Phillips, *cum laude* at Vermont Academy and a three-letter man there, is now a sophomore at Yale.

When our six daughters were still very young I used to remind them that doctors, dentists, and plumbers took most of their father's money, and that it might be a good thing to have these services represented in our family. It was not to be. Our first three to wed, Rachel, Mary, and Joan, married chemical engineers, and our fourth, Billie, found herself a business executive. Bill Van Note knew of my interest in acquiring a doctor for a son-in-law, and the first Christmas after he had married Rachel he presented me with a gift-wrapped gallon jar of Absorbine Junior, made in the laboratory where he then worked. "Here's a little something as a return on your investment," he remarked.

Our daughters Ann Louise and Jane have not married. Ann, a graduate of New York University, is a business executive who seems to have inherited all her mother's talents and abilities. She is now personnel director for the Community Service Society in New York, and is a genius in settling disputes, organizing departments, and for plain hard work. Explaining why she chose to remain single, Ann once said to me—with her tongue in her cheek, I think—"Somebody has to help earn the money to finance your remarkable clan of grandchildren through college, and perhaps a bit later on look after you."

Jane, like all our children, makes her own decisions. With degrees from Ursinus College, the University of West Virginia, and Johns Hopkins University, she is today busy and happy as a supervising nurse with the Board of Education in Denver, Colorado. Lillian maintains that she has the healing in her hands that she—Lillian—has also found in mine.

Our twenty-one grandchildren—eleven girls, ten boys—have renewed the youth of their grandparents, and some of them have even contributed materially to my theological training. Before she was ten, Rachel's daughter Gretchen prepared and sent to me an album of sacred pictures clipped from magazines, the collection enhanced by appropriate Bible verses. On the last page she wrote, "And now, Grandfather, I hope that looking at these pictures and reading these verses will do you great good." The little girl's hope was fully realized, as I assured her at the time. Now she and her brother, William Gardner Van Note, Jr. ("Dutch"), our eldest grandchildren, are both married, and it was my privilege to officiate at their weddings. Dutch, after three years with the Marines, returned to marry his high-school sweetheart, Ann Eichorn. As a straight "A" student, he is now completing his course at Clarkson College. Gretchen was married on her twenty-first birthday to Robert Dix, a Massachusetts Institute of Technology senior. Having graduated, he is now finishing his remaining six months of government service while Gretchen goes on to graduate from Simmons College in Boston.

Our daughter Billie's eldest of seven living children, Philip Clark ("Rusty"), is our first Eagle Scout. Recently, while I was recovering from a major operation, Rusty's seven-year-old brother Stevie spelled out the Apostles' Creed in clean-cut block letters, signed it "By Stevie Roy," and mailed it to me at my hospital. Though the words were familiar, my grandson gave them a twist that was all his own. Touched as I am by all my children's and grandchildren's efforts on my behalf, I heartily appreciated Stevie's contribution and the thought behind it.

9

Daniel, my older boy, ran true to the Poling ministerial tradition from the outset, but when his brother Clark first became concerned about what he was going to do with his life, he announced, "I want to be a lawyer." I rather liked the idea. Perhaps since I had not gotten there myself, I had hopes that one of us would. But Clark also impressed me as having natural talents for the law. He had always been a good extemporaneous pleader, beginning in the days when he used to develop cases as to why I shouldn't spank him, and when he said that he was determined not to be a preacher, I went along. "I'm going to break this vicious Poling circle of father to son," was the way he determinedly put it—with a grin.

However, as Clark developed his plans, I realized that in spite of all he said and even believed at the time, he was preparing for the ministry. During my Marble Collegiate Church days I once heard sounds of violence in our living room. Running in, I found Daniel sitting on his brother's chest. After I tore the warriors apart and demanded an explanation, Daniel answered, with a snort, "Aw, he's all the time talking about peace and brotherhood, and I'm sick of it. I told him it was soft stuff, and he dove into my belly."

This was Clark, the beneficiary of a year's education at Oakwood, the Quaker school at Poughkeepsie. The incident was symbolic of a lot that followed. Though he was philosophically a pacifist and became a man of peace, Clark was never a practicing pacifist. A mystic and a realist, he followed Jesus and sought to know His will, but though he knew many sincere Christian pacifists, he was finally as committed against the absolutist position as was his father.

An experience that doubtless helped to turn Clark toward the ministry came the summer he and his sister Ann served as senior counselors at the *Christian Herald's* children's home at Nyack. His understanding and love for children and his interest in making his life count for human gains and a fuller life for others were certainly broadened that summer. I remember his saying to me, "These kids have so little that Mont Lawn is heaven to them. Their gratitude at times nearly tears you apart. I don't know just where or how, but I'm going to keep close to little people."

From Clark's headmaster at Oakwood I learned that he was not overly pious—that he was even a prankster who took a night ride through the girls' dormitory in a laundry basket!—but still had a high sense of responsibility. A few years later, after Clark had left us, Headmaster Reagan told me that he remembered the boy above all for one experience. "My own small son had died," he said, "and I had returned to my office just to get acquainted with it again and to be alone there. When I started home, I found Clark waiting at the door. He was then president of the student body. I thought I could not discuss school matters with him that night, but he spoke only twice to me. He said, 'I have waited to walk home with you, Mr. Reagan.' When we reached the house, he opened the door for me and said only, 'Good night, Mr. Reagan.' But what a good night your boy gave me! I could face it better after that walk with him."

One Friday afternoon when Clark was in his third year at Oakwood, I received a telegram from him: MEET ME AT GRAND CENTRAL ELEVEN TOMORROW. VERY IMPORTANT. DON'T TELL MOTHER. I'M NOT GOING HOME. LOVE, CLARK.

That was the first telegram I had ever received from him, and to say the least it left me uneasy; and the more I wondered about what sort of jam he might have gotten into, the less composure I had left. Saturday morning, Clark was almost the first passenger through the gate. I did not see his usual smile, nor did I hear the quick, nervous laugh that was so characteristic of him. However, we kissed. Poling men are reared in that ancient form of salutation—and we don't make it a side-swiping, double-cheek affair, but an unsanitary smacker full on the mouth.

"Let's go to your office," Clark said. "You didn't tell Mother?"

Assuring him that I had not said a word, I took the boy directly to my study in the Marble Collegiate Church. As it is today, that narrow room was then a secluded spot, safe enough for any disclosure, and so never locked. Therefore I was not reassured when Clark shoved a chair under the knob of the door I closed. Coming to my desk, Clark dropped into a chair facing me, lowered his chin into his hands, and searched my face. I remember that moment as one of the most uncertain of my life. I thought of many things. What could it be that would cause a boy to shut out his mother and his home? I was far from a happy father as I watched Clark's dark eyes, but one mistake I did not make: I did not ask a question. I did not begin the conversation.

At length Clark came to life. "Dad, what do you know about God?" he asked.

What a relief! I was glad the question took me by surprise, that I had no chance to prepare an answer for him. For that question of a boy in one of his first major emotional and intellectual experiences, perhaps only a father's intuitive response was enough. I know now that my answer was the only one that could have satisfied the asker. Whatever else it lacked, it was completely honest:

"Mighty little," I said. That startled him. Then I went on. "Mighty little do I know about God—less now than I thought I knew when I sat where you are sitting. But, Clark, what I do know by the test of experience—sickness and health, sorrow and joy, death and life—what I do know about God has changed my life."

There we began, and for several hours we explored the great matter. Afterward, we had our late lunch in a restaurant and went home together. Exactly why he didn't want his mother to know, I am not sure, but I imagine he had feared another conclusion to the interview—one that might have made her unhappy. Whatever the case, that homecoming was one of the happiest of a long series. Lillian looked at us and said right off, "Something fine has happened, hasn't it? I can tell." Though I had to keep my promise of verbal secrecy, the new intimacy of father and son could hardly be concealed from Lillian's sensitive awareness.

Later, Clark came again to my sanctum at the Marble Collegiate Church. This time he said flatly: "I don't believe the virgin birth." Again I had no "prepared text" for him; I had to speak out of my knowledge of him rather than from the wisdom of books or the creeds of the Fathers. Again I was first of all my boy's father, and I said, "Well, then that settles it. If you don't, you just don't. You cannot *make* yourself believe anything even if you greatly desire to believe it, any more than you can make yourself happy or make yourself fall in love. But, are you sure, very sure, you are ready to say that? Intellectually sure?"

Clark's brow contracted. "What do you mean by that, Dad?"

"I mean that unless you have read the books, unless you have listened to the masters of thought in this field—unless you are both intellectually and spiritually sure that you are justified in your conclusion—your affirmation that you do not believe will bring you unnecessary confusion and embarrassment. Now, are you still ready to say it?"

The boy grinned and said, "Where are the books?"

I gave him two: *The Deity of Jesus*, by Dr. Robert E. Speer, and perhaps the most convincing, direct argument of all for the virgin birth, *Fundamentals*, by Dr. Charles E. Jefferson. For a long time that was the end of it. Not until his ordination did I know the impression his studies made on him, for we never discussed the subject again, not even when he returned my books. On that occasion he simply slapped me on the shoulder and grinned.

Just when Clark reached his decision to take his place in what he still called our "vicious circle," I do not know, but I do remember the announcement. I had gone to Detroit in 1931 to deliver a series of noontide Lenten talks in a downtown theater, and Clark came on from Hope College to spend an afternoon and a night with me. Our family believes in the small coeducational college, the church-directed school, and a wide experience, originating in Father's Dallas College, confirms our opinion. The small college best answers the needs of undergraduates, we feel, and then let the graduate work, if any, be done in one of the great institutions in the land. Clark chose Hope, the Dutch Reformed Church's college in Holland, Michigan.

In the afternoon after my address, we visited a surgeon. Afterward, we saw a movie and then had a steak dinner. Clark had been having a great deal of trouble with the wrist he had broken playing football the previous season, and he was wearing a heavy leather guard. It was apparent even before we obtained the specialist's conclusive verdict, that his football days were over, for he was too light for any line position, and his strength to his team in both tackling and passing was now gone.

I thought that his painful wrist was responsible for his unusual silences. He did little talking until we retired to our room, and then he began. We had a room with twin beds. It was late and I was ready to sleep, but Clark spared me not. Several times I was on the verge of telling him to close down and go to sleep, but each time I stopped and listened, for something was there—something still unsaid after all the saying. At length it came out, so quietly but so impressively that as long as I live I shall remember the thrill with which I heard his words. He flung his left arm with its sound wrist across to my bed; I felt his hand on my chest, and then I heard him say: "Daddy, I'm going to preach. I've got to do it!"

I wasn't sleepy then; I wasn't tired in the least. I knew that I had always wanted to hear this, even when I was so sure that he would become the first lawyer of our line. All fathers, I suppose, have a sense of fulfillment, a subtle feeling of vindication, when their sons follow after them.

The next nine years were the best of Clark's short life on this earth in terms of study, eager search, companionship, love, and the opening of a prophetic ministry.

It was during his first year at Yale Divinity School that he and I took a long walk down the abandoned ridge road from Long House. He had sent me another of his telegrams to make sure I would be on hand to see him. At the time he was serving a Methodist church in South Meriden, Connecticut, as student pastor. He arrived at Long House at night, and the next morning we took our walk—not a hike but a walk, for we were chiefly interested in undisturbed conversation.

"Dad, an old man is dying in my parish, and he wants me to say something to him. He needs me, Dad, and I haven't anything to say."

We stopped by a stone wall and Clark waited for me to speak. It was a large order he had given me, but at least the matter had been frankly stated. I began by telling him of my own difficult experience as a young minister, when I had had to help a dying mother leave her six small children and her husband. The work of a minister, I assured him, was first of all not for weaklings. But this was only a part of it. The minister had to have something to say before he could say it, something to give before he could give it. Yet there was a sure way open to him. I told my son that it was as sure and simple as "Ask and ye shall receive"—that God would not, could not forswear Himself. The South Meriden man needed the answer and he, Clark, was desperately concerned to get it for him. That settled it! "Ask and ye shall receive."

In that abandoned roadway we talked to the heart of life's mystery—to its beginning and to its end in time, which we agreed was only its greater beginning. Then we knelt together in the dry grass and dead leaves by that stone wall. Afterward I left him and walked home alone. When Clark returned later I sensed that he had his answer and that he would not disappoint his dying parishioner in South Meriden.

Though Clark gave a great deal of himself to a great many people in his short ministry, he was never to have an easy time of it with himself. When he was in his sophomore year at Yale he came again to Long House and gave me another stiff assignment. "I'm going up to Wolf Hill tonight," he said, "and I'll not be back for some time. Please don't worry about me, and keep Mother from worrying." And he grinned. We both knew this would not be easy. Wolf Hill, a granite ledge, was the summit of our property. "I may stay twenty-four hours or longer, but there are some things I want to settle, and I hope I won't be interrupted. Of course you understand."

Well, I wasn't sure I understood, but I agreed to give him his freedom. Off he went, after supper, taking a blanket and a canteen of water but firmly rejecting our advice about a few sandwiches. The night was clear, the sky filled with stars, and the moon—I was awake to see it—rose shortly before daylight. The day that followed was one of the season's finest, and the next night was another faultless one. Lillian had been reminding me for hours of the drop on the west side of Wolf Hill, a precipice she had never seen but pictured pretty convincingly in her imagination. Finally, when Clark had been gone thirty-six hours, I decided I could wait no longer. My promise of noninterference, I felt, had been sufficiently honored.

At three in the morning, just as the moon lifted, I called Fluff, our American shepherd dog, and started for the summit. Foxes yapped at us, but Fluff had long ago learned that they were too swift for her. She kept at my side. As we began the direct climb toward the ledge, my anxiety took on proportions. Why had I waited so long? Of course Clark had not meant that he would spend *two* nights on the mountain! Lillian had been right. What a fool I had been to wait so long!

Before I reached the last pitch of Wolf Mountain I shouted our son's name at the top of my voice. No reply came to me. Fluff stood quietly at my side; she had caught no familiar scent. Panic seized me as I climbed onward. Parenthood is a strange, mysterious experience. Though only a mother may know its ultimate heights and depths, a father can face poignant moments. That night on Wolf Hill, under a midsummer moon, one father knew infinite anguish.

Then, from his blanket, startled from his sleep, there rose a tousle-headed young man. In a voice that I still hear, he said "Dad!" and came to meet me. No other moment of my life was ever quite like that, nor will ever be again.

We did not wait but started down the trail. Fluff, leaping and yelping about the boy, expressed in her way what I could only feel. After our first greeting, Clark was silent until we reached the road that would take us back to the house. Then he talked. He was glad I had come, but he was glad, too, that I had not come before. "I thought that up there I might hear the Voice," he said. "I did not hear it, but some things are clearer to me now, and other things will be, I know. Yes, Dad, I'm glad I went up there."

Then Clark began to sound like his buoyant self again. "Breakfast will certainly taste good," he said—and that thought brought us both back to earth. His voice was penitent as he asked, "Is Mother worried?"

I told him that his mother had been at least considerably interested.

Walking along with the boy shoulder to shoulder, I knew that he had found himself on Wolf Hill, and knew too that to Clark our mountain was what the people of Bible times had called their Mount of Sacrifice—the place where they went to find their God.

As the divinity-school years followed the college years, our sons had less time for leisurely vacations, but I do remember a couple of wonderful days the three of us—Daniel, Clark, and I—had at Nantucket, walking in the ancient whaling town, visiting the museums, bathing in the surf, and idling on the sand. One night there, when the stars seemed low enough to touch, I stretched between my boys on the beach and listened to them as I had not listened since they were little fellows. Now each was a man in his own right, a man with his work beginning in the world. I did not know that we would never again be as we were then, but I listened even so as if it were already the last time. They razzed each other, they threw pebbles at each other across their father, they debated the problems of the universe, and they talked about their girl friends. I listened to it all, mostly in wondering silence, but when they began on theology, I felt it was time to open up.

The theological differences between Daniel and Clark were theoretical and scholarly rather than vital; they did not affect the very practical character of their ministries. Daniel was born believing; as he matured, he marshaled the facts and experiences to justify his faith. Clark, on the other hand, came into the world questioning, but he, like his older brother, found answers that confirmed his faith. Agnosticism may be either negative or positive. One agnostic will say, "I do not believe and I don't give a —care." The other will say, "I do not know, I find it difficult to believe, but I do care and I am determined to search the matter out." Clark was a man of the latter sort.

I, of course, am not a theologian, but when I heard Clark challenge his brother with a particularly radical assumption and Daniel then and there denounce Clark as a son of heresy and a Yale liberal, I ventured the prophecy that I would live to see the day when the Princeton conservative would find himself no less liberal as a sound evangelical than his argumentative younger brother. That suited neither of the boys, so they rolled me in the sand—or tried to.

And then, arm in arm, we strolled up the beach, deliciously weary and sleepy, and at last went to bed. Someday I hope to take a few of my grandchildren to Nantucket and stretch out on that beach and listen to them talk.

Clark was ordained in the fall of 1936, in the First Congregational Church of New London, Connecticut. Father came on from Oregon to make it a three-generation affair. In the afternoon there was the customary conference with its questions and voting. I listened closely when Clark was asked: "Do you believe the virgin birth?"

"My ministry stands on Jesus Christ," he said. "To me God is limitless, and for Him the virgin birth would be as simple and as profound as any natural birth. But it is not unique, for nearly every Eastern religion claims as much for its founder. Surely faith in the virgin birth is not the ultimate, or all the Gospel writers would have made the claim. Paul would have affirmed it, and Jesus Himself would not have remained silent. For me deity and the virgin birth are not synonymous. The vicarious atonement does not stand upon it. I do not disbelieve, but I am not convinced." Clark had decisively not dodged the question. With a glance in my direction, he quoted one of my favorite verses from St. Paul: "For He hath made us able ministers of the New Testament, not of the letter but of the spirit, for the letter killeth but the spirit giveth life."

There was a suggestion of appeal in my boy's glance, and he got from me the look of assurance that he wanted. Even his grandfather was satisfied—and who would not have been?

That night, during the ordination ceremony, after Clark's grandfather had led the prayer, I charged the new minister. My closing words were to have a significance in retrospect that they did not have at the time. "I would call to your attention three exits . . . the only three ways that open out from your ministry. The first is the way of physical disability or of any honorable retirement. The second is the way of repudiation. The third is the way of triumph. . . . May you so preach and so minister . . . that when at last your earthly sun shall set, no cloud shall float upon your sky."

Now my two sons were both with me in my calling, even as I had followed the calling of my father. I could not reasonably have expected it and I had not suggested it, but I was overjoyed to find it so. Daniel was pastor of one of the oldest Presbyterian churches in the United States, at Bedford, New York, and for another year Clark would remain at Christ Church (Congregational) at New London, Connecticut.

Father expressed his own profound satisfaction with these events before he returned to Oregon. "It means more than ever you will know," he said to me, "to have been here and to find my grandsons following in the family succession."

Clark was always proud of his early associations with the Marble Collegiate Church and, whatever his immediate relationship, felt himself always a son of the Reformed Church (Dutch) in America. His happiness was great, therefore, when in 1938 he was called to the First Reformed Church (Dutch) in Schenectady, and given charge of that ancient parish. Clark reveled in the traditions of this church. For him its most sacred spot was the tower room under the spire, where the stained-glass windows told the story of the death of the church's first pastor, Domine Petrus Tessemacher. Young Tessemacher, who was the first Protestant clergyman to be ordained in the New World, was killed and scalped in the French and Indian massacre of February 8, 1690, when the little stockade settlement of Schenectady was sacked and burned. As Clark studied the life of his martyred predecessor, he conceived a plan to build in that tower room a chapel in which all people might worship. Had he lived, I am confident that he would have made his interfaith ideal a reality.

From his installation as pastor until he enlisted as an army chaplain, I watched Clark's progress with increasing pride. He took all his responsibilities with utmost joy and yet utmost seriousness, and it was evident that he considered his ministry in Schenectady his life's work. At last, I said to myself, a Poling preacher has finally broken one of the family traditions —that of wanderlust. When World War II compelled Clark to interrupt his activities and plans in his church, he put himself on record in a letter that he had but one desire so far as his future was concerned: to get through his experiences in uniform as well, but also as quickly as possible so that he could return to his congregation.

From the very beginning of my career I believed that my interests and responsibilities as a Christian minister and as a Christian citizen were indivisible, and as a youthful clergyman in Canton, Ohio, I was active in local politics. Later, as we have seen, I ran for governor of Ohio. Still to come is my story of running for mayor of Philadelphia. In all these ventures I made myself one important rule and stuck to it: I never carried partisan politics into my pulpit. If I had reason to hire a hall, I hired it and presented my views. But just as I never took politics into my churches, so I have never shrunk from public life because of my ministerial status.

As this story moves on to deal with events of World War II as I saw them, and with my relationships with Presidents Franklin Delano Roosevelt and Harry S. Truman, my thoughts go back to the other Presidents I have known either intimately or casually.

Theodore Roosevelt, famous not only for his Rough Rider exploits in Cuba but for the fact that at forty-three he was our youngest President, was a figure and a personality to capture the imagination of the nation's youth, and I was wholeheartedly one of his devotees. As a public-spirited sixteen-year-old in Portland, Oregon, I had worn the McKinley-Roosevelt campaign button even as earlier, in 1896, I had worn the McKinley-Hobart button. I was twenty-three when I finally saw Roosevelt in the flesh. The President came to Canton, Ohio, in 1907 for the funeral of President McKinley's widow. After lunch in the home of Supreme Court Justice William Rufus Day, Teddy, instantly recognizable by his rounded face and mustache and glasses, popped out of the house and began walking to the McKinley home, a few doors up North Market Street. Walking is not the word: he set a pace fit for the cinder path. Short and stocky, the President was accompanied by vice-president Charles Warren Fairbanks, an Indianan as tall and lean as Abe Lincoln must have been. Fairbanks had to stretch his long legs in order not to be left behind. The two men made a startling sight as they seemed to race, and I'm sure that only the solemnity of the occasion kept me, the young preacher, and half a hundred other Canton folk from cheering them on toward the tape.

Warren Gamaliel Harding, big of frame, handsome of face, had the true presidential mien. Perhaps only the bearded, grandly impressive Charles Evans Hughes surpassed Harding in looking as we think a President should, and he, of course, was defeated for the presidency by Wilson—by a California nose. Wilson, to my mind, looked precisely like the university professor he was. I first met Harding in 1908. As lieutenant governor of Ohio, he had already won the confidence of the state's drys by keeping certain pre-election promises when other politicians conveniently forgot them. I found him receptive to an invitation from Christian Endeavor, and the lecture on Alexander Hamilton he gave our state convention impressed us all by its literary distinction, whereas Harding the man won us by his obvious sincerity and cordiality.

When Harding became President in 1921, I regarded him as a man of honor, if not a statesman of major stature. Presently, like many another who voted for him, I began to regret that his choice of associates and friends was not always sound—but that is a story beyond the scope of this book. One of Harding's minor distinctions was that he was the last of the tobacco-chewing Presidents, a line of men that, along with the snuff takers, perhaps included a majority of the earlier American statesmen. I remember a visit with the President-elect in his office in Marion, Ohio, during which I watched in fascination as he punctuated our conversation about public and personal affairs with shots at one or the other of two brass cuspidors located at either end of his flat-top desk. Perhaps the White House became a more sanitary institution when the spittoons were retired.

My contacts with Calvin Coolidge were brief and casual. I found him as taciturn as the next man did, but perhaps a bit mysterious too, for it struck me that his perpetually serious face sometimes masked a half-smile struggling to break through. He seemed to enjoy the impression left by his solemn manner. His dead-fish hand clasp made you do all the reaching and squeezing, but I'm sure the technique eventually saved him great amounts of energy and some real pain. However, if the laconic little Vermonter sometimes gave the public a false impression of himself, he sustained his role with remarkable consistency. As time went by, everyone began telling "Coolidge stories." Today, some of these yarns have entered the body of our national legends. For example, the conversation supposed to have taken place the morning Mrs. Coolidge did not attend church. "What was the pastor's subject?" "Sin." "What did he say about sin?" "He was agin it." I first heard that one when it was still a baby.

President Hoover told me a typical Coolidge story one day in 1932. He and I were standing before a window in the White House that looked down toward the Washington Monument. At a pause, Hoover indicated the window, grinned, and said, "Cal once stood here and watched Senator Borah ride by on his morning constitutional. All he said was, 'Borah riding a horse. At the moment they seem to be going in the same direction.' " Such stories seemed to be about the only resources most of us had when we tried to find the human qualities in that elusive figure.

Herbert Clark Hoover was the first President I came to regard as a close personal friend. We had common interests in our Oregon boyhoods. Orphaned in his ninth year, Hoover left Iowa, the state of his birth, and lived for a time with one of his uncles in Newburg, a Quaker community seven miles from my village of Lafayette. Here, as a youth, he became a charter member of the Christian Endeavor Society in the Friends Church. As Oregonians, Hoover and I did not chance to meet, but years afterward we discussed these early days in which, though Mr. Hoover was ten years my senior, we were fellow members of Dr. Clark's youth movement. At our first meeting, which was when Hoover was Secretary of Commerce in Harding's Cabinet, I was struck by his reserved, even shy, manner. For a man of his eminence as engineer, international relief administrator, and government servant, he seemed both modest and embarrassed, and I felt that his manner sometimes put him at a disadvantage, both as a candidate and as a President.

During the 1928 campaign I publicly praised Mr. Hoover's opponent, the Democratic candidate, Alfred E. Smith, for his forthright stand on the prohibition issue, even though it was opposed to my own stand. Unlike the majority of office seekers during those years, the New York governor did not hypocritically try to play both ends against the middle. He was for repeal of the Eighteenth Amendment and let it be known. "There is no political expediency in the Democratic aspirant," I said. My opposition to Smith, as I carefully made clear, was in no degree based on his religious affiliation, for I took him at his word that, if elected, he would be a President who happened to be a Catholic, and not a "Roman Catholic President." When Smith issued a statement that as a public official he had never taken orders from any group or agency, religious or otherwise, I announced in the *Christian Herald:* "So far as we are concerned that settles it! We take this man at his word." But such was the feeling about the possibility of a Catholic occupying the White House that I was severely criticized for taking this position and we lost some subscribers.

I supported Hoover because I believed he was the better candidate, more fully qualified to be President, and because he was against repeal of the Eighteenth Amendment. An interesting development in the 1928 campaign began when I received a letter from Mrs. Franklin Roosevelt, written on the letterhead of the Democratic National Campaign Committee, in which she questioned Hoover's personal sincerity, stating that she had been served spiked punch at a Hoover reception. After I received a second letter from Mrs. Roosevelt on the same letterhead, confirming the charge, a conference was arranged with Mr. and Mrs. Hoover in their S Street home. Among those present beside myself were Mrs. Mabel Walker Willebrandt, Solicitor General of the United States, and Mrs. Lena Lowe Yost, a national officer of the Woman's Christian Temperance Union. The Hoovers told us that Mrs. Roosevelt's statement was false—that there must have been a misunderstanding, for they had not spiked the punch. Certainly the Hoovers had not been total abstainers during their long sojourns overseas, but they had faithfully observed the law of the United States and no liquor had been served by them in Washington.

Mr. Hoover's repugnance at the idea of getting into a controversy with a woman, particularly Mrs. Roosevelt, was great and understandable, so we decided to bring the matter into the open in this manner: I would write Mr. Hoover a letter presenting the facts as they had been brought to my attention by an unnamed member of the Democratic National Campaign Committee; Mr. Hoover would then deny the charge and leave the rest to the newspaper reporters. It was Mr. Hoover's campaign managers who decided that we should drop the matter. "He is in," they said, "and this is now too small a business to engage his attention." And so it was dropped.

My own personal relations with Mrs. Roosevelt, I might add, were ever cordial despite this incident and my opposition to her candidate, Governor Smith. My associations with her when we were fellow members of the National Child Labor Committee had left me impressed with her social vision and her understanding of the needs of human beings of all ages.

In a statement he sent to Senator William E. Borah in 1928,

Hoover wrote that prohibition was a "great social and economic experiment, noble in motive and far-reaching in purpose." Through ignorance, more often by intent, this statement was widely misquoted, and during the 1932 campaign its author was praised or condemned as the President who called prohibition a "noble experiment." Regardless of what he thought in 1928, his acceptance speech after his renomination made Hoover unacceptable to the doctrinaire drys of the Anti-Saloon League, the Prohibition party, and the Woman's Christian Temperance Union, because he advocated state, rather than national, control of the liquor traffic. One political analyst, rating candidate Franklin Roosevelt a "wet wet," opined that the President had become a "moist dry."

During the 1920s, after witnessing the lawlessness and corruption that had developed when prohibition was not properly enforced, I had come to see that changes in the law were both inevitable and advisable—changes that would help to preserve the essential gains in the national welfare brought about by the enactment of prohibition. During the second Hoover campaign, therefore, I became active in the Allied Forces for Prohibition, a temporary organization of the more flexible supporters of the Eighteenth Amendment. With the help of a personal letter from our candidate, I was able to get all but a small number of the 211-man executive committee of the Allied Forces to endorse Hoover for President. Taking notice of this achievement, which seemed to answer the adamant drys' rejection of Hoover, one Midwestern newspaper had the frightful idea that if Hoover was re-elected, he would do well to make me his Secretary of State. Well, my friend the President was not re-elected, I did not replace Henry L. Stimson in the State Department, and all too soon the Eighteenth Amendment was repealed. Sincere but adamant drys refused to budge an inch and all was lost.

Another colorful figure belongs in my gallery of Presidents. Even though he didn't win his race, he made a great showing in a period when the war situation abroad was becoming more and more ominous for the United States, and after he lost to that master campaigner, Franklin Roosevelt, he went determinedly and devotedly on with his work of alerting our nation to the perils of isolationism. I refer, of course, to Wendell Willkie.

I campaigned for and with him, and in the *Christian Herald* covered his development as a world figure. His record appealed to me. I knew that as a schoolteacher in Kansas he had promoted the High Y Club, and that he had been a lay preacher in the Episcopal Church. In the course of an interview I once asked Willkie this question: "Just what does religion mean to you?"

His big handsome face clouded with thought for just a second, and then a broad smile flashed at me. "Why, Poling, religion means just about everything to me." It wasn't a glib answer. He believed!

Another time, interviewing him in his home in Rushville, Indiana, I commented on the fact that his Sunday-morning appearance at a rodeo had been widely reported in the press, whereas his visits to churches, if any, had not been mentioned.

"You know and the whole country knows that I am a churchman," he answered, "and I do not intend to exploit my religion, or allow it to be exploited, for any reason whatsoever."

"But just because you are a candidate," I countered, "surely that is no reason why you should discontinue your participation in public worship."

He got the point and grinned. Thereafter he went back to what had been his Sunday morning routine before the hectic campaign: He went to church.

Wendell Willkie, defeated in elections but victorious in life, left this world much too soon.

I first met Franklin Delano Roosevelt in 1929 when he was governor of New York. The occasion was the annual luncheon of the Greater New York Board of Trade, of which organization I was a vice-president. James Roosevelt brought his father to his place at the head table and helped him out of his wheel chair. After offering the invocation, I sat near the governor, and, though I recall that he presently made a scintillating speech to the large gathering, after all these years I remember even more my fascination at the way he used cigarettes. He smoked and he didn't.

Often he would crush out a partially smoked cigarette and then take out another. Before even lighting it, he might add it to the collection in the ash tray. To a confirmed nonsmoker like myself, there was something hypnotic in Roosevelt's performance.

Presently the man on my left, General Edwards, commander of the First Army, stationed then on Governor's Island, said, "Say, man, this is unusual. Here are three of us who are not smoking." And so it was. The man on my right, Police Commissioner Harris, was another nonsmoker. General Edwards looked warily at the column of gray fog that was rising above the governor. "I tried to learn it when I was a kid, but I always got sick," he said. "When this room gets loaded, if you see me get up and leave in a hurry, don't think I'm retiring in line of duty. I'm just going to the men's room."

The general stuck it out till the governor finished his speech, but the moment the applause began, he ducked away from the swirling clouds of smoke and disappeared.

When Roosevelt became President, I went on the attack. I felt that he had been unwise not to accept the outgoing President's invitation to confer about the state of the Union; that if the conference had taken place, the financial debacle of the first New Deal administration could have been avoided. I regarded Roosevelt's dealings with gold as unsound. I was emphatically opposed to Keynesian economics and deficit financing. I was not in favor of repealing the Eighteenth Amendment. In a word, I was opposed to the New Deal. But on September 1, 1939, when Hitler declared war on Poland, I took a long look at the prospects ahead, and from then on Roosevelt's war leadership had my all-out support.

As it happened, I did not offer the President my services; they were requested. Out of the blue, in the spring of 1941, Stephen Early, the President's secretary, telephoned me in Philadelphia and asked me to come immediately to the White House. I did not see the President on this first visit. Instead, it was Mr. Early who explained the reason for the sudden call.

At that time London had gone through the appalling experience of the Nazi aerial bombings and the great fire that was the result. The British church leaders, who had seen their great old churches bombed to rubble, their very civilization threatened, were having difficulty reconciling the realities of Britain's desperate defense of her homeland with the pacifist and neutralist attitudes of many of our American churches and their leaders.

Our Ambassador in England, John G. Winant, had telephoned the White House and asked that I be sent across to advise with him in the situation. Winant I had known intimately for years, ever since he became governor of New Hampshire in 1925. One of the wise and realistic men of the prohibition period, he had been a strong supporter of Herbert Hoover. After three terms in the governor's mansion, he had gone to Geneva as an official of the International Labor Office. After that he had become our Ambassador. Of all the men I have known in public office, John Winant stays in my memory as one of the most selfless and dedicated.

"John says you are the one who can help us out over there," Steve Early told me. "How soon can you go?"

Dazed with the suddenness of the assignment, I murmured something about my obligations to the *Christian Herald* and to my church.

"We want you to fly across tomorrow morning," Mr. Early said, and without further ceremony, and with no specific instructions concerning my mission, he passed me on to William Hassett, the bookish and delightful Vermont newspaperman who had just come to the President's secretarial staff.

With frantic use of the telephone I made arrangements for my Philadelphia church officials and my *Christian Herald* and Christian Endeavor associates to meet me for dinner that night in New York City. And immediately, of course, I went into a long-distance consultation with Lillian. She rose to the occasion as always and gave me her blessing. My arrangements in New York were completed in time for me to take the midnight train back to Washington, and I was on Bolling Field in time for the early-morning take-off.

It was my happy experience to be associated with Bill Hassett through all the rest of the Roosevelt years, and on into Mr. Truman's administration. A devout Roman Catholic, Bill was always a discriminating, understanding, and loyal friend, and I think the President could not have had a more efficient or faithful associate. Of all my missions for the President or for the Chief of Chaplains of the Army, Bill Hassett and his office handled my travel arrangements. Before I was finished with these assignments I had crossed the Atlantic fourteen times by air, the Pacific four times, and flown twice around the world, logging better than two hundred thousand miles in all.

I was no hero about my first flight across an ocean, and when our bomber reached Gander, Newfoundland, but could not go on because of heavy weather, I began to wish my friend Winant had not been so confident of my helpfulness as an interchurch diplomat. One of my fellow passengers, an Air Force veteran of World War I, did a lot to make the lay-over time pass agreeably. James Harold Doolittle, better known as Jimmie Doolittle, the following year became the living symbol of America's determination when he led the great bombing raid that struck Tokyo from the aircraft carrier *Hornet*. Not a giant physically, certainly, Doolittle was quiet and considerate of others, with a particular quality of self-confidence that carried over to those associated with him. He was impressively a leader.

After waiting five days for the weather to improve, and then making one false start, we finally took off for Prestwick, Scotland. The entire flight was made above the overcast and we never once saw the Atlantic. From Prestwick I took a train to London, arriving there on a Sunday evening. My first view of the battered streets and blasted buildings profoundly depressed me. At the time of the Armistice in 1918 I had rejoiced in the all but universal feeling that another world war would be impossible. Now, as I beheld all about me the tragic devastation of the new conflict, I was again faced with the seeming paradox of war itself. As an American churchman representing the united church and carrying some hastily acquired letters from the Federal Council of Churches, what was I to say to my brothers in the churches of Britain? To agree that war was a hideous wrong would be only to state the obvious. What, then, would be my message?

At its heart was this conviction—I held it with all my heart in 1941 and I so believe today: War is sin, and man has made it. War is not God's visitation of wrath upon weak and sinning man. To say that war is God's work in any part, or is His intention, is to speak blasphemy. The man who blames himself when the blame is his is on the way to achieve a worthy character. That principle holds true for a nation of men. But I knew that God was with men who entered with Christian conscience into the unspeakable ordeals of war, even as I knew that He did not leave alone those others who, in Christian conscience, renounced war. In general, this would be my message. As to my specific assignments in London, I waited on directions from John Winant.

After the firing of World War I had died away, I had been distressed to see that America was overwhelmingly opposed to participation in the League of Nations and international activities for peace. Though we had spent vast treasure and precious lives to help win the war, we turned our backs on what then became the more crucial task. I believe that the best that may be said for us during that period is that we helped to lose the peace. We assumed that we could keep apart from what we called "Europe's quarrels," which were in reality the opening skirmishes of World War II.

Today, we have no excuse. World War II taught us that to keep America out of war, war must be kept out of the world. Steadily, rapidly, the world has grown smaller. Trade routes cross and tangle. New inventions, constructive as well as destructive, bring the continents closer. The great human needs and the extensions of social progress are uniting people as never before. The world's bitter racial and religious antagonisms are coming to be recognized, like the sin of war itself, for what they are: the self-punishment of man rather than the will of God. In such a world, no more than any other nation, can the United States remain apart. Here, then, is the lesson for each of us, and for our country. We must accept our destiny, not in sterile fear or in self-pity, but with the propagating power of a marching faith. Then we shall partake of Christ's victory, the victory that triumphed over a cross and rose from a tomb.

Facing the situation I knew existed in London, I determined to scuttle the credo of defeatism that one misguided clergyman expressed in these words: "It makes no difference who wins the war if God loses it." I would not say that we could sow evil and reap good, nor would I maintain that a righteous peace—Christ's peace—would come automatically out of an unholy and sinful war. I would say only this: that Christ's peace must come *after* the war or it would never come at all, and that we all had better be about the business of seeing the war through as quickly as possible.

During my hurried visit to the White House I had not seen President Roosevelt. I was quite touched, therefore, when I arrived in London and found a personal cable from him awaiting me; in it, he expressed his appreciation for my quick response to his call and wished me well in my mission.

I had not seen my friend John Winant for several years, and now it seemed to me that he had matured considerably, though without aging. As we sat in my hotel room discussing my forthcoming first meeting with the church leaders, Winant crossed his long legs and I noticed a wartime detail. "John," I said, "are you aware that you have a large hole in the sole of your shoe?"

He looked at me a little sadly and showed me the hole in his other shoe. "But it doesn't really matter," he said. "I had dinner with the King last night, and he has holes in his shoes too."

Later in my stay I took Winant to a meeting of the clergymen of the Free Churches. He addressed the gathering of forty or more with deliberation. He was always a deliberate speaker, sometimes painfully so. On this occasion he seemed shy and embarrassed as he spoke to the churchmen, yet he achieved a kind of quiet eloquence and won his audience with his deep earnestness. One of his remarks was classically perfect, and it could well have been modified to become his epitaph when he took his life two years after the war was won: "You English have said so little. You have done so much. It is all part of a soldier's faith—to have known great things and to be content with silence."

After the meeting, as we drove back to the Embassy, I told my friend how deeply moved I had been by what he had said. After a silence, he said thoughtfully, "Dan, I do not know how men live at all—how they can survive—without faith, faith in God, a faith that lives within them."

The explanation of John Winant's suicide I do not possess, although I was with him in New York only two days before he died. He was alone in his Concord, New Hampshire, home when the deed was done. Civilian soldier that he was, and veteran flier of World War I, he too was content with silence. I will be forever convinced that John Winant was in a momentary period of mental illness that terrible night in 1947 when he hurled one pistol at the wall because it would not fire, and then shot himself with the second. Nor will I ever doubt, knowing John as I did, that God at last went with him into the darkness and silence that he drew upon himself.

In my efforts to bring the churches of England to an understanding of the position of our American churches, I met with the Archbishop of Canterbury, Dr. Temple; Dr. J. H. Rushbrooke, president of the Baptist World Alliance; a cardinal of the Roman Catholic Church; the president of the Free Church Council; and the executive committees of the British Christian Endeavor Union and other youth organizations. As a member of the Federal Council of Churches' Commission on a Just and Durable Peace, I sat in conference with the leaders of the peace movement in London. Back of all these meetings was the differing position of the churches in our two countries. In the United States the churches were not unanimous in their support of the war; in England they had suddenly become so as a result of the bombing of London and all the attendant experiences.

An added embarrassment to our international church negotiations was the presence in London of Dr. Frank Norris, a brilliant but unpredictable Baptist preacher from Fort Worth, Texas. In previous years I had admired him for his effective pulpit work in support of national prohibition, but most of his later career had filled me and many other churchmen with dismay. A man of splendid physical proportions and a magnetic personality on any platform, Norris had achieved notoriety at one point by shooting to death a Fort Worth politician who had come to his study to complain of Norris's attacks upon him. Although the slain man was found to have been unarmed, Norris's defense was that he had believed the caller had come to kill him. The case was heard in another city and the jury set the preacher free.

In 1940, after the Nazis had already occupied France, Luxemburg, Belgium, and the Netherlands, and had driven the British across the Channel from Dunkirk, Dr. Norris took it on himself to visit Berlin to get his own close-up view of Hitler's might and purpose. He returned to the United States with a souvenir that he displayed proudly: a photograph showing him riding in an open automobile with Paul Joseph Goebbels.

The British church leaders, particularly the Baptists, were appalled when Norris showed up in London shortly before I arrived. Though no one believed that he spoke for the American Protestant community, it was evident that he was a rabble rouser who might easily stir up more bad feeling between the English and the Americans. The question was, as a possible destructive force, how should Dr. Norris be "contained"? I advised that he be shown every courtesy, for I knew that what he would have to say when he returned to his pulpit in the States would influence a sizable portion of our citizens.

The red-carpet treatment was extended. Dr. Norris responded beautifully. The climax of his visit was his gracious reception at 10 Downing Street, after which he held a press conference and disclosed that he and the Prime Minister had concluded their hour of talk with a prayer session during which Churchill had wept. He also announced that he planned to urge Roosevelt to make the United States a belligerent. And indeed he cabled the White House to this effect. I saw the copy of the message that was forwarded from Washington to Ambassador Winant. Having established international amity to his satisfaction, Dr. Norris moved on to other scenes—greatly relieving official London.

Soon after his departure I visited 10 Downing Street. As I stood on the doorstep, I remembered the night, twenty-three years before, when I had come to that same entrance to see another Prime Minister.

Churchill greeted me cordially and thanked me for my efforts with the English clergymen and wished me Godspeed home. More than any other man, Winston Churchill was in the spring of 1941 the living embodiment of the world's hope for freedom and security from war and the threat of war. I was much moved when he wrote out and autographed for me his immortal statement, "I have nothing to offer but blood, toil, tears and sweat."

In my visit with Mr. Churchill I sat in the room, and perhaps, since it was an old one, at the very table where a generation before I sat with David Lloyd George. The Prime Minister spoke with appreciation and at some length about John Winant's personal courage—our Ambassador had remained in London all throughout the raids—and of his diplomatic acumen. Said Mr. Churchill, "Winant reminds me of Lincoln. He is Lincolnesque, and universally the British admire him."

The Prime Minister then went on to inquire in detail about the health and appearance of President Roosevelt. Since I hadn't seen the President on my hurried visit to the White House, I could reply only in general terms. Mr. Churchill summed up the discussion with the remark, "Your President is a man indestructible in body and in mind."

On the subject of the Baptist preacher, little was said in that interview but it was all to the point. As Churchill conducted me along the hall to the outer door, he placed his hand on my arm, looked up at me with a cherubic smile, and spoke his last words on that subject.

"Dr. Poling, did you ever kill a man?"

I shook my head. "No," I replied, "but I have been tempted."

"Well," the Prime Minister said with a chuckle, "there are times, are there not, when one may feel like doing it?"

10

My son Clark once made a wise remark about youth in general and Christian Endeavor in particular. "There will never be a real world youth movement, Dad, because we do not stay young long enough." And of course he was right. A young man must assume the responsibilities of maturity so quickly these days that his commitment to any youth movement is of short duration.

I was moved by the glimpse that remark gave me of Clark's conviction about his purpose in the world. It was no surprise to me or the rest of his family when, a few days after the Japanese attack on Pearl Harbor, he enlisted to become a chaplain in the Army.

Months before this we had had a discussion about the chaplaincy. Clark had informed me that if we entered the war, as he believed we soon would, he would not go in as a chaplain. There was an unmistakable tone of challenge in the announcement.

I grinned at him. "Are you afraid?" I asked.

That nettled him. I knew what his trouble was. He couldn't think of himself occupying some more protected place than other men, or of accepting any special consideration granted the ministry. "If you go in," I told him, "you'll go where you, Clark Poling, can count for the most. I am sure of that. In the nature of things that will be the Chaplain Corps. And to relieve your mind about the lack of danger—statistically, you'll have the finest chance in the world to be killed, even though you won't carry a weapon. The death rate for chaplains in 1918 was one out of ninety-six, the highest for any officer group save only the Air Force."

Clark seemed impressed by my statistics. We did not discuss the point again, but his change of mind about the chaplaincy did not surprise me.

His decision to enter the Army was not a gesture of immaturity; Clark not only had his church to think of, but his own family.

In 1939, he had married a Philadelphia girl, Elizabeth Jung, the daughter of August Jung, a Presbyterian clergyman, and now he was the father of an infant son, Clark Poling, Jr., or "Corky."

Early in 1942 Betty Poling's parents and Lillian and I went to Schenectady for the farewell supper given by the First Reformed Church. It was held in the Sunday-school auditorium, I remember, and Clark, standing beneath the Christian Endeavor monogram, made a simple but moving statement of the conviction that had led him to serve in his country's uniform. The communion service that followed made that evening unforgettable. I stood with Clark at the altar he so greatly reverenced, and with him ministered to the officers and members whom he so deeply loved. Realist though Clark always was, he was a mystic too, and that evening in blessing the emblems and in distributing the bread and wine to the worshipers, he came in to the innermost heart of his calling. Betty had made the decision with him. There was a calm radiance in her face as she faced what the future would bring.

Though there followed weeks of waiting before Clark went to Camp Shelby, Mississippi, for his period of training, the formal farewells were spoken this night. Always I will be happy to remember that Clark's official ties with his congregation were not severed. Given a leave of absence, he continued to be the minister of the First Reformed Church for the rest of his time on earth. For Clark, the continuity of his sacred relationship was the surest sign that he would return to his church, and the fact that his church officials refused to accept his resignation moved him profoundly.

I next saw Clark in November, 1942, after he had received his commission as a first lieutenant and his orders for overseas. He came to Philadelphia with his wife and two-year-old son for a few days to say good-by to us. We had our pictures taken together, Clark wearing an overcoat that made him look very much the soldier and chaplain. I took him to my church and he preached from that historic pulpit, doing his best to assure my congregation that the Army would not corrupt its sons and daughters. History, in its odd way, was repeating itself, for this was substantially the message I had given American parents after my experiences in France in 1918. Said Clark, "If your sons received good home training and example, if you taught them to pray and gave them the experience of the church, you may reasonably expect them to return as forthright as they were when they went away. The Army is a cross-section of America. Men do not become either saints or sinners just by putting on the uniform. Nor do women."

Another evening before he left, Clark brought up a subject that had long been troubling me. Now I learned that he had given it a great deal of thought too. "You must be very considerate of Daniel," he said. "It is harder for him to stay than it is for me to go. It takes greater courage for him to do what he is doing than it does for me to do what I am doing." Clark was thinking of Daniel's invalid son, an almost helpless spastic boy.

Daniel had dreamed of the chaplaincy too, and only a clear understanding of his duty had kept him out of uniform. Each brother was loyal to the spiritual mandate within himself, and this, of course, is the final test of true courage.

Late in 1943, after enjoying a happy and successful pastorate as senior minister in the First Presbyterian Church in Wheeling, West Virginia, Daniel generously stepped out of his own career to help me in mine. This was the beginning of the period when my war missions took me on consecutive, almost constant assignments overseas, and I was greatly touched when my elder son came to my side as co-minister of Baptist Temple. It was not an easy decision for Daniel to make, for he was pastor of a fine church in Wheeling and immensely popular in his city, having been voted its Man of the Year.

After our farewells in Philadelphia, unexpectedly, I had one more day with Clark—and with Betty and Corky. I went to Boston and the three of them came in from Camp Miles Standish to meet me. We ate breakfast together at the City Club. Corky's table manners were nothing to brag about and this caused his father an anxious moment or two. Clark was always concerned that his son should be at his best in public. Perhaps he also feared that I might get a poor impression of my grandson's home training. However, having been given this unlooked-for additional day with Clark, I was in a mood to overlook a little spilled cereal.

Clark had never taught Corky to salute, but the boy had learned by observing. As we walked together in Boston's wintry overcast, I watched him solemnly and awkwardly helping his father return the salutes of enlisted men. Smiling, I recalled the story Betty had told me about Corky marching around at home in his father's heavy G.I. shoes. He would march until he had to rest—and then he would simply squat down on the high backs of the shoes, ready to go again when his strength returned.

How well I remember the details of that day. During the morning we visited the headquarters building of the World's Christian Endeavor Union, where Corky, as usual, enjoyed riding in the elevators. When the noon hour arrived, Corky helpfully agreed to remain with two young Endeavorers while Clark, Betty, and I took one of our family friends, the actress Martha Scott, to lunch. Afterward, we enjoyed seeing Martha in a matinee of her new play, *The Willow*.

That afternoon and evening passed all too quickly for me. After our family supper, I went to the bus station with Clark and his little family, and there I spent my last hour with my son. I like to remember him as he stood watching Corky trudge up and down between the crowded benches of that waiting room. Although young Corky believed that he was on his own, Clark's eyes strayed never far from him.

I had a final glimpse of Clark. Seated in his bus, he leaned past Betty and Corky and waved to me, smiling. Then the bus was gone and it was dark, but the smile remained—and has to this day.

Clark's letters had always given me much of him. The one Lillian and I received a few days after that Boston visit not only told us that he had gone on from Camp Miles Standish to his unidentified port of embarkation but brought his concerns vividly before us:

> Dearest Dad and Mother:
>
> In order for you to check on whether my letters are getting through, I will number each one and you can keep a record. Mother's letter, which she gave to me in Philadelphia, slipped in with my orders, has been read, and is a very beautiful letter....
>
> So far I have stood up pretty well against the sharp arrows of loneliness. I miss Betty and Corky terribly and I find myself turning unconsciously as though to tell Betty something. It is not so much the physical side of marriage that counts, as the constant comradeship with all the taken-for-granted little details of living together that makes for happiness.
>
> Corky is often in my mind. I have dreamed about him several times. The worst pangs come when I realize that he won't know me when I get back, and that he will be quite a different small boy. Dad made the remark that Corky might be better without me during these formative months! He must have been joking because I really have not spoiled him more than Betty. You must remember that you have seen him under most unfavorable conditions, hurried glimpses when Corky has been tired and in strange and difficult surroundings. I like to think Corky would benefit by having me to tell him stories and play with him....
>
> Did I tell you that Corky has now graduated from the "Amen" limit to the repeating stage and can go through the entire length of "Now I Lay Me Down to Sleep"? Also he can navigate through the various "bless the relatives" all by himself. He even made a responsive reading out of "Now I Lay Me," for he would continue by himself "Down to Sleep." Pretty good for a boy not two and a half years old! I love you both,
>
> Clark

After that letter I received one more. Although Clark had counted on being sent to the European theater, his orders had been changed at the last minute and he, along with three other chaplains, was headed for Greenland. His last letter to me expressed both his disappointment and his enduring faith: "Apparently I am headed for a blind alley, but, Dad, if when I get there I find one other man, then there will be three of us."

Betty went back to her home in Schenectady, where she expected soon to have her second baby. She shared her last letters from Clark with Lillian and me:

> Dearest: I can't write a "noble, brave" letter. I would be a little self-conscious writing that sort of letter to you. All I can say is that always I will love you and hold our happy memories in the most sacred part of my thoughts until that time when we shall be together again....

The last words of all came after Clark's nameless ship had carried him away into the North Atlantic:

> There is a part of my mind that is quite satisfied with the turn of events that send me to the safe but lonely post we have talked about. However, you know there is another part of me that is disappointed. Perhaps all of us are drawn to the heroic and hazardous. I have done all and more than is legitimate to get into the thick of it.... Dearest, I love you, and wherever I go and for all time I am yours, and you are mine. Read to Corky for me and spank him, love him, keep him away from the river, and feed him the oil!

On February 11, 1943, Betty received a telegram from the Adjutant General's office in Washington informing her that Clark was missing in action in the North African area. She telephoned us this news from the parish house in Schenectady. I was disturbed, but I was able to reassure Betty and myself to a degree, for there was obviously an error in the message: Clark's ship could not have reached North African waters. There had not been time, and I knew where he was headed.

Then, though it was hard for me to leave all whom I loved while this gnawing uncertainty remained, I flew to Europe, under orders from the Office of the Chief of Chaplains. I went praying for a better word, but realizing that war is no respecter of anxious families. Eight weeks were to pass, as it turned out, before we knew for sure that Clark was gone.

Following that first word of February 11, I had a dream in which Clark came to me. It occurred on a night train taking me from London to Glasgow, soon after I arrived in England. Though no ship or men were named, a few hours before taking that train I had heard a B.B.C. announcement of a sinking in the North Atlantic in which four American chaplains had been lost. Lying asleep in my train compartment, I suddenly saw my son. He was swimming toward me. I had a vivid impression of the sea. I heard nothing, but saw his arms striking toward me, saw his straining face. I flung myself to meet him—and smashed up against the wall of the compartment. Then I was awake and shaking in my berth.

Years later, after the war was over, Clark came to me again, but this time it was a happy experience. Again, it was a dream or it seemed to be a dream. I stood on a street corner looking into the windows of a store. Inside, two men moved about, completing a display of toys. As I watched them, I heard Clark's quick, nervous laugh, and I sensed him standing so close to me that I almost felt his breath on my cheek. "Daddy," he said, "you love children, don't you?" That was all. When I turned, of course he was not there. Since that time I have had no other such experience.

On April 10, 1943, the original "missing in action" became "lost in action," and my loved ones at home finally learned something of what had happened in the early-morning darkness of February 3. Ninety miles from its destination in Greenland, the transport ship *Dorchester* had been torpedoed. She had gone down within twenty-seven minutes. Of the 904 men aboard, only 226 survived. The press and radio of the Allied world picked up the story of the four chaplains who had stood praying on the deck while the *Dorchester* disappeared. They represented three faiths. Alexander D. Goode was the Jew. Father John P. Washington was the Roman Catholic. George L. Fox and Clark V.

Poling were the Protestants. The fact that these men had linked arms, braced themselves against the rail now awash, and shared the last holy mission of their lives captured the imaginations of millions across the world.

The survivors of the *Dorchester* were profoundly moved by their part in the experience. "With utter disregard of self," one of them said later, "having given away their life jackets to four men without them, the chaplains stood together praying to the God they served for the safety of those men who were now leaving the stricken ship on all sides of them."

After I returned to America, I talked with one of the survivors, Engineer Grady Clark, in the Valley Forge Hospital at Phoenixville, Pennsylvania, where he was recovering from shock and exposure. Observing his shipboard orders, Grady had been fully dressed and wearing his life jacket when the torpedo struck. He had been picked up after floating nearly seven hours in the iceberg-chilled waters, and was perhaps the last survivor to be rescued. Grady told me that he had stood within eight feet of the chaplains. He confirmed that there had indeed been panic—a fact that the original story had reported. The chaplains had quieted the men milling around on the deck, Grady said, and they had forced a number of frightened ones over the rails or toward the lifeboats. Only two lifeboats got away. Others were smashed against the side of the *Dorchester*. He had seen the chaplains helping men to adjust their life jackets, and finally he had seen them give away their own jackets. When the engineer, in offering me all the details he could remember, mentioned Clark's laugh—he called it "contagious"—I knew then that I was hearing an authentic story. "As I swam away from the ship," Grady said, "I looked back. The flares had lighted everything. The bow came up high and she slid under. The last I saw, the four chaplains were up there praying for the safety of the men. They had done everything they could. I did not see them again." And the engineer concluded: "They themselves had no chance without their life jackets."

It was in a hotel just off Grosvenor Square in London that the essence of this story finally reached me by telegram, ending the harrowing uncertainty that had been mine ever since I had flown across from the United States. As I sat with my thoughts that reached back across the years, I was sustained by that unforgettable picture of the four men of the three faiths. Lost in action, they were found of God. They had learned the fine art of living together and so in death they were not divided. Somehow, that knowledge made me feel very close to Clark.

A few hours later I was the guest of General Eisenhower's chief of staff, Lieutenant General John C. H. Lee, bound for one of our bomber bases aboard his special train. When we met, Lee looked at me intently, then saluted and said, "Sir, there would be, I think, one thing harder for you than giving a son—not having had a son to give." That was all, but it was worth much. We retired late. As I sat on my bed in the compartment next to General Lee's, there was a knock and his senior chaplain, Father Ternan, came in. Cases such as mine were not discussed at great length in the service. Where death was constantly so near for so many, words were seldom needed. But Father Ternan knew precisely what to say. He did not seek to discuss anything; he simply said, "I shall pray for you at Mass in the morning, and for his wife and his son and his mother." After a moment of silence, he added, "Let it comfort you to remember that God also gave His Son." Then he left me.

As I sat there thinking over what Father Ternan had said, thinking again of those four men—Goode, Washington, Fox, and Poling—who stood shoulder to shoulder as the waters rose about them, each loyal to himself and to his vows, yet each with a cause that transcended all differences and divisions—I marveled at the ways of God. It seemed to me that in this service, this sacrifice, He had shown the world a unity that was of itself holy. Four consecrated men, linking their arms and their faiths, had demonstrated the unity that would presently win the war and, please God, ultimately win the peace.

Surely prayers like those of the Four Chaplains will help us to bring about Christ's peace. Prayer is as universal and yet individual as God's love. It is the open door for everyone. It may be one word, or no words at all save as thoughts may be considered unspoken words. But always effective prayer comes from the soul's sincere desire. You may pray with beads and a crucifix and I without, you may pray with a hat upon your head and I bareheaded, but we can be sure God is listening when any of His children cry.

While I was sometimes called on to perform a chaplain's duties in World War I, it was only in 1920 that I was commissioned a major in the Chaplain Corps of the United States Army. This was the period when our church leadership was dominated by sincere but misguided men some of whom went to the extremes of demanding that the chaplaincy be removed from the armed services, although some spokesmen insisted only that it be organized as a separate appendage. Supporting the wiser position of the Federal Council of the Churches of Christ in America, I remarked in a *Christian Herald* article that it would be a discouraging sight to see a clergyman following the fleet in a small boat with an outboard motor! Thankfully, the pacifists in the churches lost the round, and the chaplaincy continues to be an integral and highly efficient arm of all the armed services.

In 1942 the Army called me up for active service. Just as I was about to leave for Fort Dix, Major General William Arnold, the Chief of Chaplains, revoked the order and left me still a disappointed reservist but on call for missions at the fronts. It was as a reserve major that I went on my overseas missions, and it was as a reserve major that I was ultimately discharged from the Army in 1956—which is probably some kind of a record. I was a major for more than thirty-five years. At any rate I never lost ground. During the war years, however, when not wearing the chaplain's leaf and cross on my shoulders I substituted an armband marked C which signified my status as a correspondent accredited to the *Philadelphia Record* and the *Christian Herald*. My missions were many and varied, and always I traveled with letters from the President of the United States or the Chief of Chaplains or both. One of the President's letters, addressed to the Commonwealth of Australia, called me my country's "spiritual ambassador of good will."

While my rank in the Chaplain Corps was that of major, I possess documentary proof that I also attained the rank of brigadier general in the Algerian Camel Corps of the Army of the United States. I earned my star in the spring of 1943, and the man who gave it to me was Walter Bedell Smith, General Eisenhower's chief of staff. Like other war correspondents in North Africa that year, I had been given the rank of "assimilated" second lieutenant, the low rank being considered desirable in case any of us were captured by the enemy. Colonel Roy Parker, the chaplain who took me on my courtesy call to General Eisenhower's headquarters, professed to be sorry for me. He told General Eisenhower that I had been down-graded from major, that I was outranked by my own son—at this juncture the final word on Clark had not come through—and that he proposed to take me to the front for the sole purpose of blowing up his air mattress.

General Eisenhower laughed and turned to his chief of staff. "That doesn't seem quite the way to treat a guest, Bedell. Can't we do something about it?"

Smith agreed that the situation concerning this over-age shavetail needed adjustment. The commission that he presently drew up for me was the current service joke in North Africa. As Ike passed the commission over to me, he said, "Congratulations, General. Now when you get up to the line, pull your rank on Parker and make him blow up *your* mattress."

After the war, when General Eisenhower was president of Columbia University, I had occasion to write him a letter. In a postscript I reminded him of my "Camel Corps commission," noting that I had placed it with those of my private papers that were to be opened fifty years after my death. The general replied: "Add this letter which will confirm the story when the books are opened!"

I was sitting in a bucket seat of a C-46. It was Palm Sunday, April 19, 1943, and we were flying north from Natal, the great base in Brazil, to Miami. It was a Palm Sunday such as I had never celebrated before. It was the first since the *Dorchester* had gone down, and fresh details of that story were still coming to me from various sources. Before starting my homeward flight, I had learned that Clark's widow, Betty, had gone to the hospital in Schenectady to have her baby. Before that Sunday was over I had reached Miami, rushed to a telephone booth, and heard the happy news from Betty's mother that Corky's sister, Susan Elizabeth, named in part for Clark's first mother, had arrived safely—a Palm Sunday baby—and with her mother was in the best of health.

But now, as our C-46 roared above the Caribbean islands, I forgot the motor noise, the talk of the servicemen around me. I forgot the sorrows of the recent past, my wonders about the future. In my hand I held my New Testament, open at the Gospel of Saint Matthew. I read again the ageless account of Christ's triumphal entry into Jerusalem. "And a very great multitude spread their garments in the way; others cut down branches from the trees, and strewed them in the way. And the multitudes that went before, and that followed, cried, saying, Hosanna to the Son of David: Blessed is he that cometh in the name of the Lord: Hosanna in the Highest."

I became conscious of someone crowding my knees. Looking up, I found lanky Robert E. Sherwood steadying himself with one hand. In his other hand was a New Testament. Smiling down at me, he called my attention to the fact that his little book was open at the very passage I was reading. The serviceman next to me excused himself, and Bob Sherwood sat down beside me.

As one of President Roosevelt's speech writers and as director of the overseas work of the Office of War Information, playwright Sherwood was at this point one of the most important civilians in the war effort. Before the war, wholly because of my prohibition activities, we had not been friends. It was our devotion to President Roosevelt as our war leader that had drawn Bob and me together. We had talked out our differences and begun our friendship during my return flight from London in 1941. After that, the chemistry was right, and the intimacy that developed was a lasting one.

Sitting with me in the C-46, Bob showed me the inscription

in the front of his Testament. Headed "Dear Bob," the message commended the book as one that had inspired and guided the giver, who believed that it would do the same for Sherwood on his journeys. The signature was "Franklin." With this for a start, Bob and I discussed the President's religious life and practices.

The nation knew that Roosevelt was a warden in the Episcopal Church and came from a long line of Dutch forebears. His official relations were with the family church in Hyde Park, but generally the deeper faith of the President was not known, for it was not displayed ostentatiously for public scrutiny. His religion, Sherwood told me, was one thing Roosevelt did not discuss, adding, "He is both liturgically and personally a deeply religious man."

I had this comment of Sherwood's in mind early in 1944 when I asked the President if he would write a special Easter message on immortality for the *Christian Herald.* My request was a bit presumptuous, and I knew it, but quite apart from the natural desire of a working editor to score a scoop, I knew that should he write such a message, it would inspire and reassure many people.

Weeks passed without a reply. About all that kept my hope alive was the fact that no message came from my good friend Bill Hassett courteously telling me that I should have known better than to solicit such a contribution. And then, just in time to meet the deadline for the Easter issue, the message came. And what a message it was! I wonder if any of our other Presidents has ever approached this simple, brief, but comprehensive declaration of personal faith in immortality:

> Here in Washington, and across the Potomac in Virginia, we see many noble monuments to the glorious dead—to the Americans whose souls go marching on. But these monuments would be meaningless did they not symbolize something very profound within all of us and that is, faith in the eternally living spirit.
>
> That faith becomes all the more powerful in these tragic days of war. Out of suffering comes a renewal of the life of the spirit. Then men who have gallantly given their lives have turned

> our thought to religion—to a realization of man's dependence upon the Providence of God.
>
> The story of the Resurrection is the expression of man's highest aspiration; it is the story of man's greatest victory—his triumph over death; it is a source of consolation for those whose loved ones have given their lives and a source of inspiration for all generations yet unborn.

Much later, after Roosevelt had gone on to know the reality of his faith, Bob Sherwood told me how the message had been composed. One morning the President handed him my letter, saying, "Bob, I want to do this for Dan Poling." And then he began to talk out his ideas while Sherwood took notes. That was their working method. When the President had finished, Bob took the notes across to the old Cabinet room where he worked, put them in order, and typed up a rough draft. This he gave to the President. Roosevelt thanked him but did not discuss the project further. Bob next saw the statement, as it was revised by the President, in the *Christian Herald.*

There is a sequel to the story. The night the President died, Sherwood read his friend's declaration of faith to the grieving world. As I listened to that profoundly moving broadcast, I was glad that I had been bold enough to ask for the message. I was also happy to remember that I had had a chance to thank the President personally for giving it to me.

My friendship with Bob Sherwood, once truly begun, continued without a break, even after the war issues that first brought us together had passed into history. During the war, I had given Bob a membership card in the International Society of Christian Endeavor. He always carried it with him and renewed it each year. It seemed to me that the affiliation gave him a genuine satisfaction. The last time I saw Bob, shortly before his death, we came upon each other at the Boston airport.

I had just flown in from New York. As I passed through the gate, Bob, headed for his outgoing plane and towering above everybody in sight, swept down upon me and gripped my hand. While he held me fast, he drew out his wallet and showed me his new Christian Endeavor card. "This will get me through, won't it, Dan?" he asked, and there was a note of unusual earnestness in his voice as we moved apart.

I nodded and replied, "You'll make it, Bob."

It was only a few days later that Robert Emmet Sherwood traveled on ahead.

11

At the Cairo Conference, in November, 1943, President Roosevelt, Prime Minister Churchill, and Generalissimo Chiang Kai-shek agreed that the war against Japan would not end before the enemy surrendered unconditionally. At that conference as a correspondent and columnist for a Philadelphia newspaper, I had a chance to renew my friendship with Madame Chiang and her illustrious husband. I had first met them in Nanking, China, in 1935, and it had seemed to me then that these two sincere and loyal Christians represented the finest flowering of the Protestant missionary tradition in the Far East. Over the nearly twenty-five years that I have known the Chiangs that opinion has not changed, though today I would include President Syngman Rhee of the Republic of Korea in the statement. I did not meet Mr. Rhee until much later.

As I write these lines the future of Nationalist China is uncertain, but uncertain also is the future of the world. High above any uncertainty, however, there remains for me the assurance that to the end of the road Chiang Kai-shek and his wife will be faithful to their ideals of freedom. Their irrevocable choice was made long ago and their destiny is with God. They could have advantaged themselves beyond human calculation had they made terms first with Japan or later with the Communists, but both times they chose freedom and democracy, and they have never wavered in their loyalty.

One day in the lobby of Shepheard's Hotel in Cairo I talked

of the Chiangs with Cyrus L. Sulzberger, who was covering the conference for *The New York Times*. He told me that he and others had been impressed by the fact that the Generalissimo and his wife kept to a program of early morning devotions in the garden at the Pyramids Hotel. "As a Jew, I am interested in the faith and practice of these people," he said.

I volunteered the information that the Chiangs were active Christians and members of the Methodist Church. Mr. Sulzberger made it clear that he was less interested in the denomination than the fact, and said in effect, "It would be interesting to know whether any of the other Allied leaders give as much thought to religion as these people do."

After I had offered a comment or two on his point, Mr. Sulzberger concluded, "The others are nominal Christians, of course, but I have found none of them observing a comparable program."

Leaving Egypt, I headed for China, carrying instructions from the Chief of Chaplains to visit the chaplains of our armed forces there. In Assam, as I was about to fly into China, I suddenly collapsed with acute dysentery. Vomiting blood, I was admitted to General Hospital 20, our installation at the head of the Ledo Road, the supply route into Burma. In it were many personal friends from Philadelphia, for General Hospital 20 was the University of Pennsylvania's medical unit.

One of my bedside visitors as I recovered was my niece Kathleen Phelps, the daughter of my sister Ethel. Kathleen was a senior nurse in the Army Nurse Corps, stationed at our most advance position on the Road. Only the day before I had been taken ill, I had paid her a surprise visit at her post.

At the time Kathleen came to see me, though neither of us yet knew it, her fiancé, an American fighter pilot, was dead, having been shot down over Sicily. Shortly after I saw Kathleen, and before she yet knew of her loss, she contracted cerebral malaria. For two weeks she lay in a coma. Then, apparently recovering from this ordinarily fatal seizure, she was invalided home to Portland, Oregon. She arrived there in time to nurse her aged grandfather, my father. Her own sufferings became intense, and she survived her grandfather by only a few weeks. She was a lovely talented girl, and a perfect member of that noble company of young women who nursed the American fighting men through the tortures of World War II.

I remained in General Hospital 20 for two weeks. On release, I went on with my mission, flying over the rough mountain country of the Himalayas into China, traveling at night and at a high altitude. Such precautions were standard in flying the Hump in order to avoid the Japanese Zeros, which were based less than five minutes' flying time away. In my pocket, as I rode in the darkened freighter plane, was a medal of St. Christopher, the patron of wayfarers. A G.I. ward boy in the Ledo Road Hospital had insisted that I take his medal with me. When I reached Kunming safely, I sent the medal back with my thanks and the earnest assurance that it had been effective, even as his faith had blessed me.

In Kunming, which was then our great supply base in West China, I learned something about the spirit and quality of an American entertainer, the popular humorist and actor Joe E. Brown. I saw it demonstrated to a gathering of some two thousand servicemen who filled a hall to watch a U.S.O. show. Chinese were also present, as well as a number of women. The first performer was a Broadway comedian who evidently believed that American men automatically turned in their characters when they put on their country's uniform. He told a string of dirty stories and concluded with an obscene song whose refrain, the only printable part as he sang it, was, "I want a woman." I wondered how the fellow, with such ad-libbing as this, had ever managed to get his credentials as an overseas entertainer. (Soon after this performance, as a matter of fact, the rest of his tour was canceled.) His reception in Kunming consisted of guffaws and applause from the few that misrepresented the many. Definitely, the program was off to a poor start.

The second man up was Joe E. Brown. For minutes he entertained us with a clean and side-splitting routine. Then he waited for silence, standing at the microphone on that bare platform. He removed his hat and said quietly, "Ladies and gentlemen, the man who has to tell a dirty story to get a laugh isn't a humorist." That did it. There was an instant of dead quiet before the whole two thousand broke loose in a demonstration of cheering and applause. They fairly lifted the roof. Then this great little man with the shoe-button eyes and wide mouth went on giving his audience what it hungered for: stories and jokes that any man could laugh at without a feeling of shame. As I watched him perform, I knew that not all his effectiveness came from his actor's craft, as sure and sensitive as that undeniably was. Joe E. Brown's own son had died in an airplane training accident early in the war, and as I watched him give of himself to other men's sons, I knew that he did it with a deep sympathy and understanding of their needs. He was the most valuable of all the entertainers I saw performing before our armed forces, and he was the first prominent actor to fly the Hump.

In Chungking, now China's wartime capital, I took part in an extraordinary interfaith conference. Only two foreigners besides myself were present: the papal nuncio (a Chinese-speaking Italian) and an American Baptist missionary with half a century of service in China. The rest, both men and women, were Chinese Buddhists, Moslems, Protestants, and Catholics. The group, which had for some years been inspiring and educating China's people against the Japanese aggressors, called itself "Believers in One God." The members had this one thing in common, their belief in one God. Important among the group's activities was the preparation of weekly press releases for China's newspapers. The material was first gathered from foreign sources, then translated, digested, and pointed toward the cause of freedom and a united democratic China. In Chungking I saw as many as two hundred illiterates crowding about a man standing in a ricksha while he read and explained one of this group's releases that had been posted on a wall.

Since I could not understand Chinese, the addresses and discussions that day were carried on in English for my benefit. Particularly I remember the talk of a Moslem, a major general and one of Chiang Kai-shek's staff officers. He reminded us that his was not a religion of the sword, even though from time to time it had imposed the sword as had the other great religions. Then he told us of a shrine in the Vale of Kashmir which a sect of his faith reveres as the tomb of Jesus. Listening to his story, I recalled that some Moslems believe that after the crucifixion the resurrected Jesus was spirited away to the north of India, where he taught as Master among masters until he died after a thousand years.

The Believers in One God, whose militant unity in no sense produced a uniformity, had been brought together by the senior abbot of the Chinese Buddhist faith. I found him one of the most winsome religious personalities I have ever known. A graduate of Columbia University, he was an old man in 1943, but one both vital and handsome. His serene face, his far-seeing eyes, his expressive hands cuffed in spotless white cotton, his beautifully modulated voice all contributed to the impression he gave of vast wisdom and benevolence.

The day after the conference I had a private session with the abbot. I found him a conservative, rather than a liberal, in his theology, and as to Jesus a Trinitarian rather than a Unitarian. He accepted the virgin birth and the deity of Jesus. I had heard him offer all the Believers in One God the same right he claimed for himself: freedom to worship the one God as the individual conscience directed. Now he developed the point, saying, "I must be willing to hear what you have to say, what you are *bound* to say, Dr. Poling, and also willing to be convinced by you—that is if I am to be true to *my* faith, which is the eternal search for truth." He smiled at me serenely and then added, "And I can only hope that you will be as willing." He added that there were Buddhist monks who had become Christians. Personally, I knew of no Christians who had become Buddhists.

The prayer that he offered for my safe return across the Hump to my country and kin began familiarly enough with "Our father who art in heaven," but as it went along there was a difference, and before he finished I was conscious of the mature and deeply cultured voice of the East supplicating the One who is Master of us all. Reflecting later on this man's wisdom and serenity, his absolute conviction of God's might, his piety, and his altogether winning gentleness of manner, I could understood the power of his leadership among the Believers in One God. Such a spirit as his was a blessing beyond human measurement in the war-wasted China of 1943.

A few days after my meeting with the abbot, and following the late Thanksgiving service held in the Methodist mission, I attended a reception given by our Embassy in downtown Chungking. Here I came face to face with some of the darker things in the Chinese picture.

The punch was alcoholic and I passed it by, but watched two of my missionary friends get high before they knew what was happening to them. However, they behaved decorously. That little scene was the only part of the reception that was remotely entertaining, and the punch itself was later to save the faces of two of our Embassy officials.

At that period Generals Stilwell and Chennault were in serious disagreement as to policy in dealing with the Chinese Reds. Chennault wanted absolutely no part of them; Stilwell was for integration. Certainly a brave and resourceful field commander, Stilwell, in my opinion, was no diplomat, and he erred gravely in his appraisal of the Chinese Communists.

As they returned frequently to the punch bowl, the two Embassy men began telling me their opinions about Chiang Kai-shek. Not a month before, President Roosevelt, Prime Minister Churchill, and the Generalissimo had agreed in Cairo that the war against Japan should continue until China should emerge from her long ordeal as a victorious nation. Yet here were our State Department officials talking with increasing vehemence against our ally in his own capital. To me it was a shocking spectacle.

I told the two men exactly how I felt about what they had said, and since their voices were now carrying across the room, I left them and went to a quieter spot.

The next day both men came to see me at my quarters. They were profusely apologetic. I was to understand that they had had too much of the punch, and that what they had said did not represent their "final" beliefs. They were open-minded about our Chinese ally, they said. Yes, indeed, I said to myself. I departed from Chungking heavyhearted. In the light of later events in China, what these men had revealed to me suggested at best one of the reasons China was ultimately taken over by the Communists. Officially, the United States backed Chiang and the Nationalist government, but in China, and even as directed from Washington, our support was never wholehearted. It lacked the all-out quality that Chiang himself gave to our common cause. China actually began to fall into Red hands long before the Nationalists fled with their still faithful and fighting remnants to Formosa in 1949.

By the summer of 1944, after consideration that went back through many months, I had thought through to one of the crucial decisions of my life. Serving under President Roosevelt, I had come to revere him for his moral and physical courage, for his integrity, and for what I believed to be the wisdom and effectiveness of his leadership. Three times I had voted against him, in 1932 and 1936, when I disagreed emphatically with his domestic policies, and again in 1940, before we were actually in the war, when along with some twenty-two million other Americans I had caught the world vision of Wendell Willkie. How would I mark my ballot in this year of 1944?

In July of 1943, after it was known that my son Clark had gone down on the *Dorchester*, I received the following message from the President:

> I want to express to you my deepest sympathy on the loss of your boy, but you and I have the complete faith that he did not die in vain.

In the same letter the President referred to the intemperate criticisms that were being directed against his leadership:

> Like the poor, we always have with us a minority of individuals whose selfish interests, financial or political, outweigh the complete loyalty which every American owes his country, es-

pecially in times like this. . . . However, I have some of that sublime faith that Lincoln had in the American public, and I know that the rank and file almost unanimously are with the Government and doing their bit to win the war.

Your generous expressions about me, of course, are appreciated, and I know something of what you have been doing to offset some of the vicious propaganda.

For the men and women who said that Franklin Roosevelt "lied us" into the war, I myself had found many answers—the answers of millions of people, free and enslaved, around the world. I had traveled among the nations. I had talked with their leaders and with the commanders in the war theaters. I had talked with the humble people of the world and with many of the great, and also with our G.I.s. I knew that no other man was so loved and trusted everywhere as President Roosevelt. Only by a comparative handful of people—and they were practically all my fellow Americans, enjoying our precious heritage of free speech—was it ever said that the President was a "deceiver" who had "betrayed" the nation. For most of America, and for all the rest of the world, Roosevelt was the symbol of hope, the promise of victory.

This was brought home to me again and again. When I was in Africa in 1943, I had occasion to visit a remote Berber village in the Atlas Mountains, a community out of touch with civilization save only as the French authorities occasionally went there to collect taxes. The Berbers are a non-Arabic people whose origin is shrouded in mystery. Mohammedans, they hold themselves aloof from the other peoples of their rugged land. Their women do not veil. Despite their poverty and their hard way of life, the Berbers are scrupulously honest.

The village I saw was small and desperately poor, and yet its men had made a burro trail to the ruins of one of our Flying Fortresses that had crashed in the mountains at an altitude of eleven thousand feet. The bodies of seven young Americans had been brought reverently down to the village and given a temporary burial. Every scrap of salvageable material, including currency, had also been carried down from the wreckage, and it was all being held for our party. Our officers expressed America's gratitude to the head man of the village, and the fliers' bodies were taken for burial in the army cemetery near Marrakech. The head man cordially invited us into his dwelling, a tent that opened into a cave in the rocks. Goatskins were spread upon the dirt and stone floor, but there were no other furnishings, save a few cooking utensils. One thing caught my eye: a picture on the pole that supported the tent. The only object above the level of the floor, it was the colored cover of a pictorial magazine printed in Algiers. There, more or less at the end of the world, I saw the confidence-inspiring face of Franklin Roosevelt.

The feelings this man inspired cut through all racial, religious, class, and national differences. In 1943, in Algiers, I heard General Eisenhower say in effect, "President Roosevelt is the only man who can hold the Allies together." In 1944, in Brisbane, Australia, I heard General Douglas MacArthur say substantially the same thing. Both commanders had the Russian threat in mind. There was always an uncertainty about Russia—a fear that she would negotiate a separate peace with Hitler if it was to her advantage to do so. Our battle commanders were not politicians. Their responsibility was simply the winning of the war. I caught the mood of the services from a colonel who said to me, "If Roosevelt lives only ten days afterward, he must still be re-elected."

When I made my decision to support the President publicly, I had to face certain responsibilities. All through my career I had scrupulously kept party politics out of my pulpits. That much was now easy; as a citizen in the public forum of free debate, I knew I would not be tempted to stump for Roosevelt in the Baptist Temple. But as a life-long independent Republican with a new conviction, I felt that my revolutionary, if temporary, cross-over made it necessary for me to resign both from my church and from the historic and conservative Union League of Philadelphia. In this issue as in others throughout my life, I was impressed by the intense loyalty of my friends and associates, even when they themselves were opposed—some of them violently—to my decision.

Baptist Temple refused even to consider my resignation, and that was that. The governors of the Union League protracted their acceptance over several meetings. There was an amusing sequel. A month after the Union League had finally accepted my resignation, it made my son Daniel a member. He was then my co-minister at Baptist Temple—and not a convert to my cause. Thinking that the turncoat Dr. Poling had been readmitted to the Union League, some of the city's hundred-per-cent party men let their protests be heard.

My old friend Norman Vincent Peale was another who showed his loyalty to me in this crisis period of my public life. At his invitation, I had arranged to preach at the Marble Collegiate Church in the fall of 1944. Thinking that my presence might now embarrass him and his congregation, I asked to have his invitation withdrawn. Norman was adamant. "You can't do this to me, Dan. I may not agree with you in your decision, but I will not allow you to withdraw from your preaching assignment—and I speak for the church."

Another devoted supporter in my personal crisis was Harry L. Jenkins, president of the Board of Trustees of Baptist Temple. In a public statement he noted that he and other Republicans had been gratified when, in a public forum, I supported Hoover in 1932. Urging his party not to write me off as a man of integrity and conscience simply because I had entered the opposing camp, Jenkins concluded, "Many of our Baptist Temple folk do not vote with Dr. Poling or agree with his political views in this instance, but all of its officers and members believe in him, love him, and glory in his faith and supreme courage."

With such support as this inspiring me, I took to the radio on November 3, 1944, under the auspices of the Wendell Willkie Committee Supporting Roosevelt, and told the nation why I felt Franklin Roosevelt must be re-elected. I was introduced by my friend Judge John Morgan Davis, then a member of Baptist Temple, who is presently Lieutenant-Governor of Pennsylvania.

Referring to the attacks that had been made on Roosevelt and his leadership in the heat of the campaign, I made the point that we could not afford to be merely Democrats or Republicans while our sons were united on every battlefront of the world, suffering and dying. The bitter and protracted debate that was then going on, I said, was hindering our cause. I posed the differences between the party that had become, as I believed, isolationist, and whose candidate had far departed from the ideals and principles of his immediate predecessor, Wendell Willkie, and the party whose head, as our commander in chief, had appointed such war leaders as Cordell Hull, Henry L. Stimson, Frank Knox, George C. Marshall, Ernest J. King, Douglas MacArthur, Chester Nimitz, and Henry H. Arnold. I would vote for Mr. Roosevelt, I said, because I believed that a change in our leadership would interrupt the war effort, delay the victory, and jeopardize the peacemaking that would follow it.

The final and decisive reason I would vote for the incumbent was that he was the symbol of hope in every quarter of the world, and the great uniting factor among the Allies. "While, with faith in the fundamental integrity of the American people, he waited for us to come to his leadership," I said, "he gave comfort to embattled peoples who against unequal odds fought on. Without his voice, without his faith, while we temporized and delayed, the torch of Liberty might have been put out for a hundred years.... He kept the hope of our coming... alive in heroic Britain. He refused the shame of silence in the presence of dictators. He called on us to be faithful to our past, equal to our present, and worthy of yet greater things."

It was still not easy or pleasant for me deliberately to startle and, indeed, dismay my many friends who remained in the Republican camp that year.

Less than a week after he was re-elected, the President wrote me a cordial note. It concluded with a line that touched me very much: "In these grave days I like to think that I shall continue to have a remembrance in your prayers."

In January, 1945, as I flew again to Europe, I carried this letter from President Roosevelt:

> Dear Dr. Poling:
>
> On this the fifth of your overseas journeys since the beginning of the war, you will reach countries only recently fully occupied

> by the enemy. Your visit now will be an inspiration to a multitude of people and especially to those whom you meet as President of the World's Christian Endeavor Union, as Chairman of the American and Foreign Christian Union and representing the World Council of Churches.
>
> Young men and women have borne heavy physical and spiritual burdens imposed by the dictators and only a vital religious faith can give them an adequate hope for the future. . . . I am especially glad that your relationships with the Chaplain Corps of the Army has made it possible for you to meet intimately chaplains and enlisted men in all the active theatres. Wherever you have gone this, I know, has been your first interest.
>
> Our unity at home and abroad is the supreme requirement for victory, for winning the war and the peace. Your visits have strengthened unity.

In the course of this mission I renewed my acquaintance with one of the great commanders and startling personalities of World War II. I had met Lieutenant General George S. Patton, Jr., in Algiers in 1943, and had been impressed by the sincerity of his religious practices even as I had been depressed by the childishness of some of his other actions. To me, there was something almost psychopathic about General Patton's frenzies, and even now I cannot understand the man to my own satisfaction. I know only that he was entirely sincere in his belief in God and that he loved the Lord. And yet General Patton was easily the most profane man I have ever known, in or out of the Army—and I grew up in the rugged West where "men were men" and had appropriate vocabularies. An army chaplain once wrote General Patton a letter of protest about his language at a conference where women had been present. Patton's reply was essentially this: "I do not know why I do it. Chiefly I regret my language because you and others must believe me insincere when I say that I could not remain in my position for a day were it not for prayer and my faith in God"—and the letter closed with the information that he, the commander of the United States Third Army, had spent much of the preceding Sunday writing his own commentary on the Ninety-first Psalm.

I saw Patton again in Luxemburg in 1945, just after the Battle of the Bulge. He had not mellowed in the intervening years, but neither had his faith in God grown less. From Colonel James O'Neil, one of the finest chaplains and truest Christians in the service, I received a copy of the general's memorable prayer for battle weather. Jimmy O'Neil told me how Patton, with all his characteristic fervor, had ordered that prayer written, after continual rain had reduced visibility to zero, made aerial observation of enemy movements impossible, and generally threatened the entire Third Army front. The army presses ran day and night to get out the little cards with the prayer on one side and Patton's Christmas greeting to his soldiers on the other. An attractive card it was. I have carried my copy ever since Jimmy O'Neil gave it to me. This was the prayer:

> Almighty and most merciful Father, we humbly beseech Thee, of Thy great goodness, restrain these immoderate rains with which we have had to contend. Grant us fair weather for battle. Graciously hearken to us as soldiers who call upon Thee, that armed with Thy power, we may advance from victory to victory and crush the opposition and wickedness of our enemies, and establish Thy justice among men and nations. Amen.

And General Patton greeted his men thus:

> To each officer and soldier in the Third United States Army I wish a Merry Christmas. I have full confidence in your courage, dedication to duty, and skill in battle. We march in our might to complete victory. May God's blessing rest upon each of you on this Christmas Day.

That prayer and greeting had the ring of Joshua and David at their militant best. They were words to make men strong—and they did. From Luxemburg I sent home a newspaper story to the effect that ordinary mortals might no longer believe that God started rains in answer to prayer, but that along the Rhine I had found some two hundred and fifty thousand soldiers who firmly believed that He stopped the rains in answer to their prayers. The only doubters, I said, seemed to be among the officers, especially a few chaplains, but there were no doubters at Patton's headquarters!

It is a matter of history that the rains did subside almost as soon as that prayer came from the presses. Battle weather came and stayed for an unprecedented ten days, during which General Patton's army swept the Germans back to the Rhine and presently beyond it.

"I hate the man's guts," a sergeant commented, giving me his appraisal of the general, "but when we go into battle, he's the only one I want for my commander."

Yes, George Patton was a remarkable human being, and one I shall not fully understand until I meet him again, just around the corner. Not long after I left Luxemburg, I heard one of Patton's former staff officers pay an unforgettable tribute both to his faith and to his qualities as a soldier: "If there is any delay when he gets to the gate, Saint Peter will get the shock of his long career, but don't worry—George will go through!"

In a general hospital near Bastogne I had a memorable conversation with a young G.I. from Georgia. He had been badly burned in his tank, and he was dying. What was more, he knew he was dying. The medical major assured me that talking would not hurt him. "It may help him a lot," he commented. The chaplain had said to me, "He wants to discuss something with you. He remembers when you spoke at a Sunday-school convention in Savannah. He was just a kid then, but he heard you with his father. Ever since he heard you were coming here he has been waiting. In fact, he has stayed alive to have this visit with you."

So began one of the most moving of my many talks with our servicemen overseas.

The boy's shaven head was bandaged. His eyes were dark and sunken, his lips cracked and fevered. Now and then the nurse came and moistened them with cotton dipped in a solution. Always he smiled and turned his head to thank her. Otherwise, his eyes seldom left mine during the next half-hour.

"Sir," he began, "I am not afraid to die. I've settled that. But one thing keeps bothering me: all that I'm going to leave behind. I've had a lot of time to think about that, and I can't get away from it. I guess you'd call it feeling sorry for myself." He smiled so infectiously that I smiled back at him.

"Sir, did you ever feel that you just couldn't get over losing some things—even for heaven?" And the boy smiled again, only now there was an infinite hunger in the strong face.

"Yes," I said, "I know the feeling. I knew it first when they spoiled my old swimming hole in Oregon. They built locks on the Yamhill River and sank the place I loved under six feet of water. I just couldn't get over it, son. The channel where my pals and I dived for mussels, and the sandbank where we lay in the sun and talked, were gone forever."

The boy from Georgia smiled softly and turned his head with understanding. "You make me think of my catfish lines in the river at home," he said.

"I was living in the East when it happened," I went on. "A few years later when I went back I thought at first I couldn't even look at the place, but my curiosity took me right there. And then everything was different. I had the old swimming hole, again—had it, forever."

The boy on the bed was breathing faster, and his eyes were intense.

"It was like this. The channel where we dived for the mussels and the sand where we lay in the sun were not under the water. They were in me! I hadn't left them behind; I had brought them along! They—and a thousand other memories of beautiful things—are all with me. I can never go back to them, but I have brought them along."

The boy waited and then said, "But—"

I interrupted. I knew just about what he would have said. "I've thought of that too," I continued. "I used to fear death, not because of what I knew about it, but because of what I didn't know. It was fear of the unknown, and that fear is the only final, baffling fear."

He nodded his assent. I wondered then whether I could put into words what had become very real to me, so real that it is an experience as comforting as the grip of a friend's hand. I had never tried to say it before, but the boy from Georgia was waiting—and I had gone too far to turn back.

"In 1935 I received word that my father was seriously ill," I said. "I was in Singapore then. The twelve thousand miles that separated us were the most appalling frustration that I had ever known. My father recovered, but a few years later, when my mother died, I suddenly discovered that there were now no separating distances and no dividing oceans. After she died, and ever since, we have been together. And today it is like that with the son I lost. As I think of those whose physical presence I shall never know again, always I think of them and know them as with me, and there is no interference, no interruption, and no end of knowing."

John was listening, though his thoughts seemed to be far away. "I've had that same feeling about Ray, my buddy," he said. "Ray was killed by a mine on Utah Beach the day we landed. Just before it got him, he yelled to me, 'Down! Machine-gun nest!' He was thinking of me, sir. I crawled to him, but there was nothing I could do."

The boy was speaking with increasing difficulty, but I knew he had something to say that couldn't wait, and I didn't interrupt. He went on, as though fascinated by his own words and the ideas behind them. "His head wasn't hurt. I put my face against his. Then I knew he wasn't there. But, sir, I knew that he was somewhere! His body was smashed, but he wasn't. I can't tell you why I knew it, but nothing else made sense. Every day now, that feeling is stronger. Ray isn't dead. He's around! Tell me" —and his voice rose—"am I kidding myself? Am I crazy?"

I shook my head. "No, you're not kidding yourself. You must have learned in school, John, that nothing in nature is ever annihilated. Forms change and patterns of life, but life itself goes on. I can't explain the details, but I do know that a mine couldn't stop Ray. To think that a law which operates everywhere else ceases to operate in life's highest expression—the human spirit—just doesn't make sense."

The boy from Georgia strained to lift his head from the pillow. "Then you believe," he whispered, as though half afraid to give his thought a voice. "You do believe that they wait for us and that we shall know them?"

"Yes," I replied, "I believe that, because I believe that it is after what we call death, that life—your life and mine and

Ray's—really begins. I believe that this life on earth is but our childhood. And, of course, if you and I live beyond the grave, if you and I do go on, then that which makes it possible for us to know each other now—the 'you' of you—goes on, too, and just as we remember here, we shall recognize each other there. I can't prove it, John, but I believe it—I am very sure about it. Yes, and my belief has become my experience. John, it is as real to me as this bed you're lying in—and more real."

He turned his head a little, as though listening to another voice than mine, and whispered, "I believe it too, and it makes God very friendly—just like your own father."

I felt that I had stayed long enough, but when he recognized my intention to leave, an eagerness came into both his face and voice. "No, please don't go yet. Tell me something more."

I summed up for him the thoughts of one man who, after his lifetime of experience, had found his answer to the great fear: "John, all the beauty I have ever known, and all my friendships, all that I have well remembered, I have brought along with me. Only 'things' are left behind. I am sure, so sure that I no longer question. Although I do not know the country to which I travel, I shall have friends awaiting for me there who do know it and I shall not be lonely."

Now I knew that I had finished my visit. The wasted, feverish face before me was as beautiful, in its way, as any sunset. The boy pushed his burned right hand, which was bandaged as big as a toy balloon, across the sheet, and I reached out my hand and steadied it. Then he said, "Sir, please pray."

I prayed with him and for him, and my inspiration came from the words that were those of the enduring message, "Let not your heart be troubled: ye believe in God, believe also in Me . . . I go to prepare a place for you."

The boy did not open his eyes as I stood up to go, but he said, "I'm taking them all along, sir, and I'll be seeing you!"

After my return from Europe in the spring of 1945 I had my last visit with President Roosevelt—nine days before he went on his final trip to Warm Springs, Georgia. I had gone to the

White House to see William Hassett on business that did not require an interview with Mr. Roosevelt. As I was leaving through the front reception room I was called back. The receptionist said the President wished to see me.

When I entered his office he was seated at his desk and smiling. He was alone. I thought he looked unusually well—better than at any time within the past year. His face had a ruddy color. I understood later that this may have been a symptom of his high blood pressure. That day it seemed definitely a look of health. I thought the President's voice was stronger than when I had last heard it.

As he pushed himself back from his desk, crowded with the gadgets he loved, I was fascinated again, as always, by the effect he gave of great physical strength in his arms and shoulders. Partly it was his deep chest, partly it was the way he held his head. That suddenly uptilted chin not only bespoke confidence and optimism but it bred the same in others. He was a man whose spirit more than made up for his physical handicap.

"What do you mean, Poling," he demanded, laughing, "coming here and not stopping in to see me?"

For no more than that he had called me back, but I was grateful for the chance to see him again. I was not with him more than five minutes, and we talked about nothing of importance. But always I shall remember his last words to me, for they were the same that I had heard from two other memorably confident men. In 1918, in an underground headquarters on the Western Front, an American battalion commander had said to me, with a wave of his hand, "I'll be seeing you." That man, my friend Colonel Griffiths, had died at Cantigny two weeks later, but his soul went marching on.

In Luxemburg, only a few weeks before I saw the President, a boy from Georgia had bade me farewell with the same words. He knew even as we parted that his life on earth was ending, but he spoke without fear in the sure faith that death for him was an open door into eternal life.

And now the President, lifting his right hand and smiling, said, "I'll be seeing you, Poling!"

And I shall see him—and Colonel Griffiths and the lad from Georgia. The truth, the deep conviction in the President's Easter statement of a year earlier was for him a prophecy. As I left him, heartened by his appearance of physical well-being, I was wrong insofar as his life on this earth was concerned. But I was not mistaken when I nodded my head in affirmation at his "I'll be seeing you," and he was not mistaken when he spoke those words.

12

During World War II, and later in the Korean War, in my opinion our greatest soldier and military leader was General Douglas MacArthur. As the years have passed since the truce agreement was made with the Communists at Panmunjom, my opinion has not changed. No matter what consideration led President Truman to relieve MacArthur of his command in April, 1951, the actual effect of his decision throughout the Far East was tragic. And I am obliged to state my conviction despite the enduring regard I have for Mr. Truman, both as a man and as a President, that the MacArthur recall was a major mistake.

Impetuous, stubborn to a fault, courageous without giving or asking quarter, frank, loyal to his friends, indefatigable, intuitive, and completely dedicated to his country's welfare as he saw it, Harry S. Truman was a magnificent leader who courageously took up the unfinished tasks of the President who had preceded him, and dealt impressively with the new challenges that occurred during his own administration. When Mr. Truman became President after serving as vice-president for only eighty-two days, a veritable wave of despair had swept our nation, and indeed the world. I did not know him well then, and so I agreed with the all but unanimous opinion that he could not possibly measure up to his appalling responsibilities as Franklin Roosevelt's successor. But this dynamic man from Independence, Missouri, did measure up. Whatever the historical perspective may eventually do for Harry Truman, we Americans of today know that he faced courageously and acted decisively upon more grave problems than any President who had preceded him since the Civil War, including Roosevelt himself.

Two weeks before he entered the White House, Mr. Truman did not know that the atomic bomb even existed. Yet he made the decision to use it in Japan, and he believes that in so doing he shortened the war and saved half a million lives. "I didn't hesitate a minute and I have never lost any sleep since," he said afterward, in typical style. With the same directness, President Truman threw himself into the task of organizing the United Nations. He offered economic and military aid to Greece and Turkey—the Truman Doctrine—and he established the Marshall Plan, which helped bring about economic recovery in the Western nations of Europe. Mr. Truman gave the Kremlin its first, and up to now only, major propaganda and tactical defeat—the Berlin airlift. He guided the United States into the North Atlantic Treaty Organization. In one of the most dramatic and characteristic of all his lightning-like decisions, he met the Communist aggression in Korea on June 25, 1950. This would be record enough for any man, but to it must be added his personal triumph in the presidential election of 1948. As he came from far behind to win in that race, confounding opponents and political pundits alike, his spirit captured the imagination of the Republic.

For me and for many others, then, Harry Truman by the test of things accomplished will ever be one of our greatest Presidents. But having acknowledged this, honesty requires me to add that his trusted advisers in matters concerning Asia often had little idea of what was going on there, and errors, omissions, and blunders followed one another until we lost China's mainland to the Communists. The recall of Douglas MacArthur from the Korean battlefield I shall always regard as the worst of Mr. Truman's errors—and the decision must be attributed directly to him because he himself claimed it. In fact he was incensed when his entire responsibility for the decision was questioned. "He was insubordinate and I fired him, just like Lincoln fired

McClellan," the President said, as reported in the newspapers; "Sure I knew there would be a lot of stink about it, but I didn't give a damn. It was the right thing to do and I did it."

But to uncounted millions of people in the Philippines, in Japan, in China, in Korea, it was not the right thing to do, and I can say this from my personal, on-the-scenes observations and experiences in these places.

My admiration for MacArthur the soldier began during World War I. It was in Nancy, France, in 1918, that I watched Colonel MacArthur, then of the Forty-second (Rainbow) Division, as he received the star that made him a brigadier general. To me, as I then saw him for the first time, he was already an extraordinarily impressive figure: a man who, though still in his thirties, had the bearing which suggested the superb confidence of the born leader.

We did not meet at that time but became friends after the war when MacArthur was made chief of staff of the Army—the youngest man in history to be so designated. Over the years I continued to be impressed by MacArthur's achievements. In 1932, when President Hoover ordered out the troops to disperse the "Bonus Marchers"—the fifteen thousand unemployed veterans who had descended on Washington to make their grievances known—in defiant and forceful fashion—General MacArthur acted with typical decisiveness, and the marchers were quickly dispersed. Though the affair produced much criticism of the President and the general, there can be no doubt that MacArthur's action averted the imminent breakdown of law and order.

In 1935, during my first trip around the world on a Christian Endeavor mission, I visited General MacArthur in the Philippines. Japan had then begun the military and political operations in China that would soon lead to undeclared war, and President Roosevelt had given MacArthur the task of training the Philippine soldiery and preparing the Islands' defenses. At the time of my visit, MacArthur was the toast of the Islands—a man whose solid military and administrative accomplishments were matched by his obvious dedication to the cause he served.

My next meeting with the general came two years after the Japanese military machine had swept us from the Philippines. Japan had the upper hand when, on MacArthur's invitational orders, I flew to his headquarters in Brisbane, Australia, in 1944. My mission included meetings with the troops, conferences with chaplains, and six Sundays of preaching in Scots Church, Melbourne. This was the period just before the great offensive against Leyte, where the American victory would pave the way for the general to redeem the historic pledge he had made two years before to the Philippine people, and indeed to the world at large: "I shall return."

Many critics there have been of General MacArthur's seeming vanity and his undoubted histrionic flair, but to me it has always seemed that his egoism was firmly based not only in moral integrity, in his assured sense of purpose, in his belief in his destiny, but also in a comprehensive knowledge of the job to be done.

I particularly prize my memory of that Brisbane visit because I had the opportunity to meet for the first time the woman whom the general called "my bravest"—Mrs. Jean MacArthur. My good friend Colonel Ivan L. Bennett, MacArthur's senior chaplain, had already spoken to me about Jean MacArthur's personal contribution to the morale of our troops in the Southwest Pacific, and the way she had captured the love of the Australian people. She came regularly to chapel services, he said, save only when the general was away on one of his many missions, when she remained quietly at home with their son awaiting his return. After I had talked for a few moments with Mrs. MacArthur, I understood the impression she must also have made on others by her serenity and charm.

Their son, Arthur, was recovering from a severe cold at the time and she took me to his bedroom. Above this six-year-old's bed I saw the photograph of the comedian who was already a smiling hero to both of us: Joe E. Brown. From Arthur and his mother I heard the story of their escape from Bataan and their journey to Australia by submarine. As I listened to this rather frail-looking lad tell his story, I reminded myself that he had not only never seen the United States but had lived almost half his life in the thick of war. Six years later, in the American Embassy in Tokyo, Jean MacArthur told me that Arthur had once asked her wistfully, "Mother, when do you think I shall have enough points to go home?"

As we sat by his bed in the general's Brisbane quarters, his mother told her son the story of the *Dorchester*. Afterward, I filled in some of the more personal details that concerned our son Clark. Arthur wanted to know especially about Corky, Clark's son. I told him that Corky was two years younger than himself. Some weeks later, I received a short letter from Arthur, addressed to my grandson. Mrs. MacArthur told me that it represented her boy's first real attempt at putting words into sentences.

When I took my leave of General MacArthur in Australia I was more than ever convinced of both his military abilities and his qualities as a leader of civilians. The people of Australia universally regarded him as the man who had kept their country from being invaded by the Japanese. "He is our savior," one church leader told me, and I felt that his words expressed the opinion I found everywhere.

I next saw the general in 1949 when he was the supreme commander of the Allied occupation in Japan. Again I visited him on his invitational orders to address our troops and American civilians at the Easter dawn service and to confer with his chaplains. I observed not only the political and economic reforms that, under the general's direction, were liberalizing the life of the Japanese; I saw the constructive effects of religious activity. Roman Catholic missionaries had been giving Japanese communities instruction from almost the start of the occupation. Sherwood Eddy, Dr. E. Stanley Jones, Dr. John R. Mott, and other Protestant leaders had brought the message of Christ to tens of thousands of eager listeners. Within a short space of time some two hundred thousand Japanese had publicly declared themselves Christians.

The Easter sunrise service held in Tokyo in 1949 was an impressive answer to Japan's Communists, and it was perhaps the greatest Christian demonstration in all Asian history up to that time. Colonel Roy Parker, who afterward became Army Chief of Chaplains, had succeeded Colonel Bennett as General MacArthur's senior chaplain; working with Japanese Christian leaders, he made all the arrangements. The service was held on the Plaza, before General MacArthur's headquarters and facing the Imperial Palace. More than ten thousand Japanese and Americans gathered there. Three hundred Japanese youths in white silk vestments sang the "Hallelujah Chorus." As I preached my Resurrection message, "If a Man Die, Shall He Live?," to this vast gathering, I could not but feel that Japan, at least, was destined to become a great positive force in the resistance to the Kremlin's designs on Asia.

On Easter Monday I went to the Imperial Palace for a conference with Emperor Hirohito. The visit had been arranged by General MacArthur and our conversation centered on the general. The Emperor said to me, "It is the good fortune of Japan and of the world that General MacArthur is a man so wise and just."

I found the Emperor, a little man physically, not at all impressive to the eye. He was quiet and, it seemed to me, genuinely serene. When he learned that I was taking off for the Philippines the next morning he said, "Japanese soldiers did evil things in the Philippines, things I regret." And he concluded, "I desire to live the rest of my life in peace and working for peace."

I was to hear the Emperor's high praise of MacArthur from many other sources, but perhaps it was most concisely and colorfully put by a six-foot-five-inch soldier I found relaxing in a service club. He was one of the M.P.'s I had seen standing guard at the entrance to MacArthur's headquarters. With a grin, he said, "If that man is half as good as he looks when he goes by me, then he belongs on top of the world where that Buddha sits," and he pointed to a statue of Buddha in a corner of the club.

But while our policy was sound and well administered in Japan, we lost ground in China, in Korea, and to a lesser extent in the Philippines. The ruthless nature of the Communist program became clear in the Philippines under tragic circumstances.

With Colonel Joy Dow of the United States Army I was making a tour of the Pacific islands, visiting army installations as a member of the President's Commission on Religion and Welfare in the Armed Services. Colonel Dow was a close friend of the family of the late President Manuel Quezon, having accompanied the body of the President, who had died in the United States during the war, back to the Philippines for burial with full military honors. President Quezon had been known as the George Washington of the Philippines because of his achievements in bringing about his nation's independence.

On the afternoon in 1949 before she was murdered, I visited with gentle Doña Aurora, widow of President Quezon. I sat with this gracious lady and her elder daughter, Maria Aurora, in her modest home in the town of Quezon, a suburb of Manila named after the president.

Doña Aurora was a remarkable woman. She was the active head of the national Red Cross and was associated with many welfare organizations and programs. She was universally loved and revered. Maria Aurora, at age thirty, was a practicing lawyer and a community and political leader.

Doña Aurora told me of the eagerly anticipated trip she was to take the very next day to Baler, her native town on the east coast of Luzon. She was to attend a fiesta, unveil a memorial to her husband, and open a new hospital. It was in Baler that she and her husband met as children.

Between Manila and Baler lay the mountainous area that was one of the strongholds of the Hukbalahaps. These guerrillas, said by some to be Communist-inspired, had spread terror through the hills of central Luzon. Under the leadership of Luís Taruc, the "Huks" refused to support the government, demanded free land for the poor, and generally followed the revolutionary pattern that was even then to be seen in Burma and Indochina. But at the time of my visit there had been talk of an amnesty for the Huks and Luís Taruc himself was reported ready to "come in."

Doña Aurora smiled at any thought of danger in her trip to

Baler. "No one would harm me," she said. "No one would have reason to harm me." She was eager to have Colonel Dow and myself accompany her party to Baler but our connections for Shanghai and Tokyo made that impossible.

In a narrow defile of the mountain road the next day, she and her daughter and her son-in-law and ten of her friends died under machine-gun fire. The leader of the attack was recognized as the Huk captain in that district.

Luís Taruc, regarded by many American officers and correspondents as a patriot, was not an atheist and not, I think, a Communist. He claimed Doña Aurora as a friend. With sincere words of grief, he denounced her murderers.

Looking back on that tragedy, I believe that the Communists killed Doña Aurora to destroy any hope of amnesty for the Huks and to make peace an impossibility. Communism wants no peace in any land that it does not control, and it will abide no settlement that does not further its aims. The Communists have murdered before to create dissension, and they will again.

While the Administration laudably spent billions to meet the Communist threat in Europe, in China it unaccountably insisted that Chiang Kai-shek's government accept Communists in strategic posts and ultimately forced Chiang into an all-out effort to create a coalition government with the Communists. While the Russians strengthened the Chinese Reds with the vast supplies of Japanese war materials they had captured in Manchuria, the United States failed to support the Nationalists with adequate supplies of food, weapons, planes, and ships.

It is undoubtedly true that supplies were often misdirected and that venal men, among them war lords who compromised Chiang's leadership, stole and plundered. But repeatedly the Generalissimo asked that we supply competent administrative control officers. We forced on the Generalissimo the "cease fire" which immobilized his armies for more than one year during which the Communist forces were regrouped under Russian generals. In the opinion of many American leaders, both military and civilian, this cease fire came when the Generalissimo had the enemy bottled up in China's two great river valleys.

Finally, our State Department issued the White Paper which is, I think, a document of diplomatic infamy. For better or worse, Nationalist China was still our faithful ally. Yet we not only cut off all aid to Chiang but stripped our friend of just about the last garment of personal integrity and leadership—and did this while he with us faced a common foe. It is difficult not to believe what I've heard many British officials and industrialists, both in London and Hong Kong, insist: that our State Department had at least informally agreed to recognize Communist China.

It may reasonably be asked why I, a clergyman and a religious journalist, presume to speak and write as I have on these matters. Certainly I am not a military expert. Nor have I ever been cast in any role in the field of statesmanship, save on presidential commissions and in similar advisory roles. Also, I have been defeated not once but twice for public office!

But as for the Far East, I have made repeated visits into all areas of Asia and, as already indicated, I have been associated intimately with leaders and followers, public men and private, in China, Japan, Korea, the Philippines, and elsewhere. I believe that I am competent to choose the leaders whose policies in these areas I would follow. Among them are General Douglas MacArthur, General Albert Wedemeyer, General Claire Chennault, Ambassador Leighton Stuart and his successor, Ambassador Karl Rankin, Ambassador Patrick Hurley, and Congressman Dr. Walter Judd, who for some years was a medical missionary in China and now has a continuous record of support in the House of Representatives for Nationalist China. The two pre-eminent figures in the field of Protestant Church leadership with whose views I heartily agree are Methodist Bishops Herbert Welch and Ralph A. Ward, now deceased. The former spent forty years of his life in China and among all churchmen is recognized as a Christian statesman of first rank. The latter was imprisoned and tortured by the Japanese, and after a furlough spent in the United States returned to his post.

Equally important in shaping my conclusions have been the statements made and the experiences related by the missionaries, men and women, who have poured out their lives in sacrificial ministries along the yellow rivers of China's mainland. In December of 1958, I met with nearly half a hundred of these soldiers of the Cross who spoke their grief at the report issued in Cleveland by a responsible body of the National Council of Churches of Christ in the U.S.A., the report in which their fellow religionists declared for recognition of Communist China and the admission of Communist China to the United Nations. The spokesman of this missionary group said that "betrayal" was a hard word but that it was the only word that could describe the action of this Cleveland body. On this occasion, I sat with men and women who had spent, some of them, half a century in China. I believe in their wisdom and their integrity. I think they know what they are talking about.

I went to China first a quarter of a century ago, my missionary forebears decades before that. Now in the years since, having traveled Asia extensively and intensively, having been intimately associated with the foreign missionaries and ministries of my faith, having known and conferred with the diplomats and generals, industrialists and youth leaders, with newspapermen and journalists, and with the so-called little people who are forever big in my thinking, I not only do not hesitate to voice my convictions but I also feel bound to do so. Berlin and Greece were saved but China was lost. For Europe there was the Marshall Plan and the Atlantic Pact. For the Far East I believe there should have been a comparable MacArthur Plan and a Pacific Pact.

In my article in *Look* magazine in 1949, I called for them. As I saw it then, MacArthur was the man who most effectively could have rallied the East's leadership. "China now needs all that we have given Greece and more," I wrote, "for the stakes are higher. She needs today the formula of strength with patience that has been applied successfully in Berlin and in Europe generally. Give her . . . the physical presence of men who are not defeatists, men who believe in her. Then China will yield returns to freedom and democracy of world significance and beyond computation."

No such support or leadership was forthcoming from Washington, and China passed into Communist hands in late 1949.

In January, 1950, the Red government was recognized by India and by Great Britain. In June of the same year the North Koreans began the Korean War.

I was in Korea after Seoul had fallen. With Chaplain Ivan L. Bennett, once again MacArthur's senior chaplain (and later Army Chief of Chaplains), I dedicated our first military cemetery in South Korea. The United Nations forces, chiefly American units, were face to face with catastrophe at Pusan at the extreme southern tip of the peninsula. The surrounding mountains were ringed with enemy batteries, and loud-speakers blared the boast that within hours we would be pushed into the sea. Here it was, while General MacArthur was preparing his military masterstroke—the landings at Inchon that would cut the enemy forces in two—that I had my first meeting with the leader of the beleaguered nation, Syngman Rhee, the first President of the Republic of Korea, who had invited me to Korea as his guest.

On a Sunday morning he attended the chapel services at which I spoke, and he was an unforgettable figure as he rode up in a jeep, accompanied by his good friend Dr. Helen Kim, the president of Ewa College in Seoul. An elderly, unprepossessing little man with a weathered face, he moved me deeply at first sight, for I knew something of his story. From his earliest youth he had been an unyielding patriot, determined that one day his country should be free of its Japanese overlords. In the middle 1930s he had given his eloquent but unheeded warning to the League of Nations in Geneva. "Japan is ready to move and will move to fulfill her dream of world conquest," said this exiled Korean who had known the worst kind of torture in Japanese prisons and for years had had a price on his head. The members of the League had given as little consideration to his appeal for justice and action as they had to the valedictory address that had just preceded Rhee's—that of Emperor Haile Selassie of Ethiopia, who warned that if Mussolini were allowed to continue his aggressions, his country would be only the first to fall victim to the Rome-Berlin-Tokyo coalition.

Something of Syngman Rhee's wisdom and courage I learned in the first few minutes of our meeting. Someone suggested that he had taken a great risk in coming to the Army's chapel in Pusan. He replied with a smile, "No, the enemy wouldn't look for me here. Communists don't go to church, you know."

In my later meetings with President Rhee I learned that he is the last of an ancient and honored Korean family. He met a lovely Viennese woman while he was in Europe in the 1930s, and under unusual circumstances they were later married in New York City. As I have observed it, the religious life of this long-time Christian—Rhee is a Methodist—is simple, sincere and infused with a sense of destiny.

It was on my latest visit to Seoul, while I sat at lunch with the President and Madame Rhee, that I heard from the lovely lady herself the story of their unusual courtship. She and her mother were attending the League of Nations public sessions in Geneva and were present when Syngman Rhee made his impassioned address to the League concerning Japan's intentions in the Far East. She said, "He was unforgettable and I never recovered from that experience. I wrote him a letter expressing my admiration for his courage and he replied. Then began our correspondence. When he left Geneva and returned to New York, we were engaged and I was to follow as quickly as possible. There was some little difficulty and delay arranging for my passage but eventually I sailed on a German ship—I had said that I never would sail on any German ship, but I did! When I arrived in New York Syngman was not on the dock and I was alone in a strange world. That was a devastating experience. Afterward, of course, I learned that Syngman, through the excessive kindness of his many friends, had been misdirected and misled. He was up in the morning at four o'clock to meet an afternoon boat! I had almost decided to get back on board and return to Vienna when he finally appeared." She laughed infectiously. "We were married in the Community Church by Dr. John Haynes Holmes, assisted by a Korean minister. That ceremony was performed in two languages, neither of which I understood, but," she added as she looked across the table at her smiling husband, "I have never regretted that day."

After the Korean shooting ended in what has been ever since

an uneasy truce, it continued to be my routine to return to Korea, Hong Kong, and Formosa each year, visiting our eleven *Christian Herald* homes and orphanages, meeting with officers of the international Christian Endeavor Unions in Korea and Japan. We have now in Korea more than two hundred thousand Christian Endeavor members in the churches of the great Presbyterian Synod of Korea. As I write these lines, I see on my desk an invitation from the officers of the Korean Christian Endeavor Union and from the executive official of the General Assembly of the Presbyterian Church to hold the next World's Christian Endeavor Convention in Seoul. If this invitation is finally accepted and the World's Convention of 1962 is held in Seoul, ours will be the first international gathering of such size and with such purpose to be held in this heroic and embattled land.

President and Madame Rhee have shown a gracious interest in our orphanages, and on each of my visits to the Far East it has been my privilege to meet with the President. In December of 1958, he said to me, "Always I pray God to let me live until Korea shall be a free and united nation." And to that I replied, "I join you in that prayer, Mr. President." At eighty-four, he is at this writing a candidate for his fourth term as President of the Republic of Korea.

It has frequently been remarked that Syngman Rhee is a difficult ally—one given to moving independently, even when his actions contravene previous agreements—but for him the goal of national unity is paramount and it may at times blind him to the international niceties. For Rhee—he has told me this—there can be no real peace without a final victory over Korea's enemies, no peace without unification, no peace until the pledge of support made to Korea by the victorious Allies of World War II shall be fully kept. Admittedly this may make him "difficult," but true patriotism has always been a disturbing phenomenon. What we are faced with in Syngman Rhee, I am convinced, is the modern counterpart of the American leader who inspired our forefathers with his cry of "Give me liberty or give me death."

Several years ago, during a conversation with President Rhee that followed closely on his recovery from pneumonia, I was led to do what I seldom do—pray audibly with my host. We were sitting in the living room of the presidential palace in Seoul. This is a palace in name only, since it is a structure no larger than any reasonably large American home. Rhee had just told me of his heartbreak over charges, originating in America, that he had built himself a personal fortune at the expense of his country. "Why, oh why," he asked me with deep emotion, "would any of your countrymen believe that I would steal, when all that I have and am I have given? You know that I have practically nothing of my own, and that my whole life has been given to Korea." I did know it. It was then, as we stood together, that I was moved to suggest the prayer. His face became animated. "Yes," he said, "yes, pray!"

We stood side by side, with our heads bowed, our hands clasped. When the prayer was finished, Rhee looked at me with tear-filled eyes and said somewhat plaintively, "This never happened before. Now it has happened, and I am grateful."

As for the war in Korea, Syngman Rhee believed from the first that the countermanding of General MacArthur's orders to bomb the Yalu River bridges led to our losing the final victory then and there and our being forced back to the Thirty-eighth Parallel. It will be recalled that the Yalu was in flood at the time. Had the bridges been destroyed, the flow of enemy reinforcements and supplies and the deluge of "volunteers" from Red China could never have come down upon the victorious United Nations forces in time to stop their sweeping advance. President Rhee believes General MacArthur's brilliantly conceived, and up to that hour successful, campaign would have been triumphantly completed.

My opinion is that the order from the Administration that stopped the bombing of the bridges was, in some degree, influenced by the wishes of Great Britain. In Japan, in 1949, General MacArthur told me wryly, "Our great British ally has three objectives out here—the retirement of Syngman Rhee, Chiang Kai-shek, and"—with the suggestion of a smile—"Douglas MacArthur." After his recall, I reminded him of the statement. "I didn't think that I would be the first to go," he commented with a chuckle. But perhaps it might have been foretold. The attitude of the British toward MacArthur, as expressed in constant belittling editorials and news stories I read in the *Hong Kong Post*, never changed and it was never once friendly or even appreciative of his military genius. The British even discounted the magnificent feat of the Inchon landings. Another statement that I invariably related to the countermanding of the bridge bombing was that of Secretary of State Dean Acheson that Korea was not vital to the perimeter defense of the West.

Then came MacArthur's recall. I have already indicated my own view of this matter. But my view was not original: I encountered it wherever I went in the Far East. "MacArthur did not lose face, America lost face," one of my Japanese friends said, soon after the event. "We knew the general and unanimously we had a deep affection for him. I can tell you that in Japan his recall may mean eventually the moral collapse of the resistance to Communism in Asia."

Later, a Japanese newspaperman expressed it this way: "If, in the line of his providential duty, MacArthur had lived and died here, we would have held him enshrined in our hearts. We would have built him a tomb, and his spirit would have lived among us." I suggested that possibly MacArthur's inspiration would continue in Asia even though the man had gone back to the United States. "Ah, yes, perhaps," said the newspaperman, "but to non-Communist Asia, General MacArthur was America, and America repudiated herself and recalled herself."

Even after the recall, the situation might have been saved. Had the United States sent Douglas MacArthur as Ambassador Extraordinary to Asia, say, with headquarters in Tokyo or Manila, our nation would certainly have captured the imaginations of free men everywhere and taken over the peace offensive in the Far East.

As far as the free Asians are concerned, Washington's handling of the MacArthur case has still not been satisfactorily settled. Under the presidency of General Eisenhower, on two notable occasions I have faced the embarrassment of political questions that I could not really answer. The embarrassment, I felt, was my country's rather than mine.

The first such occasion was in Korea, in 1957, the day after the memorial statue of General MacArthur was unveiled on the heights above Inchon. The statue is the work of a Korean sculptor and the gift of the grateful Korean people. On the Sunday of the unveiling, while the old battle road between Inchon and Seoul was crowded with flags and soldiers, the American commander had the task of conducting the ceremony without the presence of the two men who most clearly should have been present. One of the guests of honor was still in the United States. The other, the President of the Republic, unexpectedly chose to stay away from the unveiling because General MacArthur had not come to Korea. That morning Syngman Rhee, appearing to me like a profoundly distressed man, attended my Sunday morning services at the chapel of the Eighth Army in Seoul, in company with his wife and adopted son.

The next day, when I visited the President in his palace, this was the question I faced: "Why does not General MacArthur visit us? The statue is our expression of our love for the man we regard as our savior. Above all others he was our friend. Why did he not come here for the unveiling?"

The answer I gave my friend came from my personal knowledge of the facts. The Administration in Washington had not indicated that it desired MacArthur to make the visit. I could no more understand the reasoning behind it than could President Rhee.

The second occasion came later, while I was attending the National Christian Endeavor Convention held in Adelaide, Australia. Here the Primate of the Church of England in Melbourne asked me much the same question. "Why do not the MacArthurs, whom we love, return to this country for a visit? They came to us in a time of great danger. General MacArthur saved Australia. If he were to visit us now with his wife and son, we would receive them with honors hardly less than those accorded our Queen. Why does he not come here, Dr. Poling?"

My answer to the primate had to be the same as it had been to Rhee, unsatisfactory and baffling. Thus did the United States lose face in the Far East.

In December, 1957, visiting Syngman Rhee and his wife on my way home to the United States, I asked the President for a Christmas message for my countrymen. These are the words that he gave me: "I pray God to wake up the American people. Wake up the American people for themselves and for us and for the whole world." And then, these final words: "This I daily pray. God is my constant strength—no other."

Presently Madame Rhee called us to a simple luncheon. Small and dark and unmistakably Viennese despite her long absence from the land of her birth, Madame Rhee is still a beautiful and spirited woman after the thirty or more years during which she has shared her husband's fortunes, which, by some standards, were more often misfortunes.

After our meal, I left the palace to fly to Tokyo and back to the United States. As we always do at parting, the President and I stood for a moment with our heads bowed and our hands clasped. Thinking back over my friend's long and honorable life, reminding myself of the hardships that have been his in the service of his country, marking again the religious fervor that has carried him through it all, I could not help but ask God to let him live to see his dream of a united Korea come true.

Aside from the issues just discussed, I am glad to say that my personal relationships with President Truman were always of the happiest. I was called in to advise or help him on a number of matters. Perhaps the most important of these was his Civilian Advisory Commission on Universal Military Training. Mr. Truman invited me to join this in the fall of 1946. Karl Compton, president of the Massachusetts Institute of Technology, was the commission's chairman, and the other clergyman-member was Father John Walsh, of Georgetown University.

Though Congress rejected our recommendations for universal military training and enacted instead a modified draft law, some helpful developments, I like to think, came from the commission.

My main concern was the moral and religious aspects of the proposed legislation, but I was intensely interested in every aspect of military preparedness. After both World Wars I had seen our democracy reduce her defense forces below safe levels. I knew that the nation had sinned against her own sons by sending them into battle without proper equipment and without proper training and discipline. In the winter of 1944–1945, when the Germans made their last breakthrough in the Battle of the Bulge, I had viewed firsthand the consequences of inadequate defense. The surprise, the insufficient manpower, even the improper clothing, cost our forces forty thousand casualties. We even threw in the kitchen police and a regimental band! From my own family history I could offer a telling example of insufficient training and discipline. In the great and uplifting spiritual impression made by the story of the four chaplains on the *Dorchester*, it was generally overlooked that these four young men of God were perhaps lost for the simple reason that four soldiers had not learned to obey the inflexible requirement that every man on a ship in enemy waters must wear his life jacket at all times.

I came to appreciate the directness and comprehensiveness of Mr. Truman's control of affairs when in 1949 I published a magazine article entitled "Why Should American Soldiers Live Like Pigs?" This was based on my findings at military installations and bases in Alaska where I was appalled at some of the quarters that had been provided for our men, and even for their wives and children. Mr. Truman moved personally and swiftly to have these conditions corrected.

I was with the President briefly just after his mother died. There was not even the suggestion of the unreal or the superficial in his grief, and even now I remember the impression that came to me from him with a single look and accompanying gesture.

My associations with President Truman brought me together again with an old friend: Harry Vaughan, now an Army Major General and the President's aide. I met Harry first when his father was an elder in the Presbyterian Church and he was a

Christian Endeavor boy in St. Louis. Believe it or not, he was at that time looking forward to entering the ministry. He got as far as becoming, like his father, an elder in the Presbyterian Church.

I had occasion, too, to study closely the charges and countercharges that involved Harry with the 5 and 10 per-centers, deep freezes, and fur coats. This, I know. Financially, Harry Vaughan never profited nor did his family. He rendered his services at the White House with characteristic enthusiasm to rich and poor, black and white, high and humble, alike. I remember one instance when a huge colored sergeant with feet too big to be fitted outside the factory wrote Harry Vaughan of his trouble and then came to see him. Harry got him the shoes, huge enough to cross Pennsylvania Avenue in a stride, and dismissed the matter. A year later that sergeant sent a check to cover the cost of those shoes. Harry loved to tell that story.

He was no lily. His language may have sometimes departed from the old Christian Endeavor pattern. But in my opinion Major General Harry Vaughan fully justified the President's confidence in him.

In 1951 I received a telephone summons from the President under rather amusing circumstances. I had gone to Milwaukee for a meeting of the All-American Conference to Combat Communism, an organization of which I was then chairman, and I was working on a report with George Craig, the national commander of the American Legion and the founder of the Conference. The telephone rang, and our secretary, answering it, said, "The White House is calling you, Dr. Poling."

"Tell him the King of Siam is busy," I said. Only an hour before, one of my facetious Christian Endeavor friends had called me in my hotel room and said, "This is the President of the United States speaking."

The startled lady said, "But, Dr. Poling, it really is the President!"

When I put the phone to my ear I heard Mr. Truman having a good laugh at the King of Siam. "Dr. Poling," he said, "I'm calling you because I need the help of a Republican Baptist."

I understood the invitation as a command performance and the next day saw Mr. Truman in the White House. I found him in an angry and determined mood, bent on uncovering and destroying the corruption that there might be in his administration. The country was in an uproar of charges and countercharges about skulduggery in high places and President Truman had hurried back from a vacation in Key West. He wanted Judge Thomas F. Murphy, Daniel Bell, and myself to serve on a three-man commission to investigate corruption in government.

I of course accepted, but the commission was never actually named. Eminent judicial figures, including Judge Learned Hand, were successful in persuading Mr. Murphy, who was to have served as our commission chairman, not to leave the bench even briefly for such an executive assignment. There was then a growing feeling, originating from the Nuremberg trials, that the judicial department had been too often at the beck and call of the executive.

Caught in the middle of this judicial-executive debate, I had no opinions about it but watched with considerable interest. Ultimately President Truman was unable to find anyone else of Judge Murphy's stature to fill his place and the commission died aborning. Some of President Truman's political associates breathed audible sighs of relief.

But I remember with amusement my first interview with the President on this particular matter. He finished his explanation of why he wanted me on the commission by saying, "Anyway, I like you because you are a fellow Baptist."

Thinking back to the somewhat unique position I had held at Baptist Temple, I replied, "Well, Mr. President, I was born into the United Evangelical Church and then I became a minister in the Dutch Reformed Church. Lots of folks don't think I'm a Baptist at all."

Mr. Truman laughed. "A lot of people don't think I'm a good Baptist either," he said. "So what!"

13

One afternoon during World War II, in the course of one of my overseas missions for President Roosevelt, I arrived at our great air base at Natal, Brazil. The senior chaplain there was an old friend of mine, Rev. Sam Overstreet. I had broken the band of my wrist watch, and I told Sam I would be grateful if he drove me into the city so I could buy a replacement for it.

As he shook his head, I noticed that he was grinning. "Sorry, Dan. This is Friday and I'm about to conduct the Jewish service for Father Ryan."

In response to my startled query, Sam explained that there were seventy-two Jewish boys on the base but no Jewish chaplain or resident rabbi. To fill the need, he and the other Christian chaplains were taking turns in bringing the Jews their spiritual message. "This was Father Ryan's day," Sam told me, "but he is ill so I'm taking his place."

Well, I was no longer interested in going into Natal. I stayed right on the base and watched a New England Baptist preacher conduct a Jewish service for a Roman Catholic priest. And to give Sam credit, he did a convincing job in his unaccustomed role. The cantor was a G.I. with a fine baritone voice. The boys themselves conducted the ritualistic part of the service with proper Jewish observances but Sam gave the sermon. Though informal, it was for me an extraordinarily inspiring service.

As my travels continued, in war chapels all over the world I saw men of the three major faiths worship freely under the same roof, each man's group taking its turn. There were times in the battle areas when Protestant and Jewish boys died in the arms of Catholic chaplains; there were occasions when Protestant and Jewish chaplains gave a modified form of the last rites of the Roman Catholic Church to dying soldiers of that faith. There was an exhilarating spirit of unity in all this—a spirit that I hoped would be carried into the postwar period. To me, it seemed that this lesson of religious unity was one of the greatest incidental benefits that might come out of the war.

In 1945, after Japan had surrendered, the interfaith group my wife had founded when we moved to Philadelphia, Religion in Life, held a meeting in that city in one of the clubrooms of Christ Church. I presided that night and introduced three speakers, one from each faith.

An eloquent young Jew, a lieutenant commander in the Navy who was now completing his law course at the University of Pennsylvania, spoke first. He was followed by a Protestant chaplain who was convalescing from war wounds at Valley Forge Hospital at Phoenixville. The third speaker, a Roman Catholic, was a G.I. student at Villanova College. Arriving late, he listened to the Protestant chaplain from the rear of the room. Then he hurried to the platform. When he pushed by the hand I extended in greeting, I turned in some surprise and watched him and the chaplain embrace.

A few moments later the Villanova boy told the interfaith gathering the story behind that happy reunion. He was one of the poorest public speakers I had heard in a long time. He was ill at ease. He spoke haltingly. Yet what he said will always be with me.

"It has been eighteen months since I last saw my chaplain. Then I was looking up at him from a stretcher on Utah Beach. He had lifted me onto that stretcher, and then he helped lift that stretcher into an ambulance. A little later he got his. Now we are together again." As the young man went on with his speech, his eyes filled with tears, and I saw him trembling with emotion. "Men and women, in those days we were not Catholics and we were not Protestants and we were not Jews. We did not ask, 'Are there Jews on our right and Catholics on our left and Protestants in support?' We were just Americans—and we were scared to death." And then, in a rush of feeling, he concluded, "Men and women, we must be like that now."

There in Christ Church, all unknowing, that Catholic boy expressed in words the ideal of the interfaith memorial I had been planning and dreaming of almost from the day that I had learned the story of the *Dorchester* chaplains. As I thought again and again of how my son Clark had gone down with his three companions, it came to me that the drama of their sacrifice could best be memorialized and remembered in a shrine that would bring together the altars of their three faiths. Between the inspiration, in 1943, and the realization, in 1951, there was an arduous and often discouraging period of planning, designing, and fund-raising. Somehow, with dedicated help from more good people than can possibly be named, the work was finally finished, and the Chapel of Four Chaplains was dedicated. Today in Philadelphia, in the heart of Temple University and within the walls and beneath the sanctuary of the Baptist Temple, the Chapel of Four Chaplains stands as an enduring memorial not only to the sacrifices of four young men but to an idea and a holy purpose.

Something of what the *Dorchester* story meant to the world at large may be suggested by the fact that during the years of our work on the chapel more than four hundred thousand dollars was contributed to the project by men and women of all faiths and from every one of the United States, as well as from Hawaii, Alaska, Canada, and many European countries. So many were these gifts and such was the spirit of the givers that I became convinced that the chapel was built more with love and faith and generosity than with dollars.

On one of the chapel's walls, through the generosity of Albert M. Greenfield, a public-spirited Philadelphia businessman, a mural by the artist Nils Hogner depicts the sinking of the *Dorchester*. The figures of the four chaplains, photographic in their likeness, are life size. On the opposite wall, facing the mural, five bronze tablets carry the names of the nearly seven hundred men who went down with their chaplains. These memorial tables were the gift of the women of Philadelphia through the interfaith Religion in Life group. National flags that I brought back from overseas hang elsewhere on the chapel walls. The focal point of the room, which seats as many as three hundred people, is the three altars—Catholic, Jewish, and Protestant—within the chancel arch. Only one of these altars may be seen at a time, for each one, moving into view on a revolving platform, completely fills the arch. During the regular Sunday services the altars are displayed one after another as the platform turns clockwise; thus is the symbolism of the chapel—the common foundation of our Judeo-Christian heritage and faith—made visible to all who gather there. Each of the altars was furnished and decorated by members of its faith. While canon law prohibits the Roman Catholic altar from ever being consecrated in association with the altars of other faiths, it is nonetheless dressed for the mystery of the Mass, and quite informally laymen and clergymen of the Roman Catholic Church come to the chapel to remember the heroes of the three faiths—Washington the Catholic, Goode the Jew, and Fox and Poling the Protestants. The Roman Catholic altar, with its crucifix from Rome and its marble from Italy, was the gift of Roman Catholic laymen. The Jewish altar has above it the Ark of the Covenant containing the Torah, jeweled and exquisitely beautiful. It was the gift of B'nai B'rith. The Protestant altar was the gift of Miss Mary Louise Seltzer, of Philadelphia.

Many substantial gifts were required before the chapel could be finished in a manner worthy of its theme. The Kresge Foundation gave the sum that enabled us to have Gustav Ketterer, the noted decorator of public buildings, give his talents to completing the interior. A further gift of Dorothy and Stanley Kresge made the home of the late Harry T. Patterson, where I had lived as minister of Baptist Temple, the parish house for the chapel.

The "universal" entrance to the chapel was the last of the major elements to be financed. The fund-raising committee had reached the end of its known resources before the money for this part of the project was in hand, and it was with a heavy heart that I left the scene to fly away on another overseas mission. Returning from abroad in time to keep a speaking engagement in Minneapolis, where the national convention of the Fraternal Order of Eagles was being held, I was sick with a cold and a mood of depression was on me. I almost decided to cancel my plans. Then, as I prayed, the conviction came to me that, dead or alive, I must go to Minneapolis.

The trip had every appearance of a failure. My plane was late. My hour in the concluding session of the convention program had come and gone.

Robert Hansen, then the editor of the *Eagle*, and one of the public-spirited founders of the All-American Conference to Combat Communism, met me at the airport. As we drove into town, I opened my heart and spilled out my troubles. Bob not only listened sympathetically but pumped me dry with his questions. When we arrived at the convention hall, the governor of the state, scheduled as the concluding speaker, was in the closing moments of his message.

After he had been heard, the chairman held the convention in order and introduced me. Surely God was with me. He gave me a message and I delivered it. After I had described the chapel and its purpose, I explained the significance of the proposed universal entrance. When I had finished, Bob Hansen came to the front of the platform. In a brief but moving statement he told about my dilemma, about the work that still needed to be done, and about our lack of funds. With a roar that was unanimous, the Eagles took over the completion of that final part—the universal entrance—of the chapel.

Today a great bronze plaque bearing the names of all the chaplains of all faiths who died in World War II fills the wall at the right of the tower entrance under the Eternal Light. On the tablet is the simple statement that the Fraternal Order of Eagles made the gift. Above the stairway that leads down into the chapel these words are chiseled into the stone: THE CHAPEL OF FOUR CHAPLAINS, AN INTERFAITH MEMORIAL. HERE IS SANCTUARY

FOR BROTHERHOOD. LET IT NEVER BE VIOLATED. Above the chapel, carillon bells ring out the message of faith and brotherhood. High above and beyond the halls of Temple University, they peal their message of peace with hope triumphant even beyond time and space.

In the course of a year the chapel is now visited by thousands of people. In addition to the regular services, there are many special programs, and many visits by special groups. Practically every patriotic and religious organization of Philadelphia has made the chapel its sacred rendezvous. The American Legion launched its Back to God movement here. State governors and leaders in the national government, as well as many noted and worthy men and women in public life have been among the visitors. Distinguished scholars, Jewish and Christian, from the United States and abroad, have come to speak from this pulpit.

Free of debt, the chapel today goes forward with its work which is supported by contributions and bequests that will, I believe, eventually build an adequate supporting fund. It makes me particularly happy that my venerable friend J. C. Penney, my inspiration and organizational associate for nearly forty years, is chairman of the Friends of the Chapel of Four Chaplains, the body that draws together the chapel's supporters and handles its organizational aspects. While I have been the chapel's chaplain from the beginning, and will so remain until I die, the chaplain-in-charge is Walter H. White. This man, who came to the chapel from his service in the Navy, has been God's gift to the memorial, for he is indefatigable, a veritable genius as an organizer, and an inspiration to young and old alike.

How difficult it is for Americans to maintain in peace the unity that our sons, and we too, on the home front, achieved during the war is illustrated by the problem that faced us even before the chapel was finished and dedicated.

In the fall of 1950, at the Bellevue Stratford Hotel in Philadelphia we held the banquet that marked the conclusion of our active financial campaign. It was a gala and impressive interfaith occasion. Our toastmaster was former Supreme Court Justice

Owen J. Roberts. United States Senator Herbert H. Lehman came as the special representative of President Truman to speak for his Jewish faith. The honorable Charles P. Taft, mayor of Cincinnati and president of the Federal Council of Churches of Christ in the U.S.A., spoke for the Protestants. Our third key speaker was to have been Congressman John Kennedy of Massachusetts. He had graciously accepted our invitation to take part in the program as a spokesman for his Roman Catholic faith. Yet, bowing to the will of an eminent Catholic prelate, Mr. Kennedy disappointed us.

Two days before the banquet, Mr. Kennedy telephoned me from Washington and said that he would have to cancel his appearance. His Eminence Denis Cardinal Dougherty of Philadelphia had requested him not to speak at the banquet and not to appear. The congressman's distress was obvious as he relayed this information. All but overwhelmed with my disappointment, I reminded Mr. Kennedy that the banquet was a civic occasion, that all the faiths were participating, and that we were meeting not in a Protestant church, but on neutral ground in a hotel. The congressman replied that he understood all this and that he had done everything he could to change the cardinal's position. His speech was prepared, he said, and he would gladly forward it to me, but as a loyal son of the Church, he had no alternative but not to come. Unquestionably, Mr. Kennedy was grieved as he reported Cardinal Dougherty's decision to me, and unquestionably also, he was profoundly embarrassed.

We hastily had the banquet programs reprinted to eliminate Congressman Kennedy's name, and though many Roman Catholics were present at the dinner and participated in the evening's events, there was no spokesman for their faith—Cardinal Dougherty's ruling had come too late in the day for us even to attempt to secure an adequate replacement for John Kennedy. In the interests of the unity the Chapel symbolizes, the story behind Mr. Kennedy's failure to appear was not publicly referred to at the banquet or elsewhere, but those of us who knew were indeed heartsick. The Chapel of Four Chaplains is a symbol of a cause that is dearer to me than my physical existence. The

Chapel, as I often point out, is not an argument or a debate, nor is it in any sense an expression of theological uniformity; it has nothing to do with canon law. Rather, it is the embodiment of the concept that all men are equal in God's sight.

The late Cardinal Dougherty's attitude toward me personally was always generous and benign, but he was adamant in withholding his endorsement of the interfaith memorial. He issued no public statement, but he took from me in my campaign to complete the chapel several distinguished Roman Catholics who were my close personal friends. Though they remained my friends, they could no longer help actively in the project. Protestants generally have difficulty in understanding such manifestations of what they may regard as a narrow and limited view of Christian faith. They cannot but be disturbed by the steady withdrawal of Catholic clergymen from the National Conference of Christians and Jews, which has now become largely a conference of Jews and Protestants, and the resignation of priests from Rotary and other service clubs. But Protestants and all others should know that the Roman Catholic hierarchy ever acts as it believes it must—in loyalty to the faith that it believes was once and forever committed to its guardianship. Only in the extreme ordeals of war, it seems, will the hierarchy relax its interpretation and rigid enforcement of canon law. There was Catholic opposition even to the chapel's mural which depicted a priest of the Church dying in prayer, his own prayer, with a Jew and two Protestants.

Certain it is that Roman Catholic prelates enjoy considerable latitude in interpreting and enforcing canon law, and it was some consolation that two eminent priests of the Church personally assured me that Cardinal Dougherty's attitude in dealing with the Chapel of Four Chaplains was his own and would never have been theirs. Both these men were contributors to the altar that memorializes Father John Washington.

At the chapel's dedication, on February 3, 1951, we were again faced with the crippling effect of Cardinal Dougherty's authority. A program of distinction had been arranged. President Truman was to deliver the address of dedication to an audience that would represent all the armed services and be carried thoughout the world by radio and television. Brigadier General James O'Neil, then Deputy Chief of Chaplains of the Army, was to offer the closing prayer and benediction. Jimmy O'Neil was a close personal friend of mine; I had been with him in Luxemburg shortly after the Battle of the Bulge, when he was the senior chaplain of General George S. Patton's Third Army. I knew no Catholic chaplain I would rather have seen take part in the chapel's dedication.

A few days before the ceremony the Chief of Chaplains' office in Washington telephoned me to say that Cardinal Dougherty had requested Father O'Neil not to take part in the dedication. Later, in tears, Jimmy personally expressed his disappointment to me. "You understand, Dan," he said. Yes, I understood his predicament, but I shall always regret the thinking of the cardinal who brought it about. When President Truman learned of Chaplain O'Neil's forced withdrawal, he was incensed. He felt, as I did, that a bishop of the Church had invaded the province of the State. As Commander in Chief of our Armed Forces, the President, it seemed to us, had every right to expect the presence and participation of an army chaplain at such an interfaith occasion.

Certain that it would now be impossible to secure any other Roman Catholic clergyman to offer the closing prayer, I turned to a famous Catholic layman, General William ("Wild Bill") Donovan, who had been from the beginning an active member of the chapel's sponsoring committee and its vice-chairman. General Donovan did not disappoint us in this hour of the chapel's need. He appeared at the ceremony and introduced the President.

Mr. Truman spoke movingly about our religious heritage:

> We must never forget that this country was founded by men who came to these shores to worship God as they pleased. Catholics, Jews, and Protestants all came here for this great purpose. They did not come here to do as they pleased—but to worship God as they pleased, and that is an important distinction. The unity of our country comes from this fact. The unity

> of our country is a unity under God. It is a unity in freedom, for the service of God is the perfect freedom. If we remember our faith in God, if we live by it as our forefathers did, we need have no fear of the future.

After the dedication, as we drove the President to his special train, I asked Mr. Truman whether we might have for the chapel the Presidential Seal that had hung on the pulpit while he spoke. He seemed pleased that I had asked for it. Today, suitably framed, it hangs on one of the chapel walls. The combined vestry and study of the chapel, which, as a memorial to our son Clark, was furnished by members of our family, is now known as the Presidential Room. Mr. Truman occupied it during the interval before the exercises began, and now his chair stands against one of the walls, where we shall eventually hang a portrait of the man who not only dedicated the interfaith memorial but was the constant friend of its holy purpose.

Since the day nine years ago that Congressman Kennedy acknowledged and accepted the authority of the Roman Catholic Church and withdrew from the banquet program of the Chapel of Four Chaplains, he has on a number of occasions endeavored to make clear his personal position as a Roman Catholic in the American political scene. I have studied his statements with understandable concern, especially his view that a man's religion is a private matter and that nothing should take precedence over an office-holder's oath to uphold the Constitution of the United States. "I believe as a Senator that the separation of church and state is fundamental to our American concept and heritage and should remain so," Mr. Kennedy wrote in a widely quoted magazine article.

Commenting editorially in the *Christian Herald* on his published statements, I commended Mr. Kennedy for his forthrightness and expressed the opinion that if the Roman Catholic Church would support her faithful son in his principles and beliefs, a new era could dawn for American interfaith relationships. But there was no Catholic endorsement of the senator's position; in fact, the Roman Catholic prelates who spoke at all and the American Catholic press generally criticized it.

Facing the possibility that Senator Kennedy may become the Democratic presidential nominee in 1960, I am naturally reminded of the position I took in reference to Alfred E. Smith's campaign to become President in 1928. I believed Smith's assurances that he would be an American President, beholden to no authority but that of our Constitution. Though my acceptance of his word brought me a great deal of criticism, I was convinced of Al Smith's integrity and sure that I had taken the right position. My opposition to his candidacy was based not upon his religious affiliation but upon his declaration for repeal of the Eighteenth Amendment and on other aspects of his political philosophy.

Today, though I respectfully read what Senator Kennedy has to say, one thing in his record is unmistakably clear. The Church did claim and exercise authority over him while he was in high public office. I believe that there have been priests, and now are priests, of the Roman Catholic Church who would not exercise the Church's authority in this manner. But the fact remains that the authority itself is implicit in the Church, and that at least once John Kennedy of Massachusetts submitted, apparently against his own inclinations and better judgment, to its dictates.

I am sorry to say that there has been one other manifestation of Catholic disapproval of the chapel and all it stands for. Up to now it has been impossible to make a motion picture on the theme of the *Dorchester* sinking because the Roman Catholic Church is unwilling to have a priest of the Church shown in prayer with the clergy of the Jewish and Protestant faiths. Surely such a picture would call all races, faiths, and conditions of men to brave deeds and nobler, more unselfish living. Perhaps the difficulty standing in the way of such a picture will yet be overcome. At least that is my hope.

The spirit of the four chaplains lives on in the shrine that commemorates their heroic deed. That shrine, in an historic metropolis, has inspired thousands of people from all over the world. Our son Clark also has another memorial. Though relatively few people will ever see it because it is far from any city, it is in a spot that Clark himself loved.

As I sat in my London hotel room in the summer of 1943, just after the news of the *Dorchester* sinking had finally come through, my thoughts went back through the years of my son's life. Inevitably, there were many memories of Long House in New Hampshire where so much of Clark's childhood and young manhood had been happily spent. I recalled the two nights that Clark, already a young minister, had spent alone on Wolf Mountain, hoping that God would speak to him there, and of his disappointment and yet his satisfaction in knowing that the Spirit, though silent, was near at hand and ever present. As I relived my boy's sojourn on his "Mount of Sacrifice," I remembered, too, the long hours that Lillian and I waited for him to return to us, followed by my reunion with him there on that granite ridge. Ten years later, in the first hours of anguish at the knowledge of our loss, I determined that Wolf Mountain should somehow be made a memorial to the man who had not only loved the spot but had in part found himself there.

And so it came to pass. My friend Col. Edmund ("Red") Black, a West Point classmate of Jimmie Doolittle and builder of great airfields during World War II, became a member of the New Hampshire legislature after his retirement from the Army; it was he who introduced the bill that, by joint action of both houses, renamed the top of Wolf Mountain "Clark Summit." Each summer now, when historic old Long House is filled with children that the Christian Herald Association brings there for its summer program, there are hikes up the trail through the woods. Sitting atop the ledge, looking out across the hills and valleys of Deering and the surrounding towns all the way to the White Mountains, the youngsters hear the story of the man for whom the summit is named—the minister who went down with the *Dorchester* that another man might live, the chaplain who joined three others in a spontaneous and epic demonstration that Protestants, Jews, and Catholics are brothers when, in service to their fellow men, they meet their God.

14

In 1912 a young minister with a conviction ran for the governorship of Ohio and was defeated. Thirty-nine years later, older but perhaps not much wiser in ways political, that minister ran again with another conviction, this time for mayor of Philadelphia. Michael Foley, the Roman Catholic lawyer I asked to run on my ticket for district attorney, put it this way, "It will be good fighting, Doctor, and in a worthy cause, but I think you don't have the slightest idea of what you're in for." And Mike, as it turned out, was perfectly right.

My practical interest in Philadelphia politics began when a new city charter, calling for the consolidation of county and city offices, carried by approximately 150,000 votes, despite the opposition of both the Republican and Democratic machines. This meant that many duplicate offices would be abolished and a great deal of money saved. If this could be accomplished, there was clearly the possibility of other enlightened action by independent voters. When a committee of citizens, a nonpartisan group, approached me in the spring of 1951 with the invitation to run in the Republican primaries, I succumbed. I believed, or I sold myself the idea, that as a man who had preached good citizenship, it was time for me to practice what I preached. I was no longer an active pastor in the city, having resigned my ministry at Baptist Temple three years before, so there was no question of compromising a church by anything I might advocate.

I carried the primary contest easily and then the real fight was on. The first victory had already come when I forced Michael Foley, my running mate, onto the ticket over the will of the Republican machine. The machine had promised that I might "write my own ticket"—had promised everything, in fact, when I was persuaded to run—or I would not have agreed. It was soon apparent that these astute politicians did not believe that a parson would want to, or would know enough to, interfere with the usual political performance. When they discovered otherwise, they were at first surprised, then resentful. In the end, though various pressures obliged them to keep on publicly endorsing the program I was bound in conscience to follow, most of them gradually withdrew their support from me, though I hasten to add that some remained my loyal supporters to the very end.

The city chairman of the Republican party ultimately withdrew from his office in my headquarters, telling me he would rather see me defeated than have his party machine destroyed. "After all, politics is my business," he said. The cause of the crisis was my refusal to dismiss an employee whose family had always been Democratic although they were now supporting my candidacy. Aside from his political philosophy, this man was an estimable Christian gentleman in every way. I also insisted that no candidate on my ticket could keep his job as leader of his ward. Further, I was determined that the city-county consolidation of offices should go forward without delay. When I spoke of cleaning up various situations in the city hall, and of reorganizing the Republican party in Philadelphia from top to bottom, my doom was just about sealed as far as the old regulars were concerned.

Let it be clear that I am not indicting my party wholesale. Certain of the old-line politicians kept their pledges to me down to the last comma and period, and I shall never forget their loyal efforts to see me elected. But, just as there are Democrats and Democrats, there are Republicans and Republicans, and Philadelphia was well supplied with the second kind in 1951.

Mike Foley, though under attack from the beginning because

I had obliged the machine to accept him, was a campaigner of grace and wit, quick in debate and handy with repartee. Many was the time that the slashing attacks of the opposition broke easily on his Irish lance. He and I had not many opportunities for friendly companionship during those hectic weeks of 1951, but I will always remember one day that we took off. Mike went with me to visit Mont Lawn, the *Christian Herald's* children's home at Nyack, New York. For me, at least, that home high above the Hudson River will remain one of the most beautiful children's homes I have ever seen. Years ago, when I persuaded my associates to integrate it completely, it became the first institution of its kind to take underprivileged children of all colors, races, and faiths, wherever found in Greater New York City.

Mike had a wonderful day with me at Mont Lawn, and the climax came when we entered the swimming pool with all those shouting youngsters. The sun shone down on the many colors, and in their blendings, black and white and copper, with red hair and blond and brunet, they all but cracked the spectrum. We were splashed and ducked until we had to cry for mercy. So engrossed did we become in our pleasure that we almost missed our campaign rally that night in Philadelphia.

I enjoyed our fight. Though I was older than my opponent, Joseph C. Clark, now senior United States Senator from Pennsylvania, I outtalked him from one end of Philadelphia to the other. The only thing Mr. Clark did better than I, of course, was win the election. Clark was never a machine candidate, any more than I was, and later he had all the difficulties with his machine that I prophesied he would.

Mike Foley took our defeat in stride and went back to his large and growing law practice with perfect aplomb. And I can report that I was perfectly happy to lose. Although I went clear out—mind, soul, and body—and wanted to be elected, I believe it was God's will that Joseph Clark defeated me. To have won would have meant a complete interruption of all the activities that had engaged me for years—the Christian Endeavor movement, the *Christian Herald* with all its dependent organizations, my writing, my various ministries. Embittered not the least, my political education greatly forwarded, and my general philosophy enriched, I stepped out of politics with a clear conscience, and this time—God willing—I will stay out.

As I look back on that election, some interesting facts stand out. First, the independent voter was clearly fed up with Republican promises. That Mr. Clark would have to deal with a recalcitrant and often venal Democratic machine did not weigh heavily against him on the scales. Philadelphia generally wanted the old boys out. From what was said to and about me during and after the campaign, I knew that I was regarded as an honest man, but one who would be unable to effect the necessary purge of the reactionaries in my party. Seemingly, many voters were of the mind of a dear lady of Germantown who said, "Doctor Poling, I shall vote for you, but I am praying for your defeat." As it turned out, her prayers were more powerful than her vote, and today I know that my closest friends in Philadelphia—Catholics, Jews, and Protestants alike—were all relieved for me personally when I did not win.

Another decisive factor in my defeat was the Negro vote, although I achieved no special distinction in losing it; since the days of Franklin Roosevelt this vote has been cast against Republican mayoralty and gubernatorial candidates, and it has twice been cast against President Eisenhower. A Negro clergyman who had backed my candidacy and done all he could to win support for me, said ruefully, after the election, "There's only one explanation for it, Dr. Poling—our people have voted Democratic ever since Roosevelt emancipated the slaves."

As I recall it, I carried only nineteen of the city's fifty-one wards, but one of my chief satisfactions is that two of these were the great river wards where the population is predominantly Catholic. They voted for me, a Protestant, and even more moving was the fact that they prayed and made novenas for me. Mike Foley explained it simply enough—"They believed in you"—and I like to think that was the case.

I lost to Joseph Clark by 122,210 votes. At first glance, that was a trouncing, but in the light of other elections in Philadelphia, perhaps it was not such a bad showing after all. A year later, when Dwight Eisenhower swept the country and carried Pennsylvania by 269,520 votes, he lost Philadelphia by 160,869. When he ran for re-election four years later, he carried Pennsylvania by 603,000 and lost Philadelphia by 124,564. And, the Republican who ran for mayor of Philadelphia in 1955 lost by 132,706.

My long-time friend General William Schnader, formerly Attorney General of Pennsylvania and by a narrow margin an unsuccessful candidate for governor in 1932, the year of the first Roosevelt landslide, remarked consolingly a year or so ago, "In the light of later events in Philadelphia, Dan, your defeat was a moral and personal victory." I didn't see it quite that way at the time, nor do I today, but in any case I'm glad that the four years I might have spent in bucking the machine in city hall were given back to me, so to speak, for activities in which I had more experience and which were, after all, my prior responsibilities.

In 1953, soon after his inauguration as President, I went to the White House to have a conference with the man who had once salved my feelings by making me a brigadier general of the nonexistent Algerian Camel Corps of the United States Army. With me was Senator Karl Mundt. Our purpose was to request a presidential letter in support of the All-American Conference to Combat Communism. As chairman of the Conference's executive council, I indicated the breadth of our membership—more than fifty patriotic educational, service, fraternal, and religious societies representing more than sixty million individual members—and described the Conference's sponsorship of "Know Your America Week," a program which is now observed annually by some six thousand communities and national agencies.

Mr. Eisenhower, impressed by our constructive and far-reaching effort to combat communism in the United States, agreed to give me the letter I wanted.

Rising to go, I said, "Mr. President, down in Florida, where I was making my yearly visit to the Memorial Home Community for retired religious workers, I listened to your inaugural address with the half a hundred clergymen who live there. I wish to tell you, sir, that all of us were deeply moved by your unexpected prayer."

Mr. Eisenhower answered with one of his engaging smiles. "Sit down," he said. And then, simply and frankly, he gave us the background not only of the prayer but of his religious life in general. In effect, he said, "Our family was closely knit. We were of a simple faith, and my parents, as you know, were pacifists. But there was no break in my relationships with my home when I went to West Point. They understood and accepted my decision. At West Point, the chapel for me was the central spot, and I carried my West Point Bible through all my soldiering. But until I came to Washington I had never formally identified myself with any church. I could not have gone with my mother, but I would not have hurt her by going anywhere else. Then came the presidency. Increasingly, I knew that I had to have something added, something that I had not yet found, if I was to be sufficient for this assignment. Mrs. Eisenhower is a Presbyterian. But had she been an Episcopalian or a Methodist or a Baptist, I would have followed her. I became a Presbyterian, and I entered into my church relationship and made my confession of faith even as I began to serve my country as its President."

Going on to speak of the prayer in his inaugural address, Mr. Eisenhower said, "That was my own idea. I didn't tell anybody what I was going to do. I knew that many would think it was corny. But I wanted to pray and I did so."

"Mr. President, you may be sure that the country did not think your prayer was corny," I said.

I have been happy, generally, with the leadership that Mr. Eisenhower has given us in the White House, but for me personally, as a churchman, one of the finest expressions of his character has been his regard for the late John Foster Dulles. My own association with John Foster Dulles extended across a quarter-century of his public life, and I long ago came to esteem him as a great statesman and a sincere Christian. Years ago, I served with him on a commission of the Federal Council of Churches of Christ in America. In his chairmanship of that commission, I came to admire, respect, and love him. He was never a pacifist, but it was inevitable that he should serve with sincere men and women who were. And though he could not follow them, he could and did lead them, often into constructive paths of public service.

When I was in London in 1941 on my mission of helping to repair the broken lines of communication between the churches of Great Britain and the United States, Mr. Dulles was also there. Representing his department of the Federal Council, he was obliged to disavow the pacifist position that some of his associates in America were advocating. He did it in a quiet yet forthright way that lost him none of his friends and reinforced his reputation as an expert in delicate international negotiating.

During the years when Mr. Dulles was our Secretary of State, I repeatedly saw some of his church friends embarrass him, particularly with their resolutions calling for recognition of Red China by the United States and by the United Nations. These resolutions, which almost unanimously remained silent about the tortures and martyrdoms inflicted upon Christian missionaries and tens of thousands of Chinese Christians, seemed to me untrue in their alleged facts and unworthy in their purpose. Incredibly, the latest of them, emanating from the Social Action Committee of a Protestant denomination, attacking Mr. Dulles' handling of the China situation, and charging that the real situation had been withheld from the American people was released even as the heroic, dedicated man who had poured out his life for freedom and indeed for a Christlike world lay dying.

In 1953, as president of the Military Chaplains Association, it was my honor to write and present to Mr. Dulles the association's Distinguished Service Citation of the year. The night of the presentation I was with him in the officers' club at the Brooklyn Navy Yard. Beside him, at the head table, a place was reserved for his son Avery. I saw the keen disappointment in the eyes of the father when the son, a young Jesuit priest, could not come because of his seminary duties. In spirit and intellect, he impressed me much that night.

Now, John Foster Dulles, whom the President called one of our greatest Secretaries of State, is gone from us, but of nothing in time and space am I more certain than that his career, though ended here, continues—that he has finished but to begin. I am not an historian and I may not be present when the judgment of history is rendered on the late Secretary, but at this writing it is my conviction that his character, his ability, his complete dedication, and his achievements entitle him to rank with the greatest of all Secretaries of State—and I give him first place.

Another member of President Eisenhower's team for whom I have a high regard is Richard M. Nixon. He was a boy of fifteen or sixteen when, representing the Christian Endeavor Society of the Friends Church in East Whittier, California, he attended a missionary conference in Riverside at which I spoke. We met then, an occasion that the vice-president told me he remembered, though I was obliged to confess that I had not remembered the young Endeavorer.

It has been my exciting experience to watch Dick Nixon rise steadily in the appreciation of his countrymen. Particularly in his missions to other countries he has carried himself impressively under trying circumstances, and probably no vice-president has ever been more helpful to, or more highly regarded by, a President. Whatever the future may hold for him, he has amassed so great a wealth of experience in domestic and international affairs that it will be difficult for our country to disregard him as a political leader. He has courage, faith, ability, and he is young, even dramatically young, for his record of achievement.

In July, 1959, at the International Christian Endeavor Convention held in Philadelphia, it was my privilege to write and present to Mr. Nixon the International Youth's Distinguished Service award. It was then that we again renewed our Christian Endeavor ties. Dick Nixon was not only the president of his society in Whittier, but its pianist. I was amused when I once heard him comment that as a piano player, he was a contemporary of Harry Truman, another noted performer. With a grin, Dick added, "But Harry and I never played duets."

On the other side of the world from Washington I recently met another notable figure who is a leader in the Christian Endeavor movement—Queen Salote of Tonga. Those of my readers who saw the coronation procession of Queen Elizabeth of England in London—or watched it, as I did, on television—will remember Queen Salote riding through London in her open car, acknowledging with happy smiles the cheers of that vast crowd. Tonga is but a pinprick on maps of the South Pacific, but its queen all but stole the show.

In 1938, sailing to Melbourne, Australia, where I was to preside at the tenth World Christian Endeavor Convention, I found a letter from Queen Salote awaiting me at Suva, in the Fiji Islands. It was a cordial invitation for me and Mrs. Poling to visit her palace in Tonga, and it was signed "Queen and President," the latter title referring to her position in Tonga's Christian Endeavor Union. Unfortunately, Lillian and I had no time for the side trip, and twenty years were to pass before I finally met this remarkable woman. My visit took place at the residence she sometimes occupies in Auckland, New Zealand. Impressively handsome, Queen Salote is every inch a monarch, and she stands six feet and three inches, if you please. The line of her family runs unbroken back to the fabled past when Polynesian sovereigns were worshiped as gods. The throne she occupies in Tonga, which is now a British Protectorate, is doubtless the oldest in the world today in its direct descent. Queen Salote told me that she was a schoolgirl of seventeen when she was called home from New Zealand, forty years ago, to succeed her dying father. She took a husband who gave her two sons, one now the Crown Prince, the other her Prime Minister.

Queen Salote, who has been a widow for many years, told me that her fifty thousand subjects heartily support British Methodism, which was brought to them by missionaries years ago. Today religion is the most vital factor in the life of Tonga. Recently I saw a movie of the South Sea Islands in which the handsome natives of Tonga were shown in their mass worship led by a native pastor and a beautifully trained choral group sang the "Hallelujah Chorus." For many years Queen Salote's sister was organist for the palace Christian Endeavor society. Each year in Tonga, there is a national Christian Endeavor convention attended by practically all of Queen Salote's subjects, young and old.

Education in her islands is compulsory, and the literacy rate is one of the highest, if not the highest, in all the Pacific area. An establishment is maintained in Auckland for the considerable number of Tonganese who wish to pursue advanced studies.

"Isn't it difficult to hold such young people?" I asked the Queen. "After they catch a glimpse of the outside world, don't they want to remain in New Zealand or go out to Australia or further?"

The Queen smiled and shook her head. "They can hardly wait to get home," she said. And later, when I discussed this same matter with the Queen's secretary, I found her statement confirmed. Apparently Tonga, where the population increase is scientifically controlled, and wise agricultural policies, including land allotment, contribute to a relatively high standard of living, is a modified paradise. As I went away from my interview, I thought of another point that Queen Salote had mentioned: "Two centuries ago when Captain James Cook visited our group, he gave it the name of the Friendly Islands." To me it seemed the ideal name, and of all the places in the world that I still have not visited, Tonga is one where Lillian and I hope someday to pay a lingering call.

In this year of 1959, when I have stirred my memories of forty years ago by returning to the Marble Collegiate Church on lower Fifth Avenue in New York as Sunday evening preacher, I rejoice in the fact that my son Daniel Kring Poling is ministering with me in this oldest of North America's Protestant denominations, the Dutch Reformed Church. Daniel's church is the Fort Washington Collegiate Church, on Washington Heights, at the north end of Manhattan, and his is the youngest institution of the Collegiate Church of New York.

What a man this son of mine has become, with his veritable genius for understanding friendship, his spiritual strength, and his versatility as a preacher. As a friend of youth, he carries on what I sought to make my tradition of service to the Christian Endeavor. He is vice-president of the New York State Christian Endeavor Union. He is an adviser to educational groups and he serves as a member of a special committee of the American Manufacturers Association. Perhaps a father may be forgiven for a prideful appraisal, but I have watched and listened to Daniel and I have heard others' opinions of his work, and I know this son of ours to be a man of proportions.

Twice in his adult life Daniel has risen in a wonderful way to difficult experiences. One of these occasions involved the loss of his younger brother, Clark. As I have written earlier, Daniel, too, had wanted to become a chaplain. When that became impossible, he mastered his disappointment and his grief for Clark and committed himself even more fully to the work at home.

Daniel's other triumphant experience, fully shared by his wife Evangeline, has been the raising of his son. In 1937, when Daniel telephoned me the news that Van, his wife, had given birth to a boy, and that he had been named Daniel Alfred Poling II, I whooped with joy. But then came a warning from the baby's father. "There was an accident," he said. "The doctors can't yet say what the final result will be, but we almost lost the baby. The birth was delayed and a short cord all but strangled him. Finally, he had to be turned and brought feet first."

The accident, alas, had serious results. The birth injury, although it had no effect on the centers of the brain controlling personality and intellect, did terrible damage in the area of muscular control. Today, at twenty-two, my namesake has never taken a normal step or spoken an easily intelligible sentence. He wears heavy iron braces and must be assisted at all times. Every step, every syllable is a fresh problem for him. Though he fights like a young lion to be understood, even those who know him intimately cannot always follow what he is saying. Danny, my grandson, is a spastic—or, more properly, an athetoid.

He has made his way despite his appalling physical handicap. Who knows?—perhaps the impossibility of a normal physical life caused Danny to develop to an extraordinary degree his intellectual and spiritual capacities. His record is already one to make his hale and hearty grandfather feel humble.

When he graduated from Yonkers High School, it was with State Regents honors and the grant of a college scholarship. Since Danny could not march with his fellow graduates, the president of the class, a four-letter man, asked for and received the privilege of escorting him to his seat. Later, he brought Danny his certificate of graduation. I was moved to tears as I listened to the head of the Board of Education describe my grandson's eagerness to learn, his loyalty to the school, and his popularity with the student body.

Danny has now finished his junior year at Hunter College, in New York. He is majoring in sociology and political science. Though he is not always able to sit in the classes, he takes all the courses with tutors and student assistants. His most recent report showed six A's and one B. The B (his only one in college thus far) was in Calculus; he had to take the examination without benefit of any classroom sessions at all.

But his academic achievements were only the beginning. The indomitable spirit that made this boy a scholar also drew him into a field of social action that has tried men possessed of all their powers. Two years ago, in Highbridge Park on New Year's Washington Heights, Michael Farmer, a fifteen-year-old boy, was stabbed to death in a gang war. Fifteen boys were tried for that killing. Eight were under age and their cases were heard in Juvenile Court. Four of the older defendants are now serving prison terms. Danny brooded about that tragedy. He knew the neighborhood, for it was the home of his father's church. He determined to do something practical about the conditions that led to such crimes.

With the help of Police Lieutenant William Brennan, Danny

introduced himself to some of the leaders of the Jesters. The dead Michael Farmer had been a Jester. John M. Kenny, a Y.M.C.A. worker, helped my grandson to communicate his message. At first the gang boys laughed at Danny and even imitated his uncontrolled movements. Today, as members of his "Operation Handclasp," they are unanimous in their praise of him and incredulous at what he—despite his own handicap—has been able to do for them. They who began by jeering now vie for the right to carry Danny about the neighborhood and in and out of the clubhouse arranged for them on Audubon Avenue.

Danny needed funds to start his program. From his family and from businessmen in the neighborhood he raised the necessary first few thousand dollars. He then persuaded a landlord to rent his empty store for a boys' club. All this took time. Danny could work at the project only in his after-school hours. Further, he had to overcome the community's aversion to the gang boys. His was not a popular crusade at first.

With the working space assured, and with the Y.M.C.A. acting as sponsor and the Hunter College Department of Sociology supervising, Danny began a recreation and social program that could be meaningful to boys who were used to hanging out on street corners, waiting to harass other youths on the prowl. He rounded up contributions of rickety furniture, an old television set, a radio that could be fixed. The boys he had befriended came to the clubhouse to try their hands at leatherwork, shell jewelry, and rug weaving. Some of them began making Christmas presents for their mothers and brothers and sisters. Others used the games and athletic equipment Danny and his friends had found for the boys. It wasn't easy getting the boys interested in such things. Many of them were hardened characters.

Peggy Beattie, an art major at Hunter College, did wonders with the little that was available to make the club quarters attractive. She decorated the front window with the badge that Danny had designed—two hands clasping in a circle, surrounded by these words: "Who Builds His Community Builds Himself."

Along with the games and the handcrafts there was companionship and shared endeavors and hopes. The boys, many of them Puerto Ricans and Negroes, began to find that life offered them more than the destructive ways of hatred and gang rivalry. In December, 1958, Operation Handclasp held its first community dance. The admission charge was seventy-five cents if the attendee contributed a Christmas-tree ornament; a dollar otherwise. There was a good crowd and no trouble. Later, the boys who had done the club's wiring helped to set up the community Christmas tree in nearby Mitchell Square. Its decorations included the ornaments that had been contributed to Operation Handclasp.

As Danny looked at the results of his months of effort, he said —with one of his friends speaking for him—"Everyone told me this couldn't be done. They said I was crazy. Maybe I am, but it seems to work."

Operation Handclasp began to attract attention. There were stories about it in newspapers. In the spring of this year Joseph ("Big Joe") Rosenfield presented the story on his radio program, Happiness Exchange. Since Danny could not speak for himself in public, his father and mother spoke for him, using the script prepared by their son. They explained his conviction that juvenile delinquency will disappear when young people are given effective leadership, when their empty lives are given some constructive substance, when their antisocial actions can be recognized for what they are: the desperate measures of lonely and misguided children.

Speaking through his parents, Danny said to the radio audience: "Here am I, a boy whom some people, upon first acquaintance, think an alcoholic, a narcotic, or an imbecile; a boy who has great difficulty dressing and feeding himself; a boy who is compelled to sit in a corner of this studio like a deafmute and watch another read his creation. I do not mention this to elicit pity from your heart, but to draw determination from your soul, *determination to match my effort*. Here am I, and if I can do this much, by the Grace of God, how much more can one of you do with a normal body? With nimble hands, how much more can a group of you fashion these young lives of our town? With agile limbs, what greater strides can you take towards our goals? Perhaps this is why I have this cursed thing, to give you some idea, some clue, some inkling of what you can achieve if you will only try—try with all your might, try unceasingly, try until you succeed."

Big Joe's broadcast also featured interviews with two of the reclaimed Jesters. What they had to say about the handicapped young man who had come to them to show them a way out of the life that was heading them toward violent death or prison terms touched the hearts of the radio audience. Contributions poured in. Today, Operation Handclasp is on its way to larger and better quarters and an expanded program for the young people of Washington Heights.

I thought I knew nearly everything there was to know about youth movements, but in all humility, and with a lump as big as an apple in my throat, I confess that this grandson of mine has taught me a lesson in courage and achievement that I shall never forget.

A word or two remains to be said about Danny's parents' role in all this. All through his life they have helped him and spoken for him with a rare devotion and understanding. Especially has Danny's mother given of herself in his painful and constant struggle to reach the heights that are his goal. But there is a point not to be overlooked. Although Daniel and Evangeline have been moved by their love and compassion throughout their experience with Danny, they have never been soft with him. Wisdom is part of their love. Never once has young Danny been allowed to feel that his condition excused him from trying his utmost to compensate for it. Danny's radiance of spirit, his happiness in what he is doing, is proof again that there is a right way to raise a child, no matter how formidable the problems confronting the parents. Daniel and Evangeline and their two young daughters—both lovely, normal girls—have made Danny's difficult life a thing of triumph. For me, watching and learning, this family unity and its result have been one of the great human experiences of all my days.

15

When I was a little boy in Lafayette, Oregon, one of the first places I can remember at all, I sometimes heard a train whistle. The sound fascinated me. I had never seen a train to remember it and couldn't imagine what one looked like. That distant, mournful sound, coming and going on the wind, suggested that there was an outside world I might some day know about.

One day a boy who was older than I gave me the explanation of that awesome moaning. Probably he had never seen a train either, but his bizarre story convinced me that he had. Indians were riding above great iron wheels, making that train go, he told me, and the whistle I heard was their war whoop, which was now a cry of peace. To me, it was a thrilling explanation.

I was nearly frantic with excitement the day Father put me in the family buggy and took me to meet the train. I held Father's hand and watched the first smoke rise above the trees that rimmed the horizon. Then I heard that war whoop closer than I had ever heard it, and out from the forest it came—an amazing thing—little houses chasing each other across a field, with the smoking kitchen in front! I felt disappointed when no Indians appeared, but also considerably relieved.

The world that I first knew and can still recall was as small and uncomplicated as that. There were fewer than two hundred people in it, and I knew them all—men, women, and children. Vaguely I knew there must be people elsewhere, because letters came to us, and once I saw Father holding an important-looking yellow envelope that he called a "telegram."

Then I grew big enough to leave that small community. Today my world has grown until it includes the continents, the islands, and the oceans of the earth. When I think of all the places I have traveled to and of all the thousands of people I have met, it seems as if I must know at least someone of every color and creed the world has to offer. And when I think of capitals and great cities, the towns and small villages, I see faces—the faces and forms of those I have known and still know, loved and still love. Some of these were the humble people of the world, others were great figures, and there were many more of both sorts than I have had space to tell about in this inadequate story.

I learned a good lesson about people from one of the idols of my youth and the friend of my maturity, Will Rogers. Will was the same sort of fellow off stage as he was behind the footlights —spontaneous, original, a wit, and a thinker. In New York, during the 1920s, I saw a good deal of him. My church was at Fifth Avenue and Twenty-ninth; he lived in the old Waldorf Astoria Hotel, up the Avenue at Thirty-fourth. I had persuaded him to write a regular sermonette for the *Christian Herald* when we found that his contract with *The New York Times* would not allow him to go ahead with the idea. To me it was a disappointment; to him, busy man that he was, perhaps it was a relief.

One afternoon I sat straddling a chair in his theater dressing room, watching him put on his make-up. He had a towel spread under his chin, and every so often he would swing away from his mirror to stress a point in our discussion. A mutual friend of ours, a man very much in the public eye, had done something that brought him a good deal of criticism. Between ourselves, Will and I were attempting to determine whether our friend had really stepped off the reservation or was only the victim of a misunderstanding.

Suddenly, Will threw down his make-up stick and faced me. "Dan, you can't tell what a man is like when you are looking at him. You don't know what he sees. You have got to get around behind him and see what *he* is looking at." With that, he jumped up from his seat, snatched the towel from under his chin, and came over and stood behind me with his hands on my shoulders.

Looking over my head at the spot where he had been sitting, he said, "You've got to see what the other fellow is looking at if you're really going to know him."

I fear that I have not done as well with the principle as did Will Rogers—for he was able to say, "I never met a man I didn't like"—but I have ever kept it in mind as good counsel. And certainly, nearly if not all the men and women I have known I have liked—even when we had our differences.

More often than not, as my story has already made clear, my differences have been concerned not with personalities but with issues that I hold very important. The increasingly authoritarian development I see in American Protestantism is one such issue. Many Protestant churchmen, myself included, find a definite trend away from concern with the individual to concern with the group, away from the priesthood of the believer to the priesthood of the hierarchy.

In the May, 1959, issue of the *Christian Herald* appeared my article, "Do We Need a Protestant Separation of 'Church and State'?" It was severely critical of the National Council of the Churches of Christ in the U.S.A. for its treatment of its National Lay Committee. The parent group summarily and arbitrarily disbanded its Lay Committee in 1955 after the Committee, headed by J. Howard Pew, a distinguished Presbyterian layman, had gone into action and raised the more than six hundred thousand dollars that the Council imperatively needed.

It is with concern and deep regret that I find the National Council acting in such a manner as to discourage a healthy partnership of the Protestant layman with his clerical leader. I believe in the ecumenical movement, and I wholeheartedly second the thought of no less an ecumenicist than Dr. Henry P. Van Dusen, president of Union Theological Seminary, when he says: "The Church must center her efforts on how she can do more for the laity, rather than on how the laity can do more for the Church." Dr. Van Dusen has committed himself, as would I, to the laity as "the ambassadors of Christ in the world," and added that if the Church is to speak intelligently to the world, "it must speak through the lives and deeds of laymen."

The controversy among Protestant Christians has to do with the area of the Church's responsibility. It is not the Church's job to be the expert in every field of human endeavor. I believe that it should confine its official actions to essentially religious matters and trust the individual Protestant Christian to spell out the fine print of his life. As an example of what I consider an unwise move by the Church, I would submit the five-thousand-word "Message to the Churches," prepared by the Cleveland World Order Conference of 1958, which included resolutions supporting recognition of Communist China by the United States and admission of Communist China to the United Nations. In presenting such a message, the Conference, sponsored by the National Council of the Churches of Christ, gave further evidence of defying the earnest dissent the National Lay Committee had voiced before that committee was disbanded.

I believe that it is the Church's job to be the Church. For example, as an active member of the Federal Council of Churches, I spoke against a resolution that would have declared official opposition to the appointment, in 1939, of Myron C. Taylor as President Roosevelt's representative to the Vatican. I emphasized the fact that the appointment was personal, that Mr. Taylor was not, and without confirmation of the United States Senate, could not become an ambassador, but that surely the President, as Commander in Chief of the Armed Forces of the United States of America, must not be embarrassed in his leadership. Every one of our Allies and every enemy nation had its ambassador at the Vatican. President Roosevelt believed that he needed a listening post in Rome and that, it seemed to me, should have been enough for the Federal Council. That resolution, happily, was tabled. Later, I opposed President Truman's recommendation for an official ambassadorship to the Vatican.

Again, the Federal Council proposed a resolution that would have supported the Arab position in the still-continuing struggle with Israel. Contending that it would be clearly a disservice to the Protestant churches and to American unity for the Federal Council to take a position either for or against either Arab or Jew, I supported the motion to table. The motion prevailed.

In my view, both these resolutions reflected the wishes of a hierarchy that had cut itself loose from the wishes of the laity, and to my mind this is not the road to follow unless ecumenical Protestantism is to become a decadent faith. I submit that a reformation in ecumenical Protestantism is now in order. And it may be that this reformation is now in process.

As I look back on my years of work and travel, as minister or leader of youth groups, as magazine editor or director of charity organizations, as columnist or presidential aide, I am repeatedly struck by the mystery of how I got into all this.

When I made my decision for Christ more than half a century ago, I was in my twentieth year and I looked forward to a missionary career in China. I was unhappy, perhaps even a bit resentful, when events took me in an unexpected direction. Later on, as I got farther and farther away from my original plan, I became happy in my work and would not have chosen to change anything. Yet even today I do not feel that the control of events has been entirely in my hands. In mysterious and wonderful ways I have been directed. I have had poignant friendships and stirring experiences, great love and sadness quite as great. And always there has been God's purpose in the scheme of things.

Today, as I count my living children—seven—and my living grandchildren—twenty—I see them as branches of a tree reaching out in all directions. I give advice—I hope not too much of it. And I have my secret hopes—sometimes not so secret.

I am sure that every man in a worthy calling is honored and happy when a son follows in his footsteps. Both of our sons followed me into the ministry. Recently in a long "bull session" with Clark Vandersall Poling, Jr.—Corky—our son Clark's only son, I told him at some length of the conversation I had had with his father when Clark, Sr., was entering his junior year at Rutgers University. When we talked, Clark, Jr., was in the same phase of his academic career at Yale. In talking with Clark, Sr., I had followed the almost identical course that my own father had taken with me and with my two brothers.

My father had said: "Dan, I of course want you to look at the ministry, but not to the exclusion of other professions. Look at them all—medicine, law, business—look at them all. Study them in the light of what you think may be your strengths and weaknesesses, your likes and your dislikes, your aptitudes, family background, and all else that may even indirectly influence your future career. If you do that, my son, do it with a prayer for God's guidance. And then if you can stay out of the ministry, don't you dare go in. The ministry, as I see it, my son, must be a call that is a veritable compulsion. And finally, Dan, if I could, I wouldn't make the choice for you."

Now I said to Corky, my grandson, "That's what my father told me. That's what I told your father and your father's brother. The most vital, the supreme question to be faced by you is 'Where must I put my life to make it count for the most?' "

And we left it there. What the young man's decision will be I do not know. But I believe that it will be the right decision; that he will carefully consider all the converging factors; that, finally, he will use his best judgment; that he will—under God's guidance—put his life where it will count for the most.

A man is many things, if he lives a long time and tries to fill his days. He is too many things, I have discovered, to contain within the pages of a book. I, for instance, am a 33° Mason and a Shriner, and have served the Shrine as Imperial Chaplain, and yet I haven't mentioned Masonry in all these pages. My great grandfather was a Mason, as was my grandfather, my father, and my father's two brothers. There have been almost as many Masons in the Poling family as there have been preachers, though not quite. Masonry is a brotherhood of service and achievement, yet infinitely more than that. It is a light that shines out of the East and knows its final consummation in God's Fatherhood.

I am a member of the Board of Trustees and Chairman of the Executive Committee of the oldest life insurance company with a continuous history in the world today—the Presbyterian Ministers' Fund for Life Insurance. In our two hundredth year, we reached two hundred million dollars of life insurance written. What makes our company special is that our insurance is limited to ministers, their wives, and their children. It is the most reasonably priced insurance in the insurance world, as well it should be. This p.k. still remembers when his father earned four hundred dollars a year as a working minister; there wasn't much left over for insurance premiums.

I have also been co-chairman of the American Christian Palestine Committee and am still treasurer of its special subsidiary, the Children's Memorial Forest Fund, that raises the money among Christians to plant six million trees in Israel, each tree a memorial to a Jewish child who died in the Nazi pogrom. I shall never forget the misty afternoon when nineteen miles southwest of Nazareth, above the kibbutz that honors the name of former Justice Brandeis of the United States Supreme Court, I planted five of the first thirty thousand of those trees.

Across the pages of this book, friends and families have moved in a vastly comforting number. It has been said that a man has all the friends he deserves, but I feel that some of us have had more than we could ever deserve.

Of the many men I know today in public service, my friend J. Edgar Hoover particularly impresses me by the way he serves his country without thought of personal ambition. When subversives, fellow travelers, and those pseudoliberals who compromise the liberal movement have moved in to discredit this man it has not been necessary for him to make a personal defense. His defenders have been his fellow citizens. At once fearless and articulate, he has spelled out the menace of Communism as has no other man, and his *Masters of Deceit* is certainly the most valuable, comprehensive, and complete volume in the anti-Communist library.

In the years of my association with Mr. Hoover, it has seemed to me that he has had no less concern for giving just treatment to men and agencies falsely accused than for discovering and bringing to justice the enemies of American freedom and security. He is especially happy, I think, in his personal relationships, and he is a delightful conversationalist and generous friend. Without ostentation, he is a churchman. He has served as a trustee of the National Presbyterian Church in Washington, D.C., and his tributes to the American home, to the Sunday school, and to the youth training activities of organized religion in all the faiths have been often repeated.

Elder E. Francis Hyde has already appeared in this book, but I remember with gratitude my friendship with another elder: John Kyle—devout, pure of mind, clean of soul, successful in business, and faithful in all his assignments and relationships. His grandchildren are now the fourth generation of the Kyle family in the Marble Collegiate Church of New York, and his son, senior engineer of the New York Port Authority, follows in his father's footsteps.

Norman Klauder, a highly successful and trusted business executive and a denominational leader among all Baptists, was an officer of my Philadelphia church. Through the years he has been one of the World's Christian Endeavor Union's most highly regarded administrators. His continuing friendship for me and mine, and also that of his family, has assumed such proportions that my eyes mist as I remember him.

Dr. Charles M. Sheldon, author of *In His Steps*, said to be the most widely circulated of all books after the Bible and *Pilgrim's Progress*, was my immediate predecessor as editor of the *Christian Herald*, and he was both a noble man and a loyal personal friend.

I have known many physicians, but two in particular I wish to mention. (The first doctor I remember was the gentleman by whose side I stood as a boy of four when, opening his case, he distributed pink candies to me and my sister May. For a good many years thereafter, when doctors did not produce candy, I was sorely disappointed.) Dr. Lee Thornton was a boy in bare feet when Father met him, and he gave Father credit for launching him upon a career that made him the most popular physician in Oregon as well as city physician in Portland. Handsome, gentle, courageous, and possessed of a scientific mind, he was also the soul of understanding kindness, and once when our family larder was all but empty the great doctor replenished it.

Dr. Jack Bercovitz, who served two terms as a medical missionary in Korea, has listened to my heartbeat for more than thirty years, and more than any other member of his profession he has been my intimate friend.

There have been many unforgettable figures on the distaff side of my life and work. Those closest to me have already appeared in this book, but I cannot close without mentioning four more. Miss Blanche Whitecar, of Philadelphia, and her twin sister, Mrs. Maude Metzel, repeatedly helped in the campaign to complete the Chapel of Four Chaplains, coming forward whenever discouragements arose and almost insuperable obstacles appeared.

The late Mrs. Emily Bates, the widow of Dr. William Bates, who discovered a system of achieving better sight without glasses, placed me eternally in her debt by contributing to my activities as minister and youth leader and to the well-being of my family.

Of Miss Mae LeCount, my wife once remarked, "Whoever said no person is indispensable spoke before Mae came to our house." And that just about expresses the feeling of us all, including our grandchildren. Mae provided just about everything that Lillian, with her increasing glaucoma handicap, needed, and for nearly eight years now has been the perfect companion. Her culinary talents are incredible, and she is certainly the finest family chauffeur, male or female, I have ever known. She sees all, hears all, and, in the service of those she loves, gives all. A small granddaughter once unconsciously put me in my place as she properly located both her grandmother ("Nana") and Mae LeCount. We were at Long House in New Hampshire at the time and, ticking off the ownership of various items, Sandy said, "Nana's farm, Mae's automobile, Granddaddy's pig." Well, at any rate I was not left out.

Were I to describe the worth of my brothers and sisters, I would begin here another book, but perhaps I may be pardoned a few words about them.

Ethel, Mrs. William Hargis, was a romantic brunette, beautiful and talented, who married at seventeen. Now a striking white-haired grandmother, she continues her active public life as president of the Oregon Woman's Christian Temperance Union.

Laura, a radiant blonde who was blessed with her mother's golden soprano voice, has enriched a career in many relationships. As Mrs. Hubert Goode, she was once national president of the Women's Auxiliary of the American Legion; recently she was named Portland's Woman of the Year. She is the mother of one daughter and two grandchildren.

Mabel, the youngest of these sisters, has already appeared in this story. Today she is twice a grandmother, and her daughter Barbara and Barbara's two children are as my own.

Charles Samuel Poling, the elder of my living brothers, is a Presbyterian clergyman who has served pulpits in Pennsylvania, New Jersey, Arizona, and California. A poet, novelist, and television personality, he is also a horseman—a breeder of palominos. He served as a chaplain in both World Wars. His only son, Robert, was a pretheological student when he enlisted in the Marines and became a partial war casualty; unable to complete his academic preparation, he returned to useful civilian life.

Paul Newton Poling, the youngest of Father's and Mother's p.k.'s, is now pastor of the First Presbyterian Church in Salem, Oregon, after having served pastorates in New Jersey and Texas and been for five years a secretary of the Presbyterian Board of Education, with headquarters in Philadelphia. Two of his three sons have followed him into the ministry.

Particularly fortunate our family has been with its in-laws. My sisters' husbands have always been among my most intimate friends, as have the wives of my brothers. Hubert Goode, husband of Laura, for many years has been associated with the city government of Portland, Oregon. He, along with Mabel's husband, Walter Wood, registrar of Multnomah College in Portland, have accompanied me on some of the most unforgettable fishing expeditions of my life up to now. Ethel's husband, William Hargis, is another royal friend.

In the course of this book, I have dwelt at length on the ultimate life that continues beyond the grave. But I do not want to emphasize the values of tomorrow at the expense of today. This life is good. God made it. To disregard it, to belittle it, to disparage it, whether in pious phrases or by bringing it to a violent end, is an evil before God.

Besides, as most of us know, to journey is often better than to arrive, anticipation often happier than realization. Once I knew a wise and happy man whose deeply religious philosophy included this principle. E. Francis Hyde was nearly ninety when we met, and for another five years we were friends. He contributed much to my ministry at the Marble Collegiate Church, and fellowship with him was ever a mental and spiritual renewal for me. A talented musician, at age fifteen Francis had begun playing the organ in a New York church. He was one of the early sponsors of the New York Philharmonic Society, and was a patron of the Metropolitan Opera. For many years the vice-president of a major bank, he was also, until he died, the president of the American Bible Society. When I first knew him he had already made more than a hundred Atlantic crossings.

One evening as we sat together in my study at the Marble Collegiate Church, I asked him the obvious question: "Elder, tell me, what is your secret? You have lived nearly a century and you are still one of the most youthful men and most vital thinkers I know."

When my friend settled back in his chair, smiled, and began to talk, I sensed that I was in for a rare experience. He began, "Domine, I never reminisce!" He laughed, then, and began to reminisce, but I had caught his point: Remember the past and treasure it, but do not live in it. Francis Hyde had his memories, but they traveled with him. Always his face was front and he was on the march.

That night my friend went on to share with me the story of his life. Particularly I was interested in what he said about his companionship with his wife, whom I had never known.

"For nearly fifty years we spent practically all our summers abroad," Francis said. "I would take Mrs. Hyde to London in June, stay with her for two weeks, leave her there and return to New York for business, and then go back for another two weeks or longer, after which we would come home together. We would travel in Europe, using our London hotel as our headquarters. She loved a horse and we often rode together in Hyde Park." He smiled before he added, "Until our joints stiffened. Then we took a carriage."

My friend went on quietly with something in his voice that kept me, a man less than half his age, at close attention. "You know how I have followed the total eclipses of the sun all over the world. The year before Mrs. Hyde died—four years before you came to this church—a total eclipse happened to be visible only in the Philippines. Mrs. Hyde shook her head. 'No, Francis, I'm not going,' she said. 'Take me to London first, where I shall be comfortable and happy while I wait for you.' Then you run along and see your eclipse.' " The old man sat silent for a moment before he finished the story. "And so I crossed the Pacific and saw the eclipse—I've never missed one—and then I crossed the South China Sea and rounded India. I crossed the Indian Ocean and sailed up the Red Sea—and oh, it was hot there! I went through the Suez Canal and the blue Mediterranean, through the Gates of Hercules and past the Bay of Biscay into the English Channel.

"I found her waiting for me. Domine, that will always be the most wonderful journey of my life—save one. I did not hurry my trip, though I did not delay it either. I took things just as they came and got the most out of my adventure even as I reveled in my thoughts of our reunion in London. And when I got to London, she was there!"

Now I had his secret, and as he searched my face with his still keen eyes, he knew that I had not missed what he wanted me to understand. "Yes, yes," he said, nodding. "It is like that now. I am journeying toward her, sailing again the seas that lead always in her direction. I have work to do, interesting things to enjoy, and life is full—and always she is awaiting me. I would not hasten the event, Domine. She would be disappointed in me. But I await the hour of reunion. That will be wonderful. I am ready."

A few months after that conversation, when they went to call E. Francis Hyde one morning, he wasn't there. He had gone to his reunion.

To live like that is good. Anyone may take his life into his own hands, interrupt the divine plan for it, and shorten his career. I also believe that the divine time schedule may be kept in another and better way: I believe that it is within one's power to be immortal until his work is done.

Let me pray, then—and I do—to complete the work that is mine to finish. Let me have the strength and the courage, the faith and the time, to get my work done—well done—and to live no longer than that, please!

Neither you nor I may pass final judgment upon the work of another. We are not competent to judge. But one thing is certainly clear: The *length* of a life is not in itself the measure of a lifetime of service. Jesus was thirty-three when He was crucified. Lincoln was sixty-four when he was assassinated.

Faith in prayer and its ability to command your future and control your earthly destiny is vastly reassuring. That is a potent faith. Actually, you and I may live as long as we want to! Always life may begin—not just at forty or at eighty—but where we are at the moment. If we have faith, we will not sit out our days anticipating disaster, nor will we plan a course in life just to avoid risk and danger. It is those who sit in fear who have disaster fall upon them, while those who try to find the safe course are generally the ones who run into the most dangers. Many a life has backed away from adventure only to find misadventure.

What of my own case? Well, I shall drive the highways or fly the skies, sail in ships or ride in trains, as appointments require and schedules make necessary to finish the work undone, and always I shall know that God keeps my time table.

Apparently I have plenty of work still to finish. In Dayton, Oregon, in a quiet place above a small stream, are the graves of my father and mother, and of my young brother and two small sisters. My thoughts often go back to them. Mother was eighty-six when she died; Father was in his ninetieth year. And the Polings and Krings who preceded them were generally a long-lived lot. I had a great grandmother who died at a hundred and three. Since at a mere seventy-five I have not been ordered to lay down my editorial pen at the *Christian Herald*, or to cease with my labors for Christian Endeavor, I assume that I shall be around to add a number of new chapters to this uncompleted story of a life. When I do finish, and leave my tasks for others, I hope that my going hence will be considered only as the temporary departure of a friend who will be seen again.

Have there been times when I believed, when I *knew*, that God was stepping in to keep me at some task or other? Yes. Some might say this shows that I believe He is a God of special interests, granting to some favors that are withheld from others. But I do not think that this is so. For the prayer I pray may be your prayer too, and that of any other person who will so believe. Every good that I know of is from God. It remains only for us, all of us, to recognize that. This is the essence of my faith, and it may be yours also.

The many whom I have known and loved, and who died as I survived, no doubt reached the time and place I have yet to reach, that moment when the task, however humble, is finished, and when that which is better may be claimed. On some flight or journey or else in some quiet place my work shall be finished, and then no prayer of mine would grant me an extension of time on this earth. Nor would I pray that prayer!

I remember my father's dramatic statement of his own faith. "The greatest day of my life will be the day after they say I am dead."

Amen!

INDEX

ABOUT THE AUTHOR

Born in Portland, Oregon, in 1884, Daniel A. Poling represents the fifth generation in an unbroken line of preachers in the Evangelical Church. Soon after graduation from Dallas College in Oregon, in 1904, Dr. Poling was given his first church in Canton, Ohio. Later, he served briefly as a student pastor in Columbus, Ohio. He then became general and field secretary of the Ohio Christian Endeavor Union, and was successively citizenship superintendent, president's associate, associate president, and president of the International Society of Christian Endeavor, and president of the World's Christian Endeavor Union.

After serving overseas during World War I, Dr. Poling was called as associate preacher of the Marble Collegiate Church in New York City. He became co-minister and then minister of this church, resigning in 1930. In 1936 he became minister of the Baptist Temple in Philadelphia, resigning his pastorate after twelve years.

For more than thirty years Dr. Poling has been editor of the *Christian Herald* magazine. During World War II he visited most of the active theaters of war as correspondent, chaplain, or carrying letters of instruction from the President of the United States. The recipient of honorary degrees from a dozen colleges and universities, he has also received many awards, among them the Silver Buffalo of the Boy Scouts of America, the Cross of the Huguenot Society, a War Department citation in 1946 "For outstanding and conspicuous service as an accredited war correspondent" and, in 1947, the United States Medal of Merit "For extraordinary fidelity and exceptionally meritorious conduct." Dr. Poling was the first clergyman to receive this highest civilian award that the nation bestows.

Today a resident of New York City, Daniel Poling actively continues his career as clergyman, editor, author, and radio speaker.